Strategies of Political Theatre
Post-War British Playwrights

This volume provides a theoretical framework for some of the most
important playwriting in Britain in the second half of the twentieth
century. Examining representative plays by Arnold Wesker, John Arden,
Trevor Griffiths, Howard Barker, Howard Brenton, Edward Bond, David
Hare, John McGrath and Caryl Churchill, the author analyses their
respective strategies for persuading audiences of the need for a radical
restructuring of society. The book begins with a discussion of the way
that theatre has been used to convey a political message. Each chapter is
then devoted to an exploration of the engagement with left-wing
political theatre of an individual playwright, including a detailed
analysis of one of their major plays. Despite political change since the
1980s, political playwriting continues to be a significant element in
contemporary playwriting, but in a very changed form.

MICHAEL PATTERSON is Professor of Theatre at De Montfort
University, Leicester. He is a major British authority on German
theatre, especially twentieth-century political theatre in Germany. He
is author of *German Theatre Today*; *The Revolution in German Theatre
1900–1933*; *Peter Stein*; *The First German Theatre*; and *German
Theatre: A Bibliography*, and is editor of Georg Büchner: *Collected
Plays*. He has published numerous articles on German Naturalist
theatre, Reinhardt, Pirandello, Brecht, concentration camp theatre,
Kroetz and East German theatre.

For Kerry, Jamie and Gráinne

Contents

Contents

Part 4: The interventionist strain

Acknowledgments

Grateful acknowledgment is due to the following for permission to use copyright material: A. Alvarez; André Deutsch, London; the BBC; Faber and Faber, London; *The Independent*, London; John Calder, London; Jonathan Cape, London; Lawrence and Wishart, London; Macmillan, Basingstoke; Methuen, London; *Modern Drama*, University of Toronto; Monthly Review Press, New York; *The New Statesman*, London; Nick Hern Books, London; Peters, Fraser and Dunlop, London; *Plays and Players*, London; Suhrkamp, Frankfurt am Main; Theatre Quarterly Publications, London; Weidenfeld & Nicolson, London; Arnold Wesker. Every effort has been made to trace the holders of copyright material. Will those whom I have failed to contact please accept my acknowledgment.

I should also like to thank the following for their help and advice: Professor Judy Simons, Colin Chambers, and Frances Rankin-Hutera.

Finally I wish to acknowledge the generous financial assistance provided by the Arts and Humanities Research Board and by the Faculty of Humanities of De Montfort University Leicester.

Brief chronology, 1953–1989

1953 Joan Littlewood opens Theatre Workshop at Stratford East

1954 English Stage Company founded by Ronald Duncan and
      Neville Blond. Brendan Behan's first play, *The Quare Fellow*,
      staged by Joan Littlewood at Stratford East

1955 Anthony Eden replaces Winston Churchill as Prime Minister

      Samuel Beckett's *Waiting for Godot* (1952) performed at Arts
      Theatre, London

1956 The Suez crisis. Soviet troops enter Hungary

      First season of English Stage Company (now with George
      Devine) at Royal Court Theatre includes premiere of John
      Osborne's *Look Back in Anger*. Visit to London of Berliner
      Ensemble with Bertolt Brecht's *The Caucasian Chalk Circle*
      and *Mother Courage*. Death of Brecht. Peter Brook directs
      Paul Scofield in *Hamlet*

1957 Harold Macmillan replaces Anthony Eden as Prime Minister

      John Osborne's *The Entertainer* staged at Royal Court,
      directed by Tony Richardson. Samuel Beckett: *Endgame*

1958 Founding of European Common Market. First march by
      Campaign for Nuclear Disarmament to Aldermaston

      Harold Pinter's *The Birthday Party* flops after one week.
      Brendan Behan's *The Hostage* performed at Stratford East
      before transferring to the West End

John Arden: *Live Like Pigs* staged at Royal Court

Shelagh Delaney: *A Taste of Honey*

Arnold Wesker: *Chicken Soup with Barley* staged at Royal Court

1959 The Mermaid Theatre opens

John Arden: *Serjeant Musgrave's Dance*, directed by Lindsay Anderson

Arnold Wesker: *Roots*, directed by John Dexter

Arnold Wesker: *The Kitchen*

1960 John F. Kennedy elected US President

Centre 42 founded. Harold Pinter: *The Caretaker*

John Arden: *The Happy Haven*, directed by William Gaskill

Arnold Wesker: *I'm Talking About Jerusalem*, directed by John Dexter at the Royal Court

1961 US invasion of Cuba (Bay of Pigs). Berlin Wall erected

Peter Hall as artistic director of the Stratford Memorial Theatre, leases Aldwych and founds the Royal Shakespeare Company. John Osborne: *Luther*

1962 Cuban missile crisis. First success of the Beatles

Peter Brook's Theatre of Cruelty season. Edward Albee: *Who's Afraid of Virginia Woolf?*

Edward Bond: *The Pope's Wedding*

Arnold Wesker: *Chips with Everything*, directed by John Dexter at the Royal Court

1963 President Kennedy assassinated. Alec Douglas-Home replaces Macmillan as Prime Minister

The National Theatre opens at the Old Vic

John Arden: *The Workhouse Donkey*

Joan Littlewood: *Oh What A Lovely War*

1964 Harold Wilson becomes first Labour Prime Minister since 1951. Lyndon B. Johnson elected US President

Peter Brook's productions of Shakespeare's *King Lear* and Peter Weiss's *Marat/Sade*. John Osborne: *Inadmissible Evidence*

John Arden: *Armstrong's Last Goodnight* premiered at the Glasgow Citizens' Theatre

1965 Intensification of the Vietnam War. Anti-war demonstrations in USA. Race riots in Los Angeles

Death of George Devine. Harold Pinter's *The Homecoming*. CAST (Cartoon Archetypical Slogan Theatre) and the People Show founded. Theatre in Education initiated. John Osborne: *A Patriot for Me*. Frank Marcus: *The Killing of Sister George*

Edward Bond: *Saved*

David Mercer: *Ride a Cock Horse*

1966 Wilson announces 'standstill' in wages and prices. Mao Tse-tung: *Quotations of Chairman Mao*

Peter Brook's *US* at Aldwych. Raymond Williams: *Modern Tragedy*

John McGrath: *Events while Guarding the Bofors Gun*

Arnold Wesker: *Their Very Own and Golden City*

1967 Pound devalued. 50,000 demonstrate against Vietnam War in Washington. Six-Day War between Israel and Arab nations

Joe Orton murdered. Alan Ayckbourn's first success with *Relatively Speaking*. Peter Nichols: *A Day in the Death of Joe Egg*

1968 Assassination of Martin Luther King. Student revolt in Paris: the so-called *événements*. Riots in Chicago during Democratic convention. Russians invade Czechoslovakia. Restriction of black immigration into Britain

Abolition of Lord Chamberlain's powers of censorship. David Hare founds Portable Theatre with Tony Bicat. Charles Marowitz opens the Open Space Theatre. Red Ladder and Welfare State founded.

John Arden: *The Hero Rises Up*

Peter Barnes: *The Ruling Class*

Edward Bond: *Early Morning*

Edward Bond: *Narrow Road to the Deep North*

John McGrath: *Bakke's Night of Fame*

Alan Plater: *Close the Coalhouse Door*

1969 Nixon becomes US President. British troops sent into Northern Ireland in response to sectarian violence

Trevor Nunn takes over Royal Shakespeare Company from Peter Hall

Howard Brenton: *Christie in Love*

Howard Brenton: *Gum and Goo*

Peter Nichols: *The National Health*

John Spurling: *Macrune's Guevara*

1970 Conservative government returned to power, led by Edward Heath. First time 18-year-olds able to vote. US National Guard shoots four student protesters against Vietnam War. Marxist President elected in Chile. Women's Liberation Group and Gay Liberation Front founded

Peter Brook directs *A Midsummer Night's Dream*. David Storey: *Home*

Trevor Griffiths: *Occupations*

David Hare: *Slag*

John McGrath: *Random Happenings in the Hebrides*

David Mercer: *After Haggerty*

Arnold Wesker: *The Friends*

xiii

1971 Fighting in Vietnam spills over into Laos and Cambodia. Introduction of internment in Northern Ireland; violence escalates

Founding of 7:84 and General Will. Harold Pinter's *Old Times*

Edward Bond: *Lear*

Howard Brenton: *Scott of the Antarctic*

David Edgar: *The National Interest*

David Edgar: *Tedderella*

Trevor Griffiths: *Thermidor*

Portable Theatre: *Lay-By*

1972 Beginning of the Watergate affair. Britain imposes direct rule on Northern Ireland

John Arden and Margaretta D'Arcy: *The Island of the Mighty*

John Arden and Margaretta D'Arcy: *The Ballygombeen Bequest*

Howard Barker: *Alpha Alpha*

Howard Brenton: *Hitler Dances*

Howard Brenton, David Edgar and David Hare: *England's Ireland* performed in Amsterdam

Caryl Churchill: *Owners*

Trevor Griffiths: *Sam, Sam*

David Hare: *The Great Exhibition*

John McGrath: *Serjeant Musgrave Dances On*

Arnold Wesker: *The Old Ones*

1973 Britain joins the Common Market. Arab oil embargo; fuel crisis. Chilean president overthrown by military coup

Peter Hall takes over National Theatre from Laurence Olivier

Edward Bond: *The Sea*

Edward Bond: *Bingo*

Howard Brenton: *Magnificence*

Howard Brenton and David Hare: *Brassneck*

David Edgar and Howard Brenton: *A Fart for Europe*

Trevor Griffiths: *The Party*

John McGrath: *The Cheviot, the Stag and the Black, Black Oil*

1974 Worldwide inflation. Wilson replaces Heath, after Heath had failed to rally the nation against the miners in the so-called 'Winter of Discontent'. Violence in Northern Ireland spreads to Britain: terrorist bomb in Houses of Parliament. Nixon forced to resign over Watergate, replaced by Gerald Ford

Joint Stock and Women's Theatre Group founded

Howard Brenton: *The Churchill Play*

David Edgar: *Dick Deterred*

David Hare: *Knuckle*

John McGrath: *The Imperial Policeman*

Arnold Wesker: *The Wedding Feast* performed in Stockholm

1975 Margaret Thatcher succeeds Heath as leader of Conservatives. Fall of Saigon

Opening of the Riverside Studios, Hammersmith. Harold Pinter's *No Man's Land.* Stephen Poliakoff: *City Sugar*

John Arden and Margaretta D'Arcy: *The Non-Stop Connolly Show*

Howard Barker: *Claw*

Howard Barker: *Stripwell*

Edward Bond: *The Fool*

Caryl Churchill: *Objections to Sex and Violence*

Trevor Griffiths: *Comedians*

David Hare: *Fanshen*

David Hare: *Teeth 'n' Smiles*

John McGrath: *Little Red Hen*

Arnold Wesker: *The Journalists* published

1976 First nuclear treaty between USA and USSR. James Callaghan replaces Wilson as Prime Minister. Blacks riot in South Africa. Jimmy Carter elected US President

The National Theatre opens on the South Bank. Gay Sweatshop founded

Howard Brenton: *Weapons of Happiness*

Caryl Churchill: *Light Shining in Buckinghamshire*

Caryl Churchill: *Vinegar Tom*

David Edgar: *Destiny*

Arnold Wesker: *The Merchant* performed in Stockholm

1977 US protests about harassment of Czech dissidents

Robert Bolt: *State of Revolution*

Caryl Churchill: *Traps*

David Edgar: *Wreckers*

1978 Marxist guerrillas seize power in Nicaragua

Harold Pinter: *Betrayal*

Howard Barker: *The Hang of the Gaol*

Edward Bond: *The Bundle*

Edward Bond: *The Woman*

Howard Brenton, David Hare and Trevor Griffiths: *Deeds*

David Edgar: *The Jail Diary of Albie Sachs*

David Hare: *Plenty*

David Mercer: *Cousin Vladimir*

1979 Margaret Thatcher wins general election, pursues monetarist policies

Edward Bond: *The Worlds*

Caryl Churchill: *Cloud Nine*

1980 Reagan elected US President. Start of Iran–Iraq War

Death of David Mercer

Howard Brenton: *The Romans in Britain*

David Edgar: *Nicholas Nickleby* (adaptation)

1981 Greenham Common Peace Camp starts

John McGrath publishes *A Good Night Out*. Samuel Beckett: *Catastrophe*

Howard Barker: *No End of Blame*

1982 Falklands conflict

The Royal Shakespeare Company moves to the Barbican

Caryl Churchill: *Top Girls*

Trevor Griffiths: *Oi! for England*

David Hare: *A Map of the World* performed in Adelaide

1983 Thatcher re-elected with landslide victory

Caryl Churchill: *Fen*

Sarah Daniels: *Masterpieces*

David Edgar: *Maydays*

1984 Reagan re-elected. Thatcher confronts unions, especially in the long-lasting miners' strike

Arts Council 'Glory of the Garden' policy

Caryl Churchill: *Softcops*

John McGrath: *Imperial Policeman*

Harold Pinter: *One for the Road*

Stephen Poliakoff: *Breaking the Silence*

1985 Gorbachev becomes Soviet leader, initiates *perestroika*, a liberalization of the USSR

Edward Bond: *War Plays*

David Hare and Howard Brenton: *Pravda*

1986 David Rudkin: *The Saxon Shore*

1987 Thatcher re-elected for third term

Caryl Churchill: *Serious Money*

David Edgar: *Entertaining Strangers* performed at the National Theatre

1988 Passing of so-called Clause 28, banning the promotion of homosexuality in schools. End of conflict between Iraq and Iran

Howard Barker: *The Bite of the Night*

Howard Brenton: *Greenland*

David Hare: *The Secret Rapture*

Harold Pinter: *Mountain Language*

Timberlake Wertenbaker: *Our Country's Good*

1989 George Bush elected US President. Collapse of Communism in Eastern Europe. Dismantling of the Berlin Wall. Vaclav Havel becomes President of the Czech Republic

Caryl Churchill: *Icecream*

Introduction

This book is about a curious phenomenon. It examines the work of nine talented and innovative British playwrights who shared a laudable but strange conviction: that by writing plays and having them performed, they might help to change the way society is structured.

It is not a new conviction. Over two millennia ago Aristotle's theory of *catharsis*, that by watching a tragedy we may be purged of unhealthy emotions, ascribed a direct social benefit to drama. The Christian Church, while often distrustful of theatre, was willing to use drama as one of the means of propagating faith, giving us our modern word 'propaganda'. Eighteenth-century utilitarianism frequently justified drama in terms of its social usefulness, the German playwright Friedrich Schiller typically entitling his seminal essay of 1784, 'The theatre regarded as a moral institution'.

In the twentieth century, theatre with an intention to convert to a new way of thinking, or at least to challenge old modes of thought, became more overtly political, questioning not so much social morality as the fundamental organization of society, with the emphasis on economics rather than on ethics. Usually informed by Marx's analysis of capitalism, a number of directors and playwrights, most notably Erwin Piscator and Bertolt Brecht, sought to use the stage to propose socialist alternatives to the injustices of the world about them. In so doing they helped to define what we have now come to term 'political theatre', the actual title of Piscator's 1929 book on his work in the theatre.

All theatre is political. Indeed, it is the most political of all art forms. Most obviously, it is presented in a much more public forum than any other art. A novel may be read by more people than see a particular play; buildings and statues in public places may well be seen by many people who would never dream of setting foot inside a theatre; television daily reaches many times more viewers than the biggest theatre could accommodate in a decade. But the novel is read in private; passersby, if they notice a statue, respond individually; the television, even if watched by a group of people, is still a part of the domestic environment. As David Edgar argues: 'The inherent problem with television as an agent of radical ideas is that its massive audience is not confronted en masse. It is confronted in the atomised arena of the family living room, the place where most people are at their least critical.'[1]

The performing arts enjoy the unique distinction of bringing people together in a public place to respond communally to an artistic experience, whether to watch dance, listen to a symphony or to attend a play. And because the theatre uses words, its communication can be particularly specific and challenging. In the theatre, live actors speak out loud in front of, and sometimes even directly to, an audience, and so ideas and feelings are expressed at the same instant to a community of onlookers. Even cinema, which perhaps comes closest to live theatre in terms of its reception, offers a much more private, interior experience (one has only to consider how inappropriate it would be to heckle a film, or to compare the excited analysis of even quite mediocre plays by theatre-goers during the interval with the dulled atmosphere in a cinema intermission).

Just as the audience in the theatre cannot avoid assuming a certain communal role, so too the process of artistic creation in the theatre is a shared one. A novel, poem or painting are complete by the time they leave the creator's hands, and the accidents of publication or display will have a minimal effect on their quality. But the playwright's script is only the first stage in a complex process that will be contributed to by designers, directors, actors, wardrobe-mistresses and so on, all bringing their own creativity (or otherwise) to the final achievement, quite properly referred to as a 'production'.

Moreover, theatre depends on transcendence. On the one hand, the actors must transcend their own individuality in order to assume the role of a stranger. On the other, the audience must escape from their own self-centred preoccupations in order to become involved with the events on stage. And this process, which occurs both in the empathetic playing of realism and in the social emphases of Brechtian theatre, is an inherently political act, for the origin of political thought is in the willingness to identify with others, to share their problems, to experience transcendence.

A further important quality of theatre is its facility for juxtaposition. Most other art forms are obliged to pursue a certain linearity. Literature can only offer one line of print after another, and while the memory retains images and matches them against what is being read at that moment, words of themselves cannot actually juxtapose images. Similarly, much can be achieved in the cinema by montage, but one image still follows another, except in the rare experimental use, say, of the triptych screen. However, the theatre can place striking images side by side and offer contradictory information to stimulate our response. An actor may speak of love, and gesture to indicate hatred; a well-fed character may talk of charity, while ignoring a starving beggar at his feet. The total picture of the stage can communicate in ways that are not easily possible with the cinematic close-up.

In another sense, too, theatre is potentially a more genuinely political art form than the supposedly more democratic media of cinema and television. In both these forms, the camera dictates to us what we are to see. While naturally attempting to achieve some focus, the good stage director allows us the freedom to choose what we watch, and indeed we may see different things at each performance. Theatre invites us to look; it does not prescribe.

In terms of content, some plays are clearly more determinedly political than others, but it should be equally clear that it is impossible to parade characters interacting socially in front of a public assembled to witness these relationships without there being some political content. Thus even the silliest farce or most innocuous musical will reflect some ideology, usually that of the Establishment. In this sense, all theatre is indeed political.

The term 'political theatre' is, however, usually given a much more specific meaning, one that is used in this volume. This is defined as a kind of theatre that not only depicts social interaction and political events but implies the possibility of radical change on social-ist lines: the removal of injustice and autocracy and their replacement by the fairer distribution of wealth and more democratic systems.

There are different elements discernible in the process of writing for the political theatre. To begin with, there is the political credo of the individual playwright. There is not entire consistency in the views of the nine playwrights under consideration: Arnold Wesker, John Arden, Trevor Griffiths, Howard Barker, Howard Brenton, John McGrath, David Hare, Edward Bond and Caryl Churchill. It is almost certain that they would all subscribe to Churchill's summary of her as-piration: 'what kind of society I would like: decentralized, nonauthor-itarian, communist, nonsexist – a society in which people can be in touch with their feelings, and in control of their lives'.[2] However, their views on how this ideal state may be achieved range from the liberal pacifism of the young Arden to the committed Marxism of Griffiths and McGrath. Individual playwrights also change their political views over the years: Arden became a Marxist, Churchill became gradually more politicized, all of them have had to reassess their thinking after the popular success of Margaret Thatcher and the collapse of Commu-nism in Eastern Europe.

There is more consistency in the backgrounds of these writers: six are middle-class, and all are university-educated, with the excep-tion of Wesker and Bond, who openly distrusts the academic world. Moreover, six of them went to Oxford or Cambridge, proving that supposed relics of privilege can be breeding grounds for revolutionary thinking. There is also diversity in the views of what they believed their writing for the theatre could achieve. None is naïve enough to believe that watching a play would drive the members of the audi-ence out on to the barricades, as famously happened at the start of the Belgian uprising of 1830, when on 25 August the audience attended Auber's *La muette de Portici*, an opera celebrating the rebellion of Naples against the Spanish. It perhaps would not even affect the way they vote at the next election. As David Hare wrote, admittedly in 1991, a decade after the decline in political playwriting: 'The first mistake is to imagine that British writers . . . wish to have any greater influence on the affairs of the nation than they have already. In my

4

experience, they do not wish more than any other citizens to bring
about the fall of governments, or to force laws onto the statute book.'[3]
Richard Seyd of the socialist theatre group Red Ladder said, 'If people
don't think that capitalism is an absurd and damaging way of organising society, then very little that one does is going to change their
minds.'[4] John Arden, in 1966, was similarly modest in his claims for
the effectiveness of his theatre:

> Protest is a sort of futile activity in the theatre. It's highly
> unlikely, for instance that supposing President Johnson and
> Mr McNamara came to see this play [*Serjeant Musgrave's
> Dance*], they would say, 'Oh dear, we've got to pull out of
> Vietnam.' . . . The only thing you can do is to keep on saying
> what you don't like about the society in which you live.[5]

That said, it is clear that even the least radical of this group of writers
would hope that an audience, after seeing one of their plays, will leave
the theatre in some way changed, their political awareness heightened.
As Simon Trussler wrote in 1975: 'Most people now involved in alternative theatre probably hope that their work, however tenuously or in-
directly, will contribute to an awareness of the need for social change,
whether gradual and piecemeal or radical and profound.'[6] Two cen-
turies earlier Lessing had argued in his *Hamburg Dramaturgy*, with
reference to Molière's comedies, that these plays might not cure the
sick but they would at least confirm the healthy in their health.[7]

The aim of this volume is to examine how different writers
have used the stage to create political theatre, making special reference in each case to a significant example of their political playwriting. The nine named playwrights have been selected because they
offer a wide spectrum of writing for theatre which is clearly identified with a left-wing viewpoint. This volume lays no claim to being
a comprehensive survey of all such writing. The following significant
British writers of the period have been omitted, although each of them
may be regarded as a political playwright, at least in some of their
plays: Peter Barnes, Robert Bolt, David Edgar, Barrie Keeffe, David
Mercer, Peter Nichols, Harold Pinter, Alan Plater, Stephen Poliakoff,
David Rudkin, Tom Stoppard, Peter Terson, Charles Wood. It also

means that this study exclusively examines examples taken from the early work of the nine named political writers. Although they all (with the exception of the late McGrath) still write for the theatre, some with continuing success, their revolutionary aspirations have had to be considerably modified in response to political developments of the last two decades. The type of political theatre that this book examines had lost its impetus by the Thatcher era of the mid-1980s, and it is the preceding period of less than thirty years that is our specific concern here. Writers like Wesker and Barker may despair that – yet again – it is one of their early plays that is analysed here, but this does not purport to be a book about their whole careers. Indeed, where a dramatist's *œuvre* has already been frequently subjected to critical examination (e.g. Wesker, Arden, Bond), I have spent less time discussing their other plays than in the case of those writers who have attracted less critical attention (e.g. Griffiths, McGrath).

The main intention of this book is not primarily to analyse the political philosophies of the nine playwrights, nor to undertake the ultimately impossible task of evaluating how effective their work has been in changing public opinion. By examining important examples of their work, we shall not only discover a wide range of strategies of political theatre and offer a theoretical context for their evaluation; we shall also discuss some of the best writing for the British theatre in the latter half of the twentieth century.

It is curious, given the quality of the playwriting and the fact that this was the last time in the development of British drama that a discernible group of like-minded writers can be identified, that there have been so few attempts to consider their work collectively. There have been many excellent studies of British theatre of this period, most recently by Dominic Shellard, as the extensive bibliography testifies. There have also been valuable monographs on single dramatists, and many insightful articles on the British political theatre of the 1970s. However, comprehensive surveys of specifically political theatre are comparatively rare. Catherine Itzin's *Stages in the Revolution* charted the development of political playwriting and political theatre groups up to 1978, and John Bull's *New British Political Dramatists* of 1984 offered interesting studies of the work of Brenton, Hare, Griffiths and

Edgar. The present volume will attempt to build on much of this earlier critical enquiry, with the advantage that it draws together the major British political playwrights of the period and is in a position to discuss their considerable achievements with the advantage of hindsight.

The writers under review represent much of what is best in British theatre since the Second World War, although of course one says this because this is the theatre one knows. Particularly in the theatre, there is a disturbing amount of randomness in the long path from the writing of a script to its acceptance in the theatre by critics and public. One knows of the early failures of writers like Beckett and Pinter, who struggled on to become major influences in contemporary theatre. One can never know of all those who were discouraged by critical abuse and empty theatres to cease writing altogether. I am familiar with the work of John Mackendrick, who ended a promising career by suicide, partly in response to the unsympathetic response to his writing. But I do not and cannot know of all the others who have abandoned attempts to establish themselves as playwrights. As Irving Wardle wrote in his Introduction to *Theatre at Work* of 1967:

> If a play gets on it will not be through the operation of the
> *Zeitgeist* but because some director is drawn to it as a creative
> challenge. If it is foreign to his temperament, or if the
> challenge it presents is one he has already met and has no
> wish to repeat, then the play, through no fault of its own, is
> liable to be ignored... Staff directors... are free to follow any
> eccentrically private course without fear of reprisal; if anyone
> is blamed it will be the playwright. As it happens no glaring
> recent examples of unjustly ignored writers have come to
> light.[8]

Wardle's final assertion is questionable: if they are 'ignored', then of course they will not 'have come to light'. This concern is particularly important when one considers the predominance of male writers in this survey. Again, the fact that Caryl Churchill is the only woman playwright to have a chapter devoted to her no doubt says more about the male prejudice which affects the means of production of a theatre piece than about the intrinsic potential of women as writers for the theatre. There will also be little discussion of plays dealing with the situation of ethnic groups in modern Britain, and, perhaps less disturbingly, nothing on right-wing political playwriting.

This survey then debates those writers who would form the standard choices for an anthology of political theatre in post-war Britain. It will be a predominantly male, white, left-wing group, and this may not sound very adventurous. But perhaps a fresh look at their strengths and weaknesses will make a small contribution towards providing a critical framework within which future work for the theatre may be discussed. Perhaps, as a result, the randomness with which plays at present achieve acclaim will be fractionally diminished.

Part 1: Theory

1 Strategies of political theatre: a theoretical overview

It is the late 1960s in Britain. The heroism and suffering of the Second World War are now more than two decades away. Although victorious, the nation has had to endure severe austerity to recover from the cost of the war. It is now returning to prosperity: between 1951 and 1964 industrial production increased by 40 per cent, there were four times as many cars on the roads and thirteen times more television sets in the home. Earnings increased by 110 per cent, and the average standard of living by 30 per cent[1]. By the end of the fifties Prime Minister Harold Macmillan could justifiably claim: 'Most of our people have never had it so good.'

Benefiting from this new-found wealth, the youth of Britain, who had not lived through a time of war, began to assert themselves. Britain, which had always been regarded by America and Continental Europe as the home of tradition and conservative values, now became the home of the outrageous mini-skirted fashion of Mary Quant and Carnaby Street and of the deafening rock music of the Beatles and the Rolling Stones. The ending of conscription in 1960 meant that young men had greater freedom and more disposable income than ever before, the widespread availability of the contraceptive pill encouraged sexual experimentation, and the common acceptability of hallucinogenic drugs allowed the young to explore different states of consciousness.

Surprisingly, though, this did not lead to a society of mindless pleasure-seekers. The so-called 'hippy' youth, while unproductive in economic terms, were highly idealistic. Despite shocking their elders with their outlandish appearance of long hair and flowing clothes, and with their indulgence in sex and drugs, they adopted a high moral stance, particularly in their steadfast opposition to violence and intolerance, most notably manifest in their protests against the United States's war against North Vietnam.

There were also many young people who rejected the capitalism that had brought them the freedom and leisure to question it. Inspired by a revolutionary philosophy, loosely based on the ideas of Karl Marx and Mao Tse-tung, young intellectuals especially sought not only to oppose war but also to attempt to overthrow the capitalist system which they blamed for warfare. Against a background of consensual politics in Britain, in which Conservatives maintained the welfare state and the Labour Party gave its blessing to a mixed economy, there were at first the disillusioned mutterings of the so-called 'angry young men', to be closely followed by the much more agitational views of revolutionary young socialists. On the Continent this agitation erupted in the student riots of 1968, where, particularly in Paris, there were daily running battles between students and police, public buildings were occupied, and the French government, if not brought to its knees, was at least brought to a standstill. Across Europe youth was in revolt, most dramatically in Czechoslovakia, where the liberalizing measures of the so-called 'Prague Spring' were suppressed by Soviet intervention. In the West there was much talk of revolution but little application of revolutionary method, many calls for solidarity with the proletariat but little effort to implement it. So when the Paris students started drifting off for their summer vacation, the so-called *événements* passed into history, but not before they had inspired a generation of international intellectuals. The British version of the 1968 upheavals was suitably restrained: voluble protests against the Vietnam War, fulfilling Lady Bracknell's seemingly preposterous fears of rioting in Grosvenor Square, and the new sport of 'sit-ins', the occupation by students of university buildings in order to force democratic concessions from university authorities. Only in Northern Ireland, where Britain was, as Irish nationalists asserted, engaged in its last colonial conflict, did the street protests of 1968 lead to serious violence and the exposure of a political problem that at the time of writing has still not been fully resolved.

It was the late 1960s in Britain, and young university-educated writers were looking for a means to express their own concerns about a world that was engaged in fundamentally re-assessing itself. Some, like Howard Brenton, had personally witnessed the 1968 student uprising in Paris. All were now eager at least to rattle the gates protecting the complacent British Establishment and to attack a capitalist system that had been deliberately undermining the Labour Party's efforts to create a fairer society. The demand for change grew more urgent when a Conservative government was returned to power in 1970, a government that introduced internment into Northern Ireland and was accused of sanctioning torture of terrorist suspects, and a government that collapsed after a confrontation with the miners in the so-called 'winter of discontent' of 1973 to 1974. In the United States four student protesters against the Vietnam War were shot by the National Guard in 1970, the War itself started to run out of control as it spilt over into Cambodia and Laos, CIA activity in South America bolstered corrupt regimes and led to the overthrow of the Marxist president of Chile in 1973, and President Nixon became more and more embroiled in mounting evidence of deliberate 'dirty tricks' in the Watergate Affair. The West appeared violent, oppressive and deceitful, and while Soviet Russia hardly offered a model to aspire to, there were smaller nations that showed how well they could function on Marxist principles: Cuba, Chile (for an all too brief period), Czechoslovakia (for an even briefer period), and – the old enemy – North Vietnam, which, tiny as it was, was to inflict defeat on the colossal superpower of the United States.

Given the sense of a changing world and the apparently very real possibility of restructuring society along socialist lines, it was predictable that these writers would turn to the most public and most immediate forum for expressing their concerns and aspirations, that of live theatre. It was a particularly exciting time for the theatre, since the powers of censorship by the Lord Chamberlain had been abolished in 1968, and freedom of expression on stage could now match the new liberties being explored by society at large. Only: what style should they write in, what theatrical strategy should they adopt?

One possibility was to follow the popular artistic style practised in Communist countries, that of socialist realism. For British writers this strategy was never seriously in contention. For one thing, it depended on a consensus in the audience that the Revolution had already been achieved, that socialism and all its works were unquestionably good, and capitalism not only evil but in terminal decline. The primary purpose of socialist realist drama was to offer optimistic reassurance that the world was constantly improving, thanks to socialism. In fact, 'realism' was a crass misnomer, since the plots and character depictions were highly idealized. It was a mode that stimulated no debate, explored no contradictions. Brecht summed up the inadequacy of the style as follows: 'The passion [which] actors showed when their stage-wives were unfaithful is now shown by them when the stage-capitalist reduces wages. The public is no longer in suspense whether Romeo gets Juliet but whether the proletariat gets the power.'[2] One might add that there is in fact more suspense in Shakespeare, since it is a forgone conclusion that in socialist realism the proletariat will definitely get the power; indeed any play predicting a different outcome would have been banned in Soviet Russia.

A further well-tried strategy was that of agit-prop, abbreviated from 'agitation propaganda'. This favourite mode of socialist groups, especially in Russia and Germany in the 1920s, presented simple stories, performed by cartoon-like characters, and often incorporated songs. Again, there was no possibility of exploring contradictions or introducing subtleties. Figures were stereotyped and instantly recognizable: the capitalist with the top hat, the general with colossal epaulettes and sword. These pieces functioned well enough when performed to sympathetic audiences, helping to reinforce their socialist convictions. It was a style usually adopted by many left-wing theatre groups, CAST (Cartoon Archetypical Slogan Theatre) being the first of many, followed by Red Ladder, Belt and Braces and others, but not common amongst playwrights who wanted to explore political situations in greater depth. David Edgar adopted something of the style for his occasional pieces like *A Fart for Europe*, written with Howard Brenton about the Common Market in 1973, and *Dick Deterred*, a 1974 parody of Shakespeare's *Richard III* about Nixon, although he denounced the use of agit-prop as a serious mode of political debate, arguing that, since all major questions had been settled in advance, 'agitprop caricature is a fundamentally elitist device'.[3] As we shall see, John McGrath exploited the style for the specific use of his community work in the Highlands.

For deeper and more general discussion of political issues, however, writers turned to conventional modes of Western theatrical discourse. These divide broadly into two strands, what one might call the reflectionist and the interventionist. The reflectionist tradition asserts that the main function of art and indeed theatre is to hold up a mirror to nature and to reflect reality as accurately as possible, what Aristotle called 'the imitation (*mimesis*) of an action'. The interventionist mode asserts that, even if it were possible to reflect reality accurately, the undertaking is futile, since it is the task of the artist and playwright to interpret reality and to challenge our perception of it. As Brecht put it in his opposition between 'dramatic' and 'epic' theatre, the reflectionist allows us to say, 'Yes, that is the way things are'; the interventionist to say, 'I had never seen it in that way before.' Expressed like this, it becomes clear that it is possible for both statements to be made, and indeed it will be the contention of most interventionist writers that they are the true realists, because their insights reveal things as they truly are rather than as they appear to be.

The most extreme form of reflectionist theatre is naturalism, the attempt to represent the external world as accurately as possible. Only in the provocative proposal of Marcel Duchamp to erect a proscenium arch over the entrance to a Metro station in Paris might one achieve exact verisimilitude (and any such project would, ironically, no doubt appear to the public as avant-garde artifice rather than an attempt at authenticity). Once one enters the theatre, however, exact imitation is rendered impossible. The action is framed, not only physically by the limits of architectural space, usually by a proscenium arch, but also by the framing of the plot, which must begin at some point and end at another. The audience knows that the actors are not the people they represent, and the performers speak more loudly than in real life and almost invariably wait for their interlocutor to finish before speaking themselves. The action is lit from several hidden sources, and the actors pretend that beyond the stage is a real world from which they step, when the audience knows full well that it is in fact the backstage jumble of old scenery and props. Audience

and performers join in a game, the rules of which require that disbe-
lief is suspended. To his dismay, when Stanislavsky brought an actual peasant woman on to the stage in his production of *The Seagull*,
she undermined the naturalism of the piece, because her genuineness
drew attention to the artificiality of the theatrical conventions. It is
the same problem when directors use real animals and young children in their productions: their natural and unpredictable behaviour
is mesmerizing, compared with the well-rehearsed routines of the
adult humans. Animals and children have not learnt how to play the
same game as audience and performers. Paradoxically, naturalist theatre, which strives to come closest to reality, is justifiably termed the
theatre of illusion. Far from being real, it is merely the form of theatre
where one is least aware of its unreality.

For the purposes of political theatre, naturalism is a theatrical
style unsuited to questioning the world about us. By purporting to
present an exact copy of the world, it is not only performing a refined
conjuring trick; it is also necessarily limiting itself to individual and
observable phenomena, without the possibility of analysis or gener-
alization. As the Marxist critic Georg Lukács argued, naturalism can
only 'describe', whereas the political writer seeks to 'narrate', that
is, not merely to record events but to establish the causal connections
between events. To reproduce reality rather than to examine causes
underlying the surface excludes the possibility of the kind of analysis
that might promote fundamental social change. As Brecht said: 'The
individual feelings, insights and impulses of the chief characters are
forced on us, and so we learn nothing more about society than we can
get from the setting.'[4] In this way, naturalism, however distressing
the subject with which it may deal, leads to an acceptance of existing
circumstances.

Predictably, none of the political playwrights under discussion
attempted thoroughgoing naturalism. While some of them belonged
to the reflectionist strain, they all wished to go beyond surface representation, to be realists rather than naturalists. This is similar to
the distinction made by the Italian philosopher, Benedetto Croce, at
the beginning of the twentieth century between the chronicler, who
merely reports events, and the historian, who emphasizes what is

significant in order to discover the connection between events. Terry Eagleton indicated the importance of such coherent narrative for the political writer, for the realist 'penetrates through the accidental phenomena of social life to disclose the essences or essentials of a condition, selecting and combining them into a form and fleshing them out in concrete existence'.[5] John Berger differentiated between naturalism and realism thus: 'a distinction between a submissive worship of events just because they occur, and the confident inclusion of them within a personally constructed but objectively truthful world view'.[6] John Arden summed it up by saying: 'I draw a clear distinction, you see, between realism and naturalism. The latter means a representation of the surface of life, the former a presentation of the life itself.'[7]

Even the most realistic writers, like Wesker and Griffiths, select their material carefully. The narration of events is organized into a dramatic framework, with the plot structure following the conventional scheme of exposition, development and dénouement. The dialogue, while approaching authenticity, is written not so much to record actual speech as to offer the opportunity to debate ideas. The characters are not random individuals but, while remaining believable, operate as representatives of social types. There are several advantages to this strategy. First, it allows a measure of political analysis while having all the appeal of a story that engages us emotionally. It is, in the English-speaking theatre at least, a congenial and popular form, for, as Michael Billington has said: 'if you look at drama over the past 100 years you will find that most of the greatest writers have, in spite of constant digressions, worked inside the naturalistic mode'[8] (by which we may understand 'realistic mode', as here defined).

Secondly, by portraying recognizable characters on stage in acceptably realistic situations, the audience has the opportunity to compare their experience with that portrayed in the play. In the realistic mode we are able to see characters sufficiently like us to be able to consider their behaviour in terms of predictability.

However, the interventionist writers feel that this is not in itself sufficient. To begin with, there is the question of the reality one is attempting to reflect. Modern physics has disposed of the solid ground of a material universe and replaced it with a model of a universe in constant flux. Sociology has shown how much individuals are products of social forces. Psychology makes us aware of the levels of mediation that affect our perception of the outside world. The individual writer's perception of reality must of necessity be subjective. Any attempt to achieve objectivity effectively means accepting an established consensual view of the world about us, precisely what the political playwright wishes to challenge. So the modernist willingly embraces and acknowledges a biased non-objective viewpoint, and employs a form that challenges not only how the world is ordered, as realism does, but challenges our perception of the world itself: 'Objectivist representations disregard the subjective moment, the will of the representer who aims at the constant productive alteration of the conditions and circumstances given to him.'[9]

The words are Brecht's, the major modernist to use interventionist techniques in his theatre to political ends. Brecht's methods are now so well known that a brief summary will here suffice. As far as his characters were concerned, they were to be viewed not as unchanging and circumscribed entities but as contradictory, alterable beings, as products of social forces, implying that, if their circumstances were to change, then they too would change. The strategy of his theatre was therefore not to induce empathy with the central characters so much as to judge their behaviour within the social context. To this end he urged actors to develop an acting style critical of the role they were playing, employing so-called *Verfremdung* or 'distanciation'.

His plots were structured in such a way as to avoid the sense of inevitability that accompanies traditional linear construction. This so-called 'epic' technique told the story in leaps rather than in seamless sequential narrative, the acid test being whether it is possible within the play to change the order of many of the scenes without disrupting the narrative. The strategy here is again to alert the spectator that the events that are unfolding are not inevitable but that there are or were alternative courses of action. The action is therefore often set in the past or in an exotic, possibly fabulous location, so that the spectator may more easily contemplate events at a distance. The outcome of these events is also often revealed in advance so that the spectator may forgo suspense about the ending to focus attention on the way the plot develops.

Despite some lingering prejudice about the gloomily Teutonic quality of Brecht's work, his example in fact reawakened the possibility of the theatre being truly theatrical. No longer limited by the attempt to imitate reality, playwrights were once again able to create plays that are vigorously theatrical, exploiting the visual quality of 'gestic' action, employing songs and poetic expression, using the stage to represent exotic locations, above all rediscovering the 'fun' (*Spass*) of the theatrical event.

The primary intention of what Brecht himself called his 'pedagogy' was not to reflect reality but to challenge it: 'Reality has to be altered by being turned into art so that it can be seen as alterable and treated as such.'[10] By attempting to show reality in a new and truer light, he could claim to be a true realist. All his methods are directed towards challenging our perception of reality and towards renegotiating the function of theatre, as he saw it. Traditional so-called 'Aristotelian' theatre allegedly portrays conflicts on stage and allows them to be resolved there. The spectators respond passively, their emotions are exhausted. In Brecht's non-Aristotelian theatre the spectators are encouraged to judge and make choices, so that they enter into a critical dialogue with the stage action. Their response is active, their emotions are aroused. For this reason, Brecht was convinced that his methods were the most appropriate to generating political awareness.

The two opposing camps of the reflectionists and the interventionists, of the realists and the modernists, or in Brechtian terms, 'dramatic' and 'epic' theatre, have repeatedly argued the merits of their respective positions, never more intensely than in the famous Lukács–Brecht debate of the 1930s.[11] There were four major areas of dissent.

First, Lukács attacked modernism because of its subjectivity. If the writer perceived and responded to reality as an isolated individual, he argued, then it was impossible to offer political insights, since these must depend on a consensus. Instead, the realist offers an image of reality in which the opposition of appearance and essence, of the individual case and the general rule, of the immediacy of the senses and abstract conceptualisation etc. is resolved. The immediate effect of the work of art is to dissolve the oppositional elements into a spontaneous whole so that they can form an inseparable unity for the reader.[12]

By rejecting the attempt to record the 'appearance' (everyday reality) and insisting instead on depicting a subjectively perceived 'essence' (underlying reality), the modernist was divorcing art from the real sphere in which political action could take place.

The modernist counter-argument (an argument that has become even more emphatic in our present post-modernist age) is that there is no longer any objective reality to be reproduced, and that modernist writers are simply being more honest in acknowledging the subjectivity of their response. As Fredric Jameson puts it:

Realism, by suggesting that representation is possible, and by encouraging an aesthetic of mimesis or imitation, tends to perpetuate a preconceived notion of some external reality to be imitated, and indeed to foster a belief in the existence of some common-sense, everyday, ordinary shared secular reality in the first place.[13]

Furthermore, while in many manifestations of modernism, e.g. Expressionism, it is true that the subjectivity of the writer led to an inward-turning apolitical stance, this need not be the case. Brecht's perception of reality may have been subjective and he may have shared with other modernists a sense of despair at the sorry state of the world about him, but his Marxist convictions offered him a non-personal, objective and scientifically reasoned solution. Brecht was able to employ modernist techniques without embracing their defeatist ideology: 'It is precisely socialist writers who are able to learn highly developed technical elements from these documents of despair. They see the way out.'[14]

As is apparent from the quotation from Lukács above, the second claim for realism was that it offered a complete and coherent account of reality, a necessary prerequisite for political action.

Modernism, on the other hand, presented a fragmented vision of reality, one that failed to depict a clear chain of causality. Lukács was particularly critical of montage, which he condemned as the 'technique of juxtaposing heterogeneous, unrelated pieces of reality torn from their context'.[15]

Brecht countered that it was an ahistorical and reactionary viewpoint to insist on continuing to write within the tradition of nineteenth-century realism, that it was essential to embrace new forms and to adapt them to political ends, in fact, to develop a theatre 'for the scientific age'. In a memorable image, Brecht stated: 'If you hit a car with a coachman's whip, it won't get it going.'[16] As has been argued, it is precisely the disruption of the even flow of scenes that contains the political message that there is no inevitable process of cause and effect but that reality offers alternatives at each juncture.

The third objection Lukács made to modernism was that it was not a popular form. The masses accepted realism, whereas modernism remained unintelligible to the majority: 'the broad mass of the people can learn nothing from avant-garde literature'.[17] This assertion is borne out by daily observation. One has only, for example, to consider how the tabloid press comments on modern art to recognize that the average British citizen has little time for aesthetic experimentation. Despite wishing to influence popular thinking, playwrights like Bond and Barker have had great difficulty in being understood let alone well received by anything other than an intellectual minority.

The modernists might reply, as Brecht did, that once again new forms are needed, but that these need not present difficulties to the masses. Indeed, he would claim that by drawing on popular traditions both within Europe and in the East, and by basing a theatre on the commonplace interaction surrounding a street accident, he was offering a type of performance that was more natural and accessible than the familiar but inauthentic style of conventional realism. As John Berger argues:

> It is claimed that the style of naturalism (called realism) is the most accessible to the masses because it is nearest to natural appearances. This claim ignores most of what we now know

about the process of perception, but even more obviously it is belied by child art, folk art, and by the ease with which a mass adult urban population learns to read highly formalized cartoons, caricatures, posters, etc.[18]

To this list one might now add popular music videos and television commercials, very popular forms that make extremely sophisticated use of montage.

Finally, the major objection to modernism is that raised most eloquently by John Peter in his fine and provocative work *Vladimir's Carrot*. In essence his argument is as follows: Beckett may create stunning stage metaphors of the world, but those metaphors are not verifiable in the way that, say, the characters and incidents of Ibsen's realistic plays are, despite over a century's distance from them. We cannot reasonably be asked to comment on the veracity of the behaviour of characters who spend their lives confined to dustbins or are buried immovably in a pile of sand. One either accepts Beckett's vision or one doesn't. It is, to use John Peter's expression, 'a perlocutionary act', an assertion that is not open to debate. As such, it is dangerously irrational, fascistic even, because we are unable to question the image set before us:

> Both [*Waiting for Godot*] and the 'perlocutionary act'...
> expect and depend on, complete and unreserved acceptance;
> they both ask for a suspension of what Popper calls 'the
> critical powers of man'. Such a reaction is contrary to
> everything we have come to understand by the experience of
> art. Art of any kind is, or we think it is, the creation of other
> worlds with which we can have a dialogue. And if we are
> engaged in a dialogue we can neither suspend judgement nor
> simply submit, not even in delighted recognition or a feeling
> of identity.[19]

In Brecht's case, John Peter argues, by writing so-called 'parable plays' he created artificial worlds where the world of work, far from being the focus, is merely a theatrical setting for the imagined events of the play:

The make-believe settings often undermine Brecht's intentions, precisely because his plays have such a powerful social and political drive... *The Good Person of Setzuan* is weakened by its lack of a sense of community. People appear to know each other and they tell us what their family ties are; but Setzuan never comes across as a village where life has its ways and people have their habits and social functions. The population is no more than a backdrop, and this fatally weakens the play's argument which is about the survival or otherwise of personal integrity in a community founded on greed.[20]

In this sense, Brecht, as a modernist, is profoundly apolitical.

Just as it is a simplification to assert that in realistic theatre the audience remains totally passive and does not engage intellectually and critically in the events of the play, so it is simply not true that audiences do not question the validity of modernist images. Beckett's visions of existential despair provoke the spectator into searching for a reason to continue living. Even at his most didactic, Brecht challenged the audience to find their own answers to the contradictions revealed in his plays.

There are many valid theatrical strategies for stimulating political debate, and a whole range of them have been used in British political theatre. It is therefore worth recalling David Edgar's words:

> Bertolt Brecht once remarked that the 'proof of the pudding was in the eating,' a comment that might appear blindingly obvious until one observes that the major preoccupations of many socialist theatre workers are with the origins of the recipe, the cleanliness of the spoons, the decision-making methods employed by the chefs, and the address of the restaurant.[21]

Thus, while it is convenient and illuminating to discuss reflectionist and interventionist strains as polar opposites (and the table on p. 24 and the way this volume is arranged imply precisely that), in practice playwrights will draw on elements from both modes: the realist may accord symbolic meaning to quite realistic situations; the

Reflectionist/Interventionist: a comparative table

Reflectionist	Interventionist
Realism	Modernism
Reflection of reality	Analysis of reality
Objective	Subjective
Recognizable world	Autonomous world
Complete, rounded	Fragmented, open-ended
Usually set in present	Often set in past
Scenes linked sequentially	Montage ('epic' structure)
Human nature unalterable	Human behaviour alterable
Actions derived from character	Character derived from actions
Empathy	Distance
Psychology	Social forces
Set design imitates real world	Set design consciously theatrical
Limited to everyday behaviour and language	Uses many theatrical elements (songs, poetry, etc.)
Lays claim to being popular	Lays claim to being popular
Change urged by considering world as it is	Change urged by positing alternatives

modernist may present action and dialogue that could be taken from everyday life. It would be more appropriate to think of the two strains as the ends of a spectrum rather than as mutually exclusive categories.

At one end of the spectrum, then, we have the reflectionist strain of realism; at the other the interventionist strain of modernism. The former appealed to some British political playwrights of the 1970s because it allowed them to portray a familiar world where injustice could be easily recognized. The latter appealed to others because it seemed to offer greater possibilities of analysing the causes of this injustice. As it happens, there had been two British models of political playwriting, who had over a decade earlier been working in the two differing modes: Arnold Wesker and John Arden. They offer convenient paradigms for the varying strategies of the political playwrights we shall be considering.

Part 2: Two model strategies

2 The 'reflectionist' strategy: 'kitchen sink' realism in Arnold Wesker's *Roots* (1959)

> Optimism in art is the result not of happy endings and joyful
> exclamations but of the recognition of truths... whether the
> truth is a sad one or not.[1]

In 1959 two major political plays were performed, Wesker's *Roots*
and Arden's *Serjeant Musgrave's Dance*. Both playwrights were young
men, not yet out of their twenties. Both had enjoyed moderate
successes the previous year with, respectively, *Chicken Soup with
Barley* and *Live Like Pigs*. Above all, both writers, informed by a socialist viewpoint, expressed a profound dissatisfaction with the society around them, earning them the journalistic tag 'Angry Young
Men'. However, their strategies for communicating 'the recognition
of truths' to an audience differed profoundly. While, as we shall
see, Arden explored new forms, Wesker, like the other notorious
'angry young man', John Osborne, continued to write in a conventionally realistic mode, familiar to London theatre-goers from the
plays of Terence Rattigan and Noel Coward. Wesker retained a formal act structure with emphatic endings, realistically detailed settings, realistic-sounding dialogue and rounded characters. The major
change was to place all this in a lower-working-class setting, with all
its shabby detail, giving him the other journalistic sobriquet 'kitchen-
sink realist'. However, while *Roots* does indeed have its kitchen sink,
there is more to the play than an attempt to imitate the real life of the
Norfolk people it depicts.

In common with John Osborne, Arnold Wesker tends to be regarded as a writer who made an important impact in the 1950s, but
who has now disappeared from the theatrical scene. Indeed, as far

back as 1970, Harold Hobson announced Wesker's retirement from the theatre, while Wesker was 'in the middle of rehearsing *The Friends'*.[2] After the rapturous reception of *Roots* in 1959 ('the most promising and exciting young dramatist to come into the British theatre since the end of the war'),[3] British critics and theatre managements have tended to dismiss Wesker's later work and to revise their assessment of his early work in the light of their current disapproval. This has no doubt been due to what Wesker has to say and to how he says it, both to his ideology and to his theatrical style, each of which may now appear outmoded.

Certainly, his political thinking lacks the energy and focus of those playwrights who ousted him in popular estimation. 'It seems to me that what I've always been is a simple, old-fashioned humanist',[4] declared Wesker in an interview in *Theatre Quarterly* in 1977. Regrettably, 'simple, old-fashioned humanism' is no longer thought to be exciting or – to use an apt word – dramatic. Wesker is aware of 'the dead weight of a feeling of failure',[5] despite the fact that his credentials as a political writer are impressive. Unlike several middle-class 'revolutionary' playwrights, he has an authentic working-class background. He was born in 1932 into a poor Jewish family in London's East End. He has been incarcerated for his convictions, having been sentenced to a month's imprisonment in 1961 for his involvement in a demonstration by the Committee of 100 against nuclear weapons. In attempting to establish a link between the arts and the Trades Union movement by founding Centre 42, he made a genuine effort to make access to the arts more democratic. He has repeatedly taken up his pen to confront issues as diverse as the threat to university drama departments, apartheid in South Africa, military intervention in the Falklands or the terrorist campaign in Northern Ireland. His liberal reformism has never been voguish, and, arguably because of this, his contribution to the development of political drama in Britain has been frequently undervalued. For most critics, Wesker's standing as a play-wright is now lower than that of Osborne, whose acerbic wit seems more attractive than Wesker's gentle humanity. Jimmy Porter did not offer any clearly defined ideology, but his verbal tirades expressed an anger and frustration that was invigorating. Hence, no doubt, the place which *Look Back in Anger* (1956), despite all its shortcomings, has been accorded in the history of British post-war theatre. That Wesker has something at least as valid if not as incendiary to say will become evident.

As for the style of his pieces, Wesker has suffered on the one hand for supposedly being too limited by 'kitchen-sink' naturalism and, on the other, castigated for the unreal lyricism of a piece like *The Four Seasons* (1965). The conventional three-act structure of the plays of *The Trilogy* (1958–60) is regarded as unadventurous, the kaleidoscopic simultaneous staging of *The Journalists* (1975) as unwieldy, the mixing of styles in *The Wedding Feast* (1974) as unacceptable. Perhaps his eclecticism is another cause of his unpopularity: there will never be a 'Weskeresque' situation or 'Weskerian' dialogue. Moreover, Wesker is never afraid to debate politics and philosophy on stage, and so frequently attracts the stigma of being 'didactic'. The British public has an aversion to hearing ethical and political pronouncements made on stage. Shaw is accepted as being a great playwright *despite* his willingness openly to discuss social issues in his dialogue. Continental dramatists who debate political issues have often had a hard time finding acceptance in the British theatre. So, for example, Brecht has for many years been thought worthy but boring, and Peter Weiss's *Marat/Sade* (1964) succeeded largely because Peter Brook managed to obscure the central debate about revolutionary change with his spectacular work on the lunatic asylum setting. As Wesker himself said: 'There is a quality in my writing which makes it very un-English and which comes from my Jewish–European background.'[6]

It is certainly true that Wesker has enjoyed considerable popularity abroad: *The Friends* (1970), *The Wedding Feast* (1974) and *The Merchant* (1976) were all premiered in Stockholm, *The Journalists* was given its first professional performance in Germany in 1977, and *Mothers* (1982) was staged for the first time in Japan.

To set Wesker in the context of post-war developments in political playwriting, we shall be paying particular attention to what is still the best known of Wesker's pieces, *Roots*. In doing so, there is no implication that such an early work is representative of the whole range of Wesker's *œuvre*. As he once complained: '... I get very distressed and impatient when journalists come to regard me only as the person who has written the *Trilogy* and *The Kitchen*.'[7] Nevertheless, like it or not, Wesker is best remembered for *Roots*, which now has often the dubious distinction of regularly being a schools examination text. Moreover, this play and the two accompanying pieces which form 'The Trilogy', *Chicken Soup with Barley* and *I'm Talking About Jerusalem* (1960), are especially suited to begin our investigation into the strategies of political theatre.

It is no accident that a writer who favoured the more popular mode of realism should be one who was committed to involving working people in his theatre. In 1960 Wesker pioneered the first major attempt since the Second World War to involve the British working classes more fully in the cultural life enjoyed by the more expensively educated. Together with a number of left-wing artists and writers, he approached the British Trades Union movement with the proposal that they should 'offer [their] talents' to the working classes by inviting the Trades Union Congress (TUC) to support 'an attempt to enable works of art to be communicated to as many people as possible – especially those to whom the experience of art was unfamiliar'.[8] The response of the TUC executive was lukewarm, since they considered that their prime task was concerned with the working conditions and rights of their members rather than with cultural matters. Nevertheless, at the annual conference the following resolution was passed unanimously:

> Congress recognized the importance of the arts in the life of the community, especially now when many unions are securing a shorter working week and greater leisure for their members. It notes that the trade union movement has participated to only a small extent in the direct promotion of plays, films, music, literature and other forms of expression, including those of value to its beliefs and principles. Congress considers that much more could be done, and accordingly requests the General Council to conduct a special examination and to make proposals to future Congress to ensure a greater participation by the trade union movement in all cultural activities.[9]

This resolution was number 42 on the TUC conference agenda, the idea of Centre 42 was born, and Wesker was elected its director.

What followed was a sad echo of the words of Piscator in his *Political Theatre* of 1929: 'Like a thread running through this book and through the story of my ventures is the recognition that the proletariat, for whatever reason, is too weak to maintain its own theatre.'[10] Despite a lack of direct financial support from the TUC, Wesker and his fellow artists decided to press ahead with Centre 42 in the hope that they might 'slowly earn the confidence of the labour movement'.[11] Ironically, however, by instead becoming dependent on the money of private industry and wealthy individuals, Centre 42, like the Piscatorbühne before it, was caught in the anomaly that a would-be socialist enterprise had to depend on capitalist funding. In 1961 Centre 42 organized a festival in Wellingborough and, the following year, in six different towns but ran up considerable debts. Between 1962 and 1968 enough money was raised to acquire and convert an old Victorian engine-shed in London, the Round House, but this rapidly became a venue for avant-garde work, which rarely could have been said to have any relevance to the lives of the working classes. Disillusioned, Wesker in 1970 persuaded Centre 42 to dissolve itself.

The sigh of relief at the collapse of Centre 42 was audible not only where one might expect to hear it, on the breaths of the right wing, but also as a loud exhalation from those who stood further to the left of Wesker. John McGrath, originally sympathetic to the enterprise, branded Wesker 'the laureate of Wilsonian politics', and wrote in 1970:

> The Trade Unions have failed to provide enough money to keep the local Centre 42 'festivals' going, and the people of Wellingborough are now mercifully free to drink their pints without hectoring folk singers thrusting a supposedly superior form of culture in their faces. Wesker's crusade for Centre 42 to bring 'culture' as he understood it – Stravinsky, Ewan McColl, Royal Court plays, his own even – 'to' the working class rests on a completely false analysis. The idea, which he shares with Roger Planchon in France, that culture is a

product to be sold by culturally-conscious (therefore superior) artists and intellectuals to culturally-starved (therefore inferior) workers, is based on a bourgeois concept of culture.[12]

Now it is undoubtedly true that Wesker betrays anger about the limited vision and cultural deprivation of the uneducated. In a central speech in the first play that Wesker wrote, *The Kitchen* (1959), Paul describes his disillusion about his bus-driver neighbour: despite having been supported by Paul in his strike action, he rounds on Paul for having held up the traffic with a march against nuclear weapons: 'Like an animal he looked.'[13] The prominence given to him in *The Kitchen* implies that this bus-driver's conduct is not atypical of the British worker. The same contempt is revealed in Ada's lines in *Chicken Soup with Barley*, when she dismisses office-girls as 'lipsticked, giggling morons' and British soldiers as men who 'wanted to get away from their wives in order to behave like animals'.[14] In the same play Ronnie's view of kitchen staff is equally belittling: 'people terrified of old age, hoping for the football pools to come home'.[15] Similarly, the conscripts of *Chips with Everything* (itself a condescending title) are described as 'yobs, good-natured yobs'.[16] In *I'm Talking About Jerusalem* Dave characterizes factory-workers as follows: 'Morning after morning they've come in with a cold hatred in their eyes, brutalized! All their humanity gone. These you call men?'[17] *Roots*, too, devotes much of its action and dialogue to revealing the emptiness of the lives of the Bryant family: 'little amazes them ... They show no affection for each other', they are 'all too bored', they are 'dead'.[18] Wesker freely admits that he shares the contempt of his characters for what he has come to describe as the 'lilliputian mentality': speaking about his drama *The Journalists*, he said:

> I inherited from my parents a contempt for a certain kind of mentality which is petty, lumpen, one that diminishes or minimalizes. I've encountered it in my Air Force experience, in work, in my schooldays – and especially with journalists. And so it seemed to me that journalism was an area in which I could explore this lilliputian mentality.[19]

What is notable here is that the 'lilliputian mentality' is asserted to be as prevalent amongst the better educated as amongst the less articulate working classes. It is found especially in the word-mongers of journalism, which, after all, was based on Wesker's observations at *The Sunday Times* and not in the offices of *The Sun* or *The Star*. Any apparent contempt towards the proletariat shown by Wesker in his early plays therefore results from his very bleak view of humanity as a whole ('the recognition of truths... whether the truth is a sad one or not');[20] and it just so happened that the section of humanity he chose to depict in his early plays was the one he knew best – the working class.

In addition, while criticizing the small-minded, he retains a belief in their potential for growth and change. As Sarah says in *Chicken Soup with Barley*: 'A man *can* be beautiful. I hate ugly people.'[21] This is the balance Wesker offers: the despising of the ugliness of humanity coupled with the faith that they can be transformed. So, although *The Trilogy* shows the defeat of socialist ideals in post-war Britain, Wesker insists that his plays are not pessimistic but about survival. Sarah holds on to her belief in social change ('if you don't care you'll die'),[22] and, despite the failure of Dave and Ada's attempt at rural self-sufficiency in *I'm Talking About Jerusalem*, Ronnie will not allow Dave to disown his former vision entirely: '[Visions] *do* work! And even if they don't work then for God's sake let's try and behave as though they do – or else nothing will work.'[23] In *Roots*, it is the drunken and incontinent Stan Mann, just before he dies ignobly in a ditch, who utters one of the most valuable aspirations of the play, the hope that the young will be able to take control of their own lives: 'Them young 'uns is all right though. Long as they don't let no one fool them, long as they think it out theirselves.'[24] Finally, Beatie, while defeated by both her family's complacency and Ronnie's betrayal, achieves a sort of epiphany in her attainment of independent articulacy.

Is not this precisely the kind of elitism that John McGrath jeered at? Are Ronnie and Beatie not 'enlightened' purveyors of highbrow culture that will somehow redeem the ignorant workers and peasant-folk, lifting them from their sordid misery to the strains of Bizet's *L'Arlésienne*? Are Wesker's plays in fact a throwback to the dramas of the German naturalist Gerhart Hauptmann, in which the failure of the protagonist to transform the world about him is seen as due not to his inadequacies but to those of the people he wished to redeem?

It might seem all very likely, especially given the autobiographical nature of most of Wesker's early work ('I've been very personal in so much work.')[25] Educated away from his humble beginnings in the East End, he has often been regarded as very abrasive ('There's something about me that attracts... hostility. It's been recurrent through my life.')[26] It might therefore be inferred that, isolated by hostility, he has adopted an arrogant and contemptuous attitude to the class that he has left behind, impatient perhaps that so few have followed his own path of escape from manual labour and the slums. But such an assessment would suppose that Wesker, angry with others, is pleased with himself. That this is not the case is shown in his treatment of the figure who most closely represents himself, Ronnie (whose name – Ronald – as Hayman has noted, is an anagram of Arnold.)[27]

To illustrate this, let us examine a trivial but curious anomaly in *Chicken Soup with Barley*. In the final scene Ronnie speaks of 'Dave and Ada in the Cotswolds',[28] but we know from *I'm Talking About Jerusalem*, *Roots* and indeed from Act Two of *Chicken Soup with Barley* that they have settled in the Fens – a 'mistake' that John Russell Taylor pounces on in *Anger and After*.[29] Now, it may be that Wesker has simply been careless, although there is a world of difference between the Norfolk Fens and the Cotswolds, but Wesker is not a careless writer. *The Friends* and *The Old Ones* (1972) were rewritten five times each, and *Their Very Own and Golden City* (1966) was released only after nine drafts. For each song in his plays, Wesker appends the appropriate melody, and in *Chicken Soup with Barley* he specifies the exact holding of cards and sequence of play for the game of solo in the final scene. It seems unlikely that such a careful writer had failed to notice that Ronnie contradicts himself within only two scenes.

Of course Ronnie has not forgotten that his sister and brother-in-law are settled in Norfolk, but he is bitterly disillusioned in the final scene of *Chicken Soup with Barley*. He is wanting to score points, and so, instead of acknowledging the effort and sacrifice made by Dave and Ada in attempting to make a living in the Fens, he sneers at their supposed cosy country idyll by referring to the Cotswolds, a prosperous and very much more congenial rural setting than where they are actually living.

This is a trivial point, but it illustrates well why, in part, Wesker has suffered such critical opprobrium. There has been a tendency to assert, contrary to the evidence, that he has done something or failed to do something and then to castigate him for this. This must be borne in mind when considering a play like *Roots*.

Roots (1959)
Plot summary
Beatie Bryant, who has been living in London with her boyfriend Ronnie for three years, comes home to visit her family in Norfolk. In the first act, we see her with her sister and brother-in-law, a farm labourer. Beatie reveals how much she has learned from Ronnie and denounces the empty lives of her family. In Acts Two and Three, she is seen staying with her mother and father, also a farm labourer. Again she tells her mother how intellectually deprived the family is, and is dismayed by her father's resigned attitude when he is threatened with the sack. A high tea is prepared for Ronnie's arrival, and the family, including Beatie's sister and brother-in-law, gather to meet Ronnie, the socialist intellectual. Instead, a letter comes from Ronnie, breaking off the relationship with Beatie. Out of her anger and disappointment, she discovers a newfound articulacy.

It is frequently assumed that Beatie in *Roots* is an idealized figure and a mouthpiece for Wesker, especially as he acknowledges that she was based on his wife Doreen ('Dusty') Bicker.[30] She is often assumed to represent Wesker's own education away from the working class, expressing disdain about her ignorant family and offering them some sort of salvation with a few pieces of middle-class culture. A typical comment is that of Ronald Hayman: '[Wesker is] often more interested in what they [his characters] are saying than in why they are saying it. They are saying it in fact because he wants it to be said.'[31]

Beatie is indeed the central figure, on stage almost all the time, except briefly before her two entrances at the beginning of Acts One and Two, and she is the character with whom the audience will identify most closely. We tend to read the other characters through her eyes: we share in her frustration when Jimmy refuses to discuss his belonging to the Territorial Army ('What's he afraid of talking for?').[32] We register with her the undemonstrative and apathetic manner of the Bryant family and their petty quarrels. We note her father's refusal even to open the Union magazine at the very time that he is threatened with the sack. Mrs Bryant's pop-song does indeed sound like 'squit'.

However, Beatie's dependence on her mentor Ronnie is never obscured. Within minutes of her arrival she is citing his views verbatim, and, in the most obvious and comic piece of self-revelation in the play, she insists: 'I don't quote all the time, I just tell you what Ronnie say.'[33] This much has been noted by critics, but the self-criticism implicit in this off-stage portrayal of Ronnie deserves closer inspection. Beatie's relationship with Ronnie is similar to that between Eugene Gaillard and the 'girl with green eyes' in Edna O'Brien's The Lonely Girl (1962). He dominates Beatie cruelly, threatening to leave her if she should get fat and apparently acquiesces in her view that she will not have to continue showing an interest in intellectual matters once she has children. This contrasts unfavourably with the loving generosity of Jimmy in marrying Beatie's sister Jenny, despite her having an illegitimate child. Towards the end of the play Beatie tells her story about the girl who is forced to remove her clothes for love but is rejected by two men. The dramatic function of this ethical problem is to reveal Ronnie as a composite culprit: the wise man, whose advice is worthless; the ferryman, who forces her to strip naked; Archie, who uses and abandons her, and Tom, who stands in judgment and rejects her. Conditioned by Ronnie's dominance, Beatie is still willing to accept the blame for his betrayal, accusing herself of failing to 'help her boyfriend'.[34]

More importantly, Beatie herself is full of contradictions. She may preach caring and self-improvement but admits that she 'can't bear sick men. They smell.'[35] She certainly would not help Stan Mann with his incontinence as Jimmy does. She criticizes her family for their empty talk and gossip but makes no effort to develop or respond seriously to anything they say. In one of her rare moments of enthusiasm, Mrs Bryant asks Beatie if she has noticed her flowers, her hollyhocks, asters and geraniums. The apostle of communication answers monosyllabically: 'Yearp.'[36] Similarly, to her mother's stories about sexual abuse and about a neighbour who has gone mad, Beatie responds with a comment about bath cubes. It may be that she has heard these stories 'a dozen times',[37] but, if she believes in words as bridges, then there was an ideal opportunity for some bridge-building here. Again, Beatie has only contempt for her mother's pop-song (but knows all the words and enjoys singing it), and it is indeed an empty jingle. However, she sets against it 'a coalmining song'. First, this can hardly be very relevant to Beatie's own experience. Secondly, the lyric is almost as trite as that of the pop-song, with its opening line: 'Oh a dialogue I'll sing you as true as me life', and the chorus: 'Derry down, down, down Derry down'.[38] Are we then to imagine that Wesker wishes us to be impressed with Beatie's observation that the words of the pop-song 'don't mean anything', given the nonsense chorus of the folk-song?

It is also the case that shortly before Beatie discovers a new level of articulacy, Mrs Bryant achieves her own insights:

> When you tell me I was stubborn, what you mean was that *he* told you *you* was stubborn – eh? When you tell me I don't understand you mean *you* don't understand isn't it? When you tell me I don't make no effort you mean *you* don't make no effort. Well, what you blaming me for then?[39]

Beatie, a bundle of contradictions, is anything but an ideal figure or mouthpiece. Wesker's intention is not didacticism but the exposure of a mass of uncertainties. Even the notorious end of Act Two, where Beatie supposedly lectures her mother on the merits of classical music, should be seen much more simply as an upbeat act-ending, illustrating that cultured entertainment can be fun: it is Beatie's 'young and high' spirits[40] that persuade her mother and us of the joy of the music as much as the music itself.

'Roots' are what Beatie is seeking. She has been torn from her roots and has found nothing to replace them, just as Wesker himself was deracinated by his education. Wesker is wise enough to know that folk-songs, classical music and an appreciation of high art will not in themselves give a person roots. Beatie has been Ronnie's parrot until the end of the play when she begins to speak for herself. It is not much, to be sure, but it is a beginning.

The statement of *Roots* is complex and ambiguous and full of productive contradictions. Mass culture and the lilliputian lives of the underprivileged are condemned; but most of the glib solutions of Ronnie and Beatie are also seen as hollow. As Wesker said in a note to actors and producers at the start of *The Trilogy*: 'The picture I have drawn is a harsh one, yet my tone is not one of disgust – nor should it be in the presentation of the plays. I am at one with these people: it is only that I am annoyed, with them and myself.'[41] Wesker's annoyance with himself can only be alleviated by words, in his case usually, but not exclusively, words on a stage. For him words can be bridges, Beatie can find a degree of liberation and 'rootedness' through language. In 1976 Wesker published an essay 'Words as definitions of experience',[42] headed by a quotation from Francis Hope: 'Not to be a poet is the worst of all our miseries.' In this essay he made the proposal that a new subject should be placed on every school curriculum – the study of some thirty essential conceptual words, with approximately six weeks devoted to the study of each. This would help to define experience more accurately, so that all those emerging from school would stand an improved chance of communicating better.

It is a typically modest and practical proposal. To admit of great uncertainty is again a very topical, one might say, post-modernist position. To seek a solution to uncertainty in the use of language is un-dramatic and unfashionable, and yet precisely what is attempted daily to avoid conflict, whether within the domestic confines of a marriage or between hostile nations at peace conferences.

As someone who places faith in words, it is predictable that the strategy of political persuasion that Wesker adopts lays emphasis on dialogue rather than on theatrical image. Hence, an early play like *Roots* is a realistic piece that gives prominence to language, but Wesker's realism is by no means a banal reproduction of everyday life.

In common with many realist plays since Shaw, *Roots* opens with a stage-direction more appropriate to a novel than to a play:

> A rather ramshackle house in Norfolk where there is no water laid on, nor electricity, nor gas. Everything rambles and the furniture is cheap and old. If it is untidy it is because there is a child in the house and there are few amenities, so that the mother is too over-worked to take much care.[43]

Some of this information may be deduced by the audience (e.g. the lack of electricity by the presence of tilly lamps, referred to in the subsequent stage-direction), but they cannot know from seeing the set that 'there is no water laid on', for example, nor until the action begins can they be aware that 'there is a child in the house'. The initial stage-direction stands as an instruction to the designer, director and cast as to the nature of the environment in which *Roots* takes place.

This environment is, first, shabbily rural. Now this is a rare setting for the British theatre. Traditionally, the rustic life has tended to represent joyous escape from urban complexity and misery. I cannot think of any equivalent in the British theatre before *Roots* to the degraded lives of the rustic characters in Gerhart Hauptmann's naturalist play *Before Sunrise* (1889). When British playwrights depict lives of the socially deprived, they have tended always to see these in an urban context. Here the curtain opens on a scene of domestic mess, clothes and papers lying around, a tub with dirty underwear and a line of washing. It makes the ironing board of *Look Back in Anger* seem positively genteel by comparison. *Roots* is 'kitchen-sink' drama without even a proper sink.

The opening scene contains surprises. First, we see that the only character on stage, Jenny Beales, is wearing glasses. No rural stereotype here. Moreover, 'she is singing a recent pop song' as she washes up. We hear the child off-stage calling for a sweet. The glasses, the pop-song and the sweet are indicators of the penetration of urban living on this otherwise primitive rural community. Thus Wesker affords us the recognition that this world is doubly deprived: deprived of the basic amenities that townspeople would take for granted, and also deprived of the traditions that have allowed the country to be a special place of refuge.

The opening moments of the play therefore establish the realistic setting of the piece, a true-to-life reproduction with authentic detail and free of clichés about rural life. The impression is reinforced by the entry of Jenny's husband in blue dungarees and wheeling a bicycle. The type of work and style of transport are defined by actual stage-images rather than being described; the life of the characters is experienced and not just referred to. As Wesker said in an interview with Jill Pomerance: 'When I have people coming on with a tin bath and sweeping up and washing up, it's not simply because I want to capture real life; what I'm trying to do is demonstrate all the little things which go to make up a point.'[44] By showing us actual physical work, and giving it a point, Wesker was again being innovatory. While other writers may talk of work, Wesker actually takes us into the workplace, most notably in *The Kitchen* and later in *The Journalists*. Where is Jimmy Porter's sweet-stall, or the pits of the miners in Arden's *Serjeant Musgrave's Dance*, how does Bond's Len survive economically? Even Brecht gives us only a vague sense of the real world of work in presenting his representative figures. Characters may be called Carpenter, Policeman, Airman, or Coolie, but we are given little insight into the daily routine of their working lives.

Furthermore, there is in *Roots* no attempt made to create dramatic action where none may be expected. The one significant incident in the piece, the death of Stan Mann, takes place off stage and has little effect on the central characters. The only developments in the plot are the arrival of Beatie at the beginning and the letter from Ronnie towards the end. In this respect, the piece, to use Lukács's terms, describes rather than narrates.

Yet, despite the apparently naturalistic setting and plot, there is much artificial shaping. The play adopts a conventional three-act structure, and the dialogue is by no means a transcription of everyday speech. The dialect is hinted at rather than authentic, for otherwise intelligibility would be lost, and repetition is used as a very conscious device, as in the three references to Jimmy's indigestion: '... some people get indigestion so bad it go right through their stomach to the back'.[45] The repetition of Mrs Bryant's diagnosis is funny, and it reinforces the sense of the predictable exchanges within the Bryant household. However, it is too contrived to operate as precise observation of actual speech. Occasionally, then, Wesker sacrifices authenticity for theatrical effect. He defends such artistic intervention eloquently: 'realistic art is a contradiction in terms. Art is the recreation of experience, not the copying of it. Some writers use naturalistic means to re-create experience, others non-naturalistic. I happen to use naturalistic means; but all the statements I make are made theatrically.'[46]

In his 'recreation of experience' Wesker allows his characters not only to indulge in repetition for comic effect but also simply to say too much. There is an almost constant flow of dialogue, which, for all its dialect patterns, consists almost entirely of properly formed sentences. Although in an early stage-direction Wesker insists: 'The silences are important – as important as the way they speak, if we are to know them',[47] he indicates in the text only five 'pauses' and five 'silences'. Thus, apart from the frequently voiced criticism, discussed above, that his characters speak like Wesker rather than like themselves, there is also the risk that they are simply too loquacious to convey a sense of real verbal exchanges. It must be remembered, however, that until the impact of Beckett and Pinter was felt, playwrights did not usually dictate pauses and thus the rhythms of performance were left to their actors and directors. It would appear that Wesker leaves much of his desired effect to be achieved in performance. Of *Their Very Own and Golden City* he said: '... it needed an energy really in the production that should have been able to cover up all the structural weaknesses'.[48] In 1980 he complained: 'Directors did and still do seem to have difficulty in lifting my plays off the page.'[49] It is significant that Wesker has taken more and more to directing his own plays, or at the very least to insisting on having a say during rehearsals.

The pacing of *Roots* may therefore be more authentic in a good performance than is apparent on the page. Certainly, John Dexter's premiere at the Belgrade, Coventry, seems to have made the play work well. 'Dexter had drilled the cast to bully the audience into accepting my [sic] slow pace and silences',[50] wrote Wesker twenty-one years later, and the reviewer T. C. Worsley clearly felt much of the strength of the piece was due to Dexter's pacing:

> John Dexter, the director, has been extremely daring in his use of slowness and silence. Accustomed to slickness and speed, we may find it difficult to accept his pace at first: but he insists from the start and soon has us with him. Ponderous slowness, pointless reiteration, stubborn taciturnity, cowlike vacuity – I have never seen these so perfectly caught on the stage. But the fact that they manage to be neither boring nor depressing is the highest tribute I can pay to Mr Dexter and his admirable cast.[51]

What Tynan called 'Chekhov's method, applied not to the country gentry but to the peasants at the gate',[52] was an achievement of the production rather than of Wesker's text, for his characters speak with a fluency and roundedness that dates the dialogue. Wesker himself admitted later that Beatie's final monologue was not naturalistic,[53] and the speech-patterns of contemporary theatre have tended to become much more minimal, with an increasing emphasis placed, in realistic pieces at least, on the eloquence of the pause and the silence.

In some respects, then, Wesker was an innovatory force in British post-war political theatre. As Ronald Hayman says, *Chicken Soup with Barley* was 'one of the first serious and successful political plays to be written in England', and he quotes Kenneth Tynan's review: 'Nobody else has ever attempted to put a real, live, English Communist family on to the stage; and the important thing about Mr Wesker's attempt is that they *are* real, and they *do* live!'[54]

However, Wesker's *Trilogy* looked back rather than forward, both in terms of content and of style. The plays contain, as Christopher Bigsby points out,[55] nostalgia for the past, a yearning for the cohesive and politically aware community of the 1930s represented in *Chicken Soup with Barley* in contrast to the empty lives of post-war Britain. In terms of style, they are written as pieces of 'kitchen-sink realism', but are neither wholly authentic nor boldly theatrical. Wesker did not

offer an innovative model for the future of political theatre. Trevor
Griffiths has come closest to adopting the realistic settings and situations, coupled with verbal debate, in the style of *The Trilogy*. Without in any way intending this to be a disparaging comment, Wesker's
realistic style has perhaps found its true successor in the working-
class settings and ethical problems of television soap operas like
EastEnders.

On the other hand, the uncertainties expressed by Wesker and
his honest exploration of contradictions have again become very topical. In many ways Ronnie's assured and dogmatic pronouncements,
as repeated by Beatie, might serve as a prognosis of the revolutionary declarations of the young playwrights that were to flourish in
the 1970s. The confusion and dismay experienced by socialists like
Wesker when the USSR invaded Hungary in 1956 have been echoed
by similar questioning responses to the collapse of Communism in
Eastern Europe in more recent times. To preach a collectivist, left-
wing philosophy from the stage is now seen to be more dated than
the aspiration towards individual regeneration portrayed in *Roots*. To
acknowledge that there must now be a period of debate and reassessment is perhaps the strongest political commitment a playwright may
appropriately make.

One might do worse than to revisit Wesker's early work. In
the opening scene of *I'm Talking About Jerusalem*, Wesker offers an
amusing self-portrayal in the image of Ronnie, having opted out of
the work involved in moving Ada and Dave's furniture into their new
home. Instead, he is standing on a chair conducting music and offering suggestions to the working-men beneath him. The two removal
men complain that he talks too much, to which Ada responds: 'Sooner
he talked than he remained silent.'[56] This might serve to summarize
Wesker's position: a writer accused of standing above the working-
class, holding forth garrulously, and yet defended by the very reasonable insight that, given the injustices of the world, it is better that this
simple old-fashioned humanist should talk than remain silent.

3 The 'interventionist' strategy: poetic politics in John Arden's *Serjeant Musgrave's Dance* (1959)

> People must want to come to the theatre *because* of the
> artificiality, not despite it ... I am pleading for the revival of
> the Poetic Drama, no less.[1]

In December 1959, while nominating Joan Plowright's performance
as Beatie as one of the best of the year, *Plays and Players* awarded
'black marks to the public for failing to support *Roots* and *Serjeant
Musgrave's Dance*'.[2] Here, already, Wesker's name was linked with
that of John Arden, and the two men have shared similar experiences
in the British theatre. Both have been dismissed as having failed to
live up to the promise of their early work, and both have been involved in wrangles with the theatrical establishment in the form of
the Royal Shakespeare Company: Wesker over *The Journalists* (1975),
Arden over *The Island of the Mighty* (1972). This is where the major
similarities end. For, while Wesker could be seen in his early work to
be treading a realistic path, Arden was striking out in quite another
direction.

One significant influence on Arden was Bertolt Brecht, whose
Berliner Ensemble had toured to London in 1956. In 1970 Wesker still
seems to have been unfamiliar with Brecht's ideas. In the December
1970 entry in 'From a writer's notebook', Wesker, in discussing the
validity of an episodic dramatic treatment, refers to Aristotle but, surprisingly, makes no mention of Brecht.[3] Not only was Arden familiar
with Brecht; he went so far as to say that *Mother Courage* (1941) was
the twentieth-century play he would most like to have written.[4] To
Walter Wager's question in 1966 whether he had been influenced by
Brecht, Arden replied:

Yes, but I don't copy Brecht; I don't use him as a model. After I had started writing plays I decided that Brecht was inspired by the same sort of early drama that was interesting me: The rather conventionalized plays of the European Middle Ages, the Elizabethan writers and various exotic styles such as the Japanese and Chinese theatre. I was not interested in naturalistic Ibsenite writing.[5]

To explore two very contrasting strategies of political theatre, it is a piece of serendipity that Wesker's 'Ibsenite' *Roots* and Arden's 'Brechtian' *Serjeant Musgrave's Dance* were performed within months of each other at the Royal Court in London. Both plays have become classics of modern British theatre, appearing on schools examination syllabuses. However, while *Roots* appears now to be languishing in a theatrical limbo, *Serjeant Musgrave's Dance*, despite its initial poor reception with critics and audiences, is now regarded as a masterpiece.

Choosing to discuss one of Arden's earliest plays may, as with the choice of *Roots*, appear to contain the insulting implication that Arden has failed to develop as a playwright. It may also seem to support the prevalent critical view that his early plays, written alone, are better than those written in collaboration with his wife, Margaretta D'Arcy. *Serjeant Musgrave's Dance* is a very fine play, but it would be hard to evaluate its merits against a piece like *The Non-Stop Connolly Show* (1975), written in a quite different style and to a quite different purpose. Moreover, any book about the strategies of political theatre must make at least a mention of D'Arcy and Arden turning their backs on the theatre establishment and of their significant work with amateur groups, e.g. with Kirbymoorside schoolchildren on *Ars Longa, Vita Brevis* (1964) or at a Belfast teacher training college on *The Ballygombeen Bequest* (1972).

Nevertheless, despite these reservations, *Serjeant Musgrave's Dance*, the best-known play by Arden, forms such a useful parallel to *Roots* that it will be used here as a model of a certain type of political theatre, without in any way wishing to imply that it encapsulates Arden's achievement.

Serjeant Musgrave's Dance (1959)

Plot summary

Serjeant Musgrave arrives with three soldiers in a northern min-
ing town, apparently recruiting for the army. The town is in
unrest, with striking miners rebelling against the forces of law
and order: the parson, the constable and the mayor, who is also
the mine-owner. The soldiers lodge at an inn, and it gradually
becomes clear that they have taken part in an atrocity in the
colonies. The recruiting meeting will be an opportunity for them
to tell the English citizens what is being done in their name. At
the meeting, Musgrave dances and chants as a skeleton of a youth
formerly from the town is hauled aloft, and then threatens to kill
twenty-five of the townspeople as a reprisal for the atrocity. The
dragoons arrive and restore order violently, and everyone joins
in a dance. At the end, only Musgrave and one soldier remain in
prison awaiting execution.

We recall that *Roots* opened with a stage-direction offering such a full
description of the set that it even contained information that could
not be perceived by the audience. By contrast, the setting of the first
scene of *Serjeant Musgrave's Dance* is defined simply as: 'A canal
wharf. Evening'.[6] Such terseness does not betray a lack of theatrical
imagination; Arden is concerned to offer only enough information
relevant to the playing of the scene. As he wrote in his Introduction
to the play:

> Scenery must be sparing – only those pieces of architecture,
> furniture and properties actually used in the action need be
> present: and they should be thoroughly realistic, so that the
> audience sees a selection from the details of everyday life
> rather than a generalised impression of the whole of it.[7]

Whether Arden was aware of it or not, this exactly echoes Brecht's understanding of the function of scenery. There is no longer the pretence
that 'the fourth wall' has been removed, so that we may look into
a 'real' room. Instead, the setting acknowledges to the audience that
they are in a theatre, but by using authentic furniture and properties,

vague abstractions are avoided. So, paradoxically, a much more real experience is offered in place of the illusion of reality. While *Roots* employed two box sets representing mainly interior settings, *Serjeant Musgrave's Dance* requires eight different locations, half of them exterior. Theatre space is acknowledged to be such. Thus, towards the end of the first scene Musgrave 'makes a rapid circuit of the stage',[8] a stage-direction unthinkable in *Roots*, since Wesker's play does not openly concede that the audience is looking at a stage. Furthermore, Arden employs non-realistic devices like the split stage in Act Two, Scene Three, with action alternating between stable and bedroom, or in the transition from Scene One to Scene Two in the third act, where the prison is 'achieved by a barred wall descending in front of the dancers of the previous scene'.[9]

Characteristic of realist plays like *Roots*, too, was the sense of a world off stage, whether a crying child or the place of work from which Jimmy enters. In *Serjeant Musgrave's Dance* 'off stage' is acknowledged to be such; beyond the action on stage there is not a 'real' world but wings and dressing rooms. So in the penultimate scene of the play Arden is quite specific about the level of authenticity of the off-stage crowd: 'Noises-off indicated in the dialogue are rather unrealistic – as it were, token-noises only.'[10]

Another obvious contrast with *Roots* is the historical setting of Arden's play. One reason he gave for placing the action roughly between 1860 and 1880 was that it allowed him to have redcoat soldiers,[11] and the ballad-like effect of the strong colours of the play has been frequently noted:[12] red is the colour of the soldiers' coats and the mayor's robe, and of blood; black the colour of coal and Black Jack Musgrave, and of the Queen of Spades, the card of death; white the colour of snow and Musgrave's 'white shining word',[13] and of the bones of Billy's skeleton. Even more importantly, the historical setting allows Arden to set his chosen theme at a distance, in the same way that Brecht uses history in *Galileo* (1943) and *Mother Courage* to permit a more objective discussion of political issues than would be possible in a contemporary context. This does not derive from a Romantic view that historical situations are 'universal', but rather prompts the insight, expressed by the Brechtian director Peter Palitzsch as follows:

'the stranger the period [of a play] appears to us, the greater its topi-
cality. We say: aha – even then, when there wasn't any this or that or
the other, the appropriate questions were being asked.'[14]

Arden adds to this sense of distancing by placing the action in
an unnamed snow-bound town in winter. Isolated for some twenty-
four hours from the rest of the world, the events of the play can be
observed in a crucible. Retaining a sense of its historical context, the
piece nevertheless remarkably acquires the quality of a parable (and we
should not forget that the play is subtitled 'An un-historical parable').

Characters, too, are conceived very differently from those in a
realist play like *Roots*. More than half the *dramatis personae* of *Serjeant Musgrave's Dance* are referred to by their position or trade and
not by name (Parson, Constable, Mayor, and so on) and the Colliers are
given epithets like figures in a Morality Play (for example, Pugnacious
Collier, Slow Collier). Clearly, Arden is once again allying himself with Brecht by discovering more interest in social interaction
than in individual psychology. Indeed, Albert Hunt cogently argues,[15]
this was the major reason for the unpopularity of the play in 1959.
Arden's methods still seem to remain incomprehensible to some critics. Ronald Hayman, who wrote a brief monograph on Arden in 1968
and who discusses *Serjeant Musgrave's Dance* in his survey, *British
Theatre since 1955*, even resorts to misrepresenting Arden in order
to make his point. He quotes an interview with the playwright in
1961, where Arden stated that he did not begin with the character of
Musgrave, but that 'I decided what he had to say, and why he had to
say it, and roughly what he was going to do about it, before I worked
out the character. The character came to fit the actions.'[16] From this
Hayman quite improperly deduces that Musgrave's character is an
artificial creation without substance, a mere functionary of Arden's
ideology: 'Arden... knew what he wanted to say through Musgrave's
mouth before he knew anything else about Musgrave.' Hayman then
goes on to say that Arden like Edward Bond is 'subordinating characterization to his didactic starting point'.[17] Of course, Arden said nothing
of the sort: he decided what Musgrave had to say and do, not what
he, Arden, wanted to say through the figure of Musgrave. That the
character of Musgrave followed from his response to a situation does

not mean that this figure is put on stage merely to act out the writer's ideas.

We are perhaps sometimes misled by titles like *Hamlet* or indeed *Mother Courage* into thinking that dramas necessarily centre on the character of a major individual, forgetting that the titles are in fact *Hamlet, Prince of Denmark* and *Mother Courage and Her Children* (and indeed Arden's play is *Serjeant Musgrave's Dance* not *Serjeant Musgrave*). In other words, these plays, like all great theatre, are, to use Aristotle's phrase, 'an imitation of an action', the representation of a given situation, through which the character of the protagonist is revealed. The starting-point of *Hamlet* is not the psychological study of a rather neurotic young man's *character* but the exploration of his *behaviour* in the situation in which he finds himself. Perhaps Shakespeare, too, began by asking himself what Hamlet might say when his father's ghost told him that he had been murdered by his brother, the new king.

Now, of course it is true that Hamlet is a more rounded figure than Musgrave, a character even less clearly defined than a Brechtian figure like Mother Courage. But Arden's strategy in presenting Musgrave is to explore attitudes to violence rather than to build up a full character portrayal which demands identification and empathy from the audience. As with Brecht, Arden's treatment of character helps to create a response in the audience of cool critical appraisal.

One indicator of the way his characters may no longer be regarded as Stanislavskian creations, ignoring the 'dark hole' of the audience, is the use Arden makes of direct address to the spectator. This occurs most obviously in the final act, where the Colliers and Bargee are the only crowd members visible on stage, and so the audience is addressed as though it comprised the townspeople, even to the extent of being threatened by the Gatling gun. But before this, statements are made by characters, though they may not be treated in production as direct address to the audience, which at least acknowledge the presence of the audience in their use of simple unvarnished self-introduction (in the manner of Brecht's 'I am a water-seller in the capital of Szechuan province'):[18] 'I'm the Mayor of this town, I own the colliery, I'm a worried man.'[19] And in Act One, Scene Three, Sparky's revelation of the soldiers' mission could seem very heavy-handed if the actor were to play it naturalistically. Frances Gray describes John Burgess's treatment of this passage in his successful production of the play at the National Theatre in 1981 as follows: 'the lines were delivered quite straightforwardly to the audience as a way of imparting information which they needed to know. Ewan Stewart as Sparky faced the front and spoke without any internal agonizing after psychological motivation.'[20]

A similar effect is achieved by the use of songs in the play, again a Brechtian device, and one that in the historical context of the piece has a much greater ring of truth than Beatie's singing of a coal-mining song. Some of the songs, like Beatie's, are contained within the action, that is to say, they arise naturally out of the situation on stage; it would be inappropriate for the audience to applaud them but acceptable that the actors should. Songs of this type are, for example, Sparky's in the first scene or those sung in the pub. Other songs follow Brecht's dictum: 'Separate the songs from the rest!... The actors turn into singers. Adopting a different posture they turn to the public, still characters in a play, but now also openly sharing the views of the writer.'[21] Such songs interrupt the action, have a more obvious commenting function, and may be sung straight out to the audience, who may indeed applaud them while it would be inappropriate for the actors on stage to do so. Examples of these are Annie's ballad, which describes the life of a soldier, and the songs with which scenes end, the Bargee's in the first scene, Sparky's in Act Two, Scene One, or, most notably, Attercliffe's at the end of the play.

The naturalness with which songs are employed is facilitated not only by the historical setting of the piece but also by the slightly archaic and lyrical quality of the language (already signalled by the archaic spelling of 'Sergeant' in the title of the play). While in *Roots* Wesker generally attempts to reproduce the rhythms of everyday speech, Arden creates an artificial dialogue characterized by short sentences, archaic-sounding constructions and potent monosyllables. One might imagine how Sparky's opening lines would sound in a naturalistic piece:

SPARKY (*shivering*). Brrr. Christ, it's cold. The snow seems to come earlier every year, and the nights get longer. (*Pause.*) Why are we being kept waiting? I hate this hanging around. Once you've started out on a journey, it's better to keep on moving.

Arden's lines read:

SPARKY.   Brr, oh a cold winter, snow, dark. We wait too long, that's the trouble. Once you've started, keep on travelling.[22]

Clearly Arden's language is terse and concise compared with the redundancies of common speech or naturalistic dialogue. The construction: 'We wait too long' instead of the more usual 'We've been waiting too long' has an archaic and forceful ring to it. The inserted pause of the first version is somewhat arbitrary but is characteristic of the need of the naturalistic actor to build psychological bridges from one part of a speech to the next. Arden's dialogue may pause to allow of silent action but is not needed for psychological motivation. This was possibly another reason for the failure of the first production by Lindsay Anderson at the Royal Court, which Harold Hobson dismissed as a frightful ordeal.[23] As A. Alvarez said in his review in the *New Statesman*:

> Instead of marshalling both scenes and actors so that they moved with the dramatic concentration that Arden's writing…demands, Mr Anderson deliberately slowed everything down. Even the most trivial bits of dialogue were punctuated by those tiny pauses in which the actors turn, or move up stage, or gesture, as though about to embark on some long set speech. The talk bogged down in endless hesitation.[24]

Most importantly, naturalistic dialogue, such as apparently Anderson thought he was dealing with, would help us to form an impression of Sparky's character – his reaction to the cold and to the waiting around. Again, this is not Arden's focus. With a few swift strokes he sketches in what we need to know – that it is winter, that it is cold and dark, that there is snow, and that the men are waiting. Sparky's disapproval of waiting does not give us an insight into his character; we do not deduce from his words that he is an impatient sort of person – he is merely commenting in a general way on the wisdom of not breaking a journey for too long.

Though minimal, Arden's linguistic style develops a richness through the use of pseudo-biblical images ('Abide with Me in Power. A Pillar of Flame before the people')[25] and dialect turns of phrase ('that serjeant squats in your gobs like an old wife stuck in a fireplace'),[26] devices familiar to Arden from another German influence on his writing, that of Georg Büchner. Like Büchner too, Arden enriches his dialogue by the repetition of simple images. We have already referred to the cumulative effect of his use of colours, and in a scene like that in the churchyard, repetition is used like a refrain from a ballad. Musgrave enters with: 'Coldest town I ever was in', and asks Hurst what he saw. Hurst replies: 'Hardly a thing. Street empty.'[27] Attercliffe's reply to Musgrave's same question is identical, as is Sparky's. Where in *Roots* the same sort of repetition was used for comic effect and militated against the plausibility of Wesker's dialogue, here it is so blatant that it can be perceived only as a lyrical device, again laying no claim to being the authentic speech of soldiers but serving to reinforce the image of the isolated and depressed township.

John McGrath summed up the achievement of Arden's language as follows:

> When I first clapped eyes on the script of John Arden's *Live Like Pigs* my ears tingled with the sound of the words. Here, back in the English theatre, about to be presented on an English stage, was the language of England's submerged culture, the language of ballad, nursery rhyme, of John Clare, Gerrard Winstanley and John Bunyan, of that rich but unvalued flood of worker–writers, of Anon... And there, in that script in 1959, I was reading an English play that gloried in these suppressed linguistic resources, and threatened to renew the language of the stage. I think in years to come Arden's work will be seen as marking a fruitful turning-point in the English theatre.[28]

Even more remarkably, despite the brilliance of Arden's language, much of the effect of *Serjeant Musgrave's Dance* depends on visual images and action. While in *Roots* a situation is described and the most 'dramatic' event is the off-stage death of a minor character, Arden's play tells a story full of incident. Packed into the forty hours of the play's action are scenes of violence, including two on-stage deaths, the stunning *coup de théâtre* when Billy's skeleton is hoisted aloft, and the dancing of the Colliers and of Musgrave himself. Beatie may dance out of a jubilant recognition of the emotional impact of Bizet, but Musgrave dances because the intensity and passion of his message can only be expressed in dance and song. Arden exploits the very implausibility of an army sergeant dancing to point up the extremity to which Musgrave is driven in his desire to communicate. One is reminded here, as no doubt Arden was, of Nietzsche's opposition of the Apollonian and the Dionysian (although Arden gives a rather different gloss to the Dionysian in the preface to *The Workhouse Donkey* (1963)).[29] The Apollonian mode is that of rational thought, the Dionysian represents the irrational impulses in humankind and is expressed above all in dance. So Arden, like Musgrave, steps beyond language at the point where words are no longer adequate.

The prominence of visual images and actions again accords well with the stress Brecht laid on *Gestus*, the socially significant action as the focus of a scene. Apart from striking incidents like the hoisting of the skeleton or Musgrave's dance, there are smaller moments in the play which make an impact through the image rather than through words. Much of our understanding and response to Musgrave is developed in this way. His calling himself 'a religious man' gains considerably in credibility when we see him a few moments later reading a pocket Bible;[30] our fears about his fate are reinforced by Annie's minute-long silent stare;[31] and we begin to sense that he is no longer fully in control of events in the apparently insignificant stage-direction: 'He plunges his hand in his pocket and pulls out a quantity of money. He does a rapid count, whistles in consternation, and selects a few coins.'[32]

Serjeant Musgrave's Dance is a thoroughly theatrical piece. As Arden said in 1960: 'costumes, movements, verbal patterns, music, must all be strong and hard at the edges'.[33] There is not much in *Roots* that needs to be seen rather than heard, whereas Arden's piece would suffer immeasurably if it were followed in sound only. *Roots* would be a tedious experience if performed in an incomprehensible foreign language; *Serjeant Musgrave's Dance* would still make a lot of sense. By embracing the poetry of theatre, both in dialogue and images, Arden hoped to make a greater impact than through the use of conventional political comment in a realistic setting: 'Social criticism ... tends in the theatre to be dangerously ephemeral and therefore disappointing after the fall of the curtain. But if it is expressed within the framework of the traditional poetic truths it can have a weight and an impact derived from something more than contemporary documentary facility.'[34]

To sum up the main differences between *Roots* and *Serjeant Musgrave's Dance*, I offer the comparative table below – with all the attendant risks of simplification that such listing involves. Despite the strongly contrasting theatrical styles of *Roots* and *Serjeant Musgrave's*

Roots and *Serjeant Musgrave's Dance*: a comparative table

Roots	Serjeant Musgrave's Dance
Realistic	Brechtian
Description of situation	Telling of story
Identification and empathy	Distance and objectivity
Contemporary	Historical
Realistic setting	Minimal sets
Realistic off-stage world	Action limited to stage space
Limited cast (all named)	Large cast (many anonymous)
Rounded characters	Representative characters
Exposition of character	*Gestus*
'Fourth-wall' convention	Direct address to audience
Realistic dialogue	Poetic dialogue
Repetition for comic effect	Repetition for poetic effect
Songs within action	Many songs as commentary
Dependent on words	Visual images equally important

Dance, there are definite similarities between the political attitudes revealed in both pieces. Especially after becoming a committed Marxist after 1968, Arden held strong left-wing views:

> I hope I have made clear... that I recognise as the enemy the
> fed man, the clothed man, the sheltered man, whose food,
> clothes and house are obtained at the expense of the hunger,
> the nakedness, and the exposure of so many millions of
> others: and who will allow anything to be *said* in books or on
> the stage, so long as the food, clothes and house remain
> undiminished in his possession.[35]

The similarities between Wesker and Arden are all the more ironic, since Wesker has been accused of being too didactic, yet, as we have seen, recognizes ambiguities and complexities; while Arden, in his early work at least, has been attacked for being unclear in his statements, yet, as we shall see, reflects a genuinely committed stance. Amusingly, too, Wesker, the 'old-fashioned humanist', accused Arden of being 'a wishy-washy liberal', to which Arden responded that a liberal puts both sides of an argument because he is committed to neither, whereas, he, Arden, was committed to *understanding* both sides, no matter which side he temperamentally favoured.[36]

In fact, there are some striking similarities between Beatie and Musgrave. Both have been through recent experiences that have changed their outlook on life, both have a sense of mission to transform the world, and both of them are flawed, imperfect heroes, with whose points of view we may have some sympathy but whose methods are suspect. Finally, there is for both of them the hope, strong in Beatie's case, weak in Musgrave's, that, despite their present defeat, their message will yet be listened to.

Musgrave's transformative experience is based on an incident that happened to Arden while he was on National Service with the British troops in Cyprus. When the wife of a serviceman was murdered, the soldiers reacted by using excessive force in their round-up of suspects in the local community, killing 125 civilians.[37] In the play the victim is Billy Hicks, a native of the coal-mining town to which

Musgrave and his men go, and the army reprisals cause the deaths of five civilians.

In *Serjeant Musgrave's Dance* the army is seen not as a means of defending the populace nor even as a glorious conquering force of the Empire: it is a means of brutal repression, a way of maintaining the status quo of the fed man, the clothed man. Musgrave's regiment occupies 'a little country without much importance except from the point of view that there's a Union Jack flies over it and the people of that country can write British subject after their names'.[38] The army's business is described by the Earnest Collier: 'You go sailing on what they call punitive expeditions, against what you call rebels, and you shoot men down in the streets.'[39]

Musgrave and his three companions, disillusioned with the army and its brutality, have deserted and, while pretending to be on a recruiting campaign, are in fact returning to what Musgrave regards as the source of the evil, the British power that maintains its strength by subjugating the weak. Here he intends to exact a terrible revenge: Musgrave's logic dictates that, since five innocent people died to avenge the death of Billy, twenty-five of the townspeople must die to avenge the deaths of the colonial victims.

Of course, Musgrave's logic is a nonsense. The common townspeople are themselves oppressed, particularly at this time of a lockout from the coal-mines. If twenty-five more innocent victims are killed, who then will avenge their deaths with the murder of one hundred and twenty-five further deaths, and these in turn with the slaying of six hundred and twenty-five, and so on? Having rejected the brutality of the army, Musgrave embraces a spurious logic that is redolent of the escalation of the very militarism he purports to despise.

One might also point out that Musgrave's 'logical' plan to execute a precise number of people is quite unrealistic. Unless he could induce twenty-five townspeople to queue for their deaths in an orderly fashion, the bullets from the Gatling gun would wound randomly and unpredictably. The point is that Musgrave, while his anger may be justified, is a dangerous idealist, a driven man without a proper hold on reality. His favourite comment, repeated eight times in the course of the play, is: 'It's not material.' This is a revealing formulation: it is at one and the same time a common idiom meaning 'it's not important'; it is also an implied rejection of the material world in favour of his obsessive vision. Whether it is a full belly,[40] a dead baby,[41] the evil of warfare,[42] Sparky's death[43] or the killing of innocent civilians,[44] Musgrave's repeated response is that 'it's not material.' What is material to him is his Logic, his word[45] (and we recall that the 'logos' of the opening verse of St John's Gospel is translated as 'In the beginning was the *Word*).'

Opposed to Musgrave's idealism is a range of viewpoints. Most easily disposed of are the three representative figures of authority: the Church in the character of the Parson, the law represented by the Constable, and capitalism and the state portrayed by the Mayor, a mine-owner. They are portrayed as being entirely self-seeking, concerned only to preserve the status quo by exploiting the colliers, and, if need be, exploiting the soldiers by organizing subversive elements into the army as the Mayor suggests, so 'exporting the social question', to use a familiar phrase:

> ... *I* think we'll use 'em, Parson. Temporary expedient, but it'll do. The price of coal has fell, I've had to cut me wages, I've had to turn men off. They say they'll strike, so I close me gates. We can't live like that for ever. There's two ways to solve this colliery – one is to build the railway here. The other is clear out half the population, stir up a diversion, turn their minds to summat else. The Queen's got wars, she's got rebellions. Over the sea. All right. Beat these fellers' drums high around the town, I'll put one pound down for every Royal Shilling the serjeant pays. Get rid o' the trouble-makers. Drums and fifes and glory.[46]

Arden is not at all concerned to be fair to these corrupt and autocratic individuals. As a socialist he rejects the capitalist Establishment, and his interest is only in the most effective way of replacing their hegemony with a fair and democratic system. As he said in an interview in 1991 with reference to *The Non-Stop Connolly Show*:

A lot of critics of those plays... have said we have given no
space for the capitalists and the imperialist elements who
express themselves and who, by taking a 'type' figure called
Grabbitall to represent all these groupings, we have
completely ignored the 'on the other hand' possibility. We've
always said that our 'on the other hand' is between different
sets of socialists.[47]

On the other hand, then, are the dissenting figures. One of the
most striking is that of the Bargee. Politically, he is an anarchist without any loyalty to anyone or anything but himself. When Musgrave
seems to be in control, he seizes a rifle as a gesture of support, shouting; 'When do we start breaking open the boozers? Or the pawnshops
and all – who's for a loot?'[48] Minutes later, when the Dragoons arrive, the Bargee uses the same rifle to place Musgrave under arrest.
As a theatrical figure he serves to undercut the gravity of Musgrave's
conduct with grotesque parody, as in his posturing behind Musgrave's
back during the Serjeant's prayer which ends Act One, or in the 'Fred
Karno' drilling of the drunken Colliers in Act Two, Scene Two.

His function in the play is reminiscent of Brecht's proposal that,
during a piece of high tragedy, two clowns should wander about the
stage, commenting on the scenery or suggesting changes to the light-
ing.[49] Arden himself recalled the pleasure of witnessing the anarchic
behaviour of an artiste in a gorilla costume during the performance of
a Dublin pantomime.[50] While admittedly the Bargee does not disrupt
the theatrical process to the same extent, his function is nevertheless
that of the traditional Fool, a zany, self-sufficient figure, who operates as a distancing device, undercutting the seriousness of the dramatic situation. He is amoral but not wholly nihilistic. The song he
repeatedly sings is 'Michael Finnegan', who loses his beard ('Poor old
Michael Finnegan'); then, after 'Begin agen', the same verse is repeated
ad infinitum. Whatever happens, the Bargee, whose actual name, significantly, is Bludgeon, is a survivor, who will always 'begin agen'.
One suspects that, as with the disreputable Sawney family in *Live
Like Pigs* (1958), Arden was strongly attracted to the anarchic figure
of the Bargee, just as Brecht refused to disown his youthful creation

of the rumbustious and amoral Baal. But in the same way that Brecht eventually came to recognize that anarchy, while attractive, would not solve social problems, so, too, Arden seems to have ended his flirtation with figures like the Bargee. Significantly, when John McGrath, with Arden's approval, rewrote the play in 1972 as *Serjeant Musgrave Dances On* for the 7:84 company, the Bargee was omitted, and the originally parodistic 'Amen' to Musgrave's prayer was spoken sincerely by a miner quietly hewing coal in the shadows.

Musgrave's own men also represent different political viewpoints. Sparky is an easy-going extravert, always ready with a song or a card-trick. His motives for revenge are purely personal, because Billy was his 'mucker'. Not possessing a coherent ideology or a real sense of commitment, he is the fellow-traveller of the revolution, ready to abandon his mission when the opportunity presents itself in the form of Annie. Hurst is another contaminated figure of revolution; he is the terrorist who has murdered an officer: '*I* thought up some killing, I said I'll get me own in. I thought o' the Rights of Man. Rights o' the Rebels: that's *me!*'[51] It is he who tries to seize the opportunity to gun down the crowd, until forcibly prevented by Musgrave: 'The wrong way. The wrong way. You're trying to do it without Logic.'[52] Finally, Attercliffe is a pacifist, who rejects war in all forms, and who, at the end, tries to stop Musgrave shedding more blood. At the time of writing, Arden obviously had strong sympathies with Attercliffe's point of view: 'Complete pacifism is a very hard doctrine: and if this play appears to advocate it with perhaps some timidity, it is probably because I am naturally a timid man.'[53] It is also Attercliffe who is given arguably the most telling line in the play: 'You can't cure the pox by further whoring.'[54] Yet Arden's sympathy for Attercliffe and his pacifism does not go so far as to suggest that this is the ideal programme for change. Significantly and ironically, it is Attercliffe who kills Sparky, which suggests that, once embroiled in a corrupt system, it is impossible to avoid violence, however honourable one's intentions.

Those who openly embrace violence for political ends are the miners, led by the Earnest Collier, Walsh. Their grievances and resulting commitment to change could ideally be a power that Musgrave could harness in his overthrow of authority. But the Colliers understandably view the normally repressive redcoats with suspicion, and it is hard to see how it could be otherwise, given that Musgrave openly admits that he is seeking the deaths of twenty-five, when there seem to be only three figures of authority in this small town. Equally, Musgrave is suspicious of what he sees as the limited objectives of the miners. Musgrave wants an apocalypse; they just want jobs with decent wages. It comes as no surprise, therefore, that the Colliers dance in celebration of the defeat of Musgrave and his men. Later the more committed Marxist Arden no doubt regretted portraying these workers as manipulated drunkards of blinkered vision, and this was 'corrected' in McGrath's rewriting of the play. However, as it stands, the striking miners cannot be seen to offer any clear political solutions.

To find the major positive element in the play we need to follow the clue given by Arden in his preface: 'a study of the roles of the women, and of Private Attercliffe, should be sufficient to remove any doubts where the "moral" of the play lies'.[55] The two women, Mrs Hitchcock and Annie, given the structure of nineteenth-century English society, cannot occupy a central role in a political drama. However, though never sentimentalized, they are both portrayed as strong, resourceful individuals, with a very generous streak, whether it is the bringing of a glass of port and lemon to condemned men or Annie's offering of her body to weary soldiers. In his warning to Annie not to seduce any of his men and so distract them from their mission, Musgrave says: 'if you come to us with what you call your life or love – *I'd* call it your indulgence – and you scribble all over that plan, you make it crooked, dirty, idle, untidy, *bad* – there's anarchy'.[56] In the final scene Mrs Hitchcock reminds Musgrave of his words: 'here we are, and we'd got life and love. Then *you* came in and did your scribbling where nobody asked you. Aye, it's arsy-versey to what you said, but it's still an anarchy, isn't it? And it's all your work.'[57] Against Musgrave's failed programme of revolution Mrs Hitchcock sets 'life and love'. It is easy to see how this might be construed as 'wishy-washy liberalism', a complacent opting out of political struggle in favour of 'the quiet life'.

However, even in this early play, Arden's commitment to radical change can hardly be in doubt. The question is not whether change is necessary, but how it can be best effected. Many varying view-points are explored: anarchy, terrorism, political activism, pacifism. Musgrave's own dangerous idealism is at the centre of the play, but then, as with Medea and Macbeth, dramatic interest is aroused less by rightness of attitude than by the energy of intense passion. So Musgrave, despite his evident wrong-headedness, is the focus of our attention, and although his crazed scheme fails, Attercliffe's final line: 'D'you reckon we can start an orchard?'[58] suggests that their desperate act of defiance may yet bear seed.

Arden's strategy, then, is to declare a commitment to over-throwing capitalism and imperialism and to consider a number of ways towards that goal. He seeks to achieve this by reviewing possi-bilities not prescribing programmes: 'Sheer propaganda in the theatre is a bore and completely uncommitted play-writing is also a bore . . . I don't regard it as the business of a dramatist to try and tell the audi-ence to accept his views.'[59] No particular road to change is advocated, since this is not the function of theatre; but whatever path is chosen, he wishes us never to lose sight of the fundamental humanity which prompts the desire for change: life and love do not scribble over the plan, they are the sustaining force behind it.

In not losing sight of human values, Arden is closer to Wesker's thinking than perhaps either man was prepared to concede. It is an atti-tude that is reminiscent too of Brecht's championing of *Freundlichkeit* (friendliness, compassion), which must inform all revolutionary activ-ity. In his 1964 essay, 'Brecht and the British', Arden praises Brecht for portraying 'the fallibility of humanity and also its potential majesty'.[60] In *Serjeant Musgrave's Dance* Arden himself achieves just that.

Part 3: The reflectionist strain

4   The dialectics of comedy: Trevor Griffiths's *Comedians* (1975)

My plays are never about the battle between socialism and
capitalism. I take that as being decisively won by socialism.
What I'm really seeking is the way forward. How do we
transform this husk of capitalist meaning into the reality of
socialist enterprise?[1]

This 'decisive' victory, anticipated by Trevor Griffiths in an interview in 1976, was characteristic of the optimism of most of the playwrights discussed in this volume. By the early 1970s when most
'Angry Young Men' – if indeed they ever existed outside the minds
of journalists – were becoming placid middle-aged men, a new generation of playwrights began to emerge in Britain. This 'second wave' of
left-wing writers, born after 1940, were largely persuaded of the imminent demise of capitalism. Yet, within three years Margaret Thatcher
would win the British general election and initiate widely acclaimed
radically right-wing policies, and within less than a decade and a half
Communism would collapse in Eastern Europe. In hindsight, the prediction by Malcolm Sloman in Griffiths's *The Party* of 1973 sounds
hopelessly inaccurate: 'There'll be a revolution, and another, and another, because the capacity for "adjustment" and "adaptation" within
capitalism is not, contrary to popular belief, infinite.'[2] If not infinite,
capitalism's ability to sustain itself is clearly destined to continue well
into the twenty-first century.

   This is one reason why the majority of Griffiths's plays now
seem dated, with *Comedians* as an example of a play that will, excep-
tionally, stand the test of time and that shows Griffiths at his best. The
other reason is that, like Wesker, he has written in a predominantly

65

reflectionist, realistic style, which now appears theatrically unadventurous. Apart from *Comedians*, Griffiths's major plays divide roughly into two types of realistic portrayal, those that deal with specific topical issues and those that examine more general approaches to socialism ('in a world way' rather than 'in a particular social way',[3] although obviously the two types are not mutually exclusive). In the first category is his play about the National Front, *Oi! for England* (1982); in the second category are historical pieces like *Occupations* (1970) and *Thermidor* (1971), and the depiction of British socialism in the play *The Party* (1973).

Griffiths began his playwriting by contributing pieces for the fringe, collaborating with Brenton and Hare in Portable Theatre's *Lay-By* (1971). Despite returning to work with them later in the decade on *Deeds* in 1978, he soon went his own way, partly no doubt because his own less privileged background of Northern English working-class, comprehensive school-teaching and journalism rather than Oxbridge made him impatient of writers and audiences who urged subversion from a position of affluence and status. 'I am not interested in talking to thirty-eight university graduates in a cellar in Soho',[4] he stated in an interview in 1978, and in an attack on British left-wing intellectuals, the Trotskyist John Tagg in *The Party* articulates Griffiths's own view:

> You start from the presumption that only you are intelligent and sensitive enough to see how bad capitalist society is. Do you really think the young man who spends his whole life in monotonous and dehumanizing work doesn't see it too? And in a way more deeply, more woundingly? ... You lose contact with the moral tap-roots of socialism ... You see the difficulties, you see the complexities and contradictions, and you settle for those as a sort of game you can play with each other.[5]

In similar vein, five years after *The Party*, David Hare admitted in his 1978 lecture: 'The urban proletariat in this country knows better than we ever can that they are selling their labour to capital; many of them know far better than we of the degradations of capitalism.'[6]

Fringe theatre seemed to Griffiths to be too much of a debating society between already committed groups: 'One of the reasons I wrote such a short time for the fringe is because I realised how impotent it was as a mouthpiece to the whole of society.'[7] Again like Wesker before him, he tried to engage a wider audience, and so, like Wesker, used the reflectionist strategy of accessible realism. Griffiths, however, did not attempt to follow Wesker's failed model of Centre 42, but instead attempted to address a broader constituency by embracing the new media of television and film. Abandoning what he regarded as the enclosed world of fringe theatre, he pursued an agenda of what he has called 'strategic penetrations'. He undertook to undermine establishment views from within rather than to attack them from the margin: ' "Strategic penetrations" is a phrase I use a lot about the socialists and Marxists in bourgeois cultures...I simply cannot understand socialist playwrights who do not devote most of their time to television.'[8]

His pieces for television, which earned him the BAFTA Writer's Award in 1982, include *Bill Brand* (1976), a thirteen-part serial about a Labour MP and the compromises he has to make once elected, and *Through the Night* (1977), which deals with the experiences in a National Health hospital of a woman suffering from breast cancer. In addition to his work for television, Griffiths wrote the screenplays for Warren Beatty's *Reds* (1981), a sympathetic portrayal of Communism in Soviet Russia, and for Ken Loach's *Fatherland* (1987), set at the time of the miners' strike in Britain in the 1980s.

Griffiths is well aware of the compromises that have to be made when writing for television, and, even more so for Hollywood movies. He confided once that he always deliberately wrote several minutes too much for any television piece, so that he, and not some anonymous script editor would be asked to make the cuts to fit the required slot, thus allowing him to retain some control over his work.[9] Griffiths was certainly not blind to the processes of operating within a dominant commercial system. As Sloman in *The Party* says of his forthcoming play for television: 'Somehow or other, when it's written, it will be squeezed and tugged and shunted and fattened and primped until it finally slurps and slithers into the ninety minute...hole...your masters have graciously reserved for it.'[10] Nevertheless, Griffiths attempted, in a way that none of his fellow political playwrights did, to infiltrate a political agenda into mainstream television.

David Edgar, for one, was sceptical about the effectiveness of such intervention:

> The inherent problem with television as an agent of radical
> ideas is that its massive audience is not confronted en masse.
> It is confronted in the atomised, a-collective arena of the
> family living room, the place where people are at their least
> critical, their most conservative and reactionary ... The danger
> of a project like *Brand* is that, by the end of thirteen episodes,
> the audience is identifying with Brand exclusively as the pivot
> of the story (my hero right or wrong) and sympathising with
> his views and actions only insofar as that is necessary to the
> experience of following the story.[11]

Weakened as the effect of any one television offering can be, the incontrovertible fact remains that a play in the theatre will be seen by a few thousand at most, while the same play on the small screen will be watched by millions. It has been estimated that only 5 per cent of the United Kingdom population attends theatre, opera or ballet, while 98 per cent watch a substantial amount of television.[12] So Griffiths writes in his preface to *Through the Night*: 'To argue ... that television is part of a *monolithic* consciousness industry whose work of truly radical or revolutionary value will never be produced is at once to surrender to undialectical thought and to fail to see the empirical evidence there is to refute such an argument.'[13] Certainly it is true that Griffiths's strategic penetration has succeeded in the sense that many television soap operas have now appropriated political themes. Issues of public health are debated in *Casualty* and of crime and deprivation in *The Bill* with a vigour that reminds us how totally apolitical their forerunners like *Emergency Ward 10* or *Dixon of Dock Green* were. It remains, of course, debatable whether this reflects a raising of political consciousness in the public or is merely an example of the Establishment's ability to absorb and emasculate genuinely political comment.

Here our concern is with the strategic use of the stage for political ends and not the abandonment of it in favour of another medium. Griffiths continued, while scripting for film and television, to write for the stage despite his recognition of its limited audience. Part of his motivation, he freely admits, is that writing for the stage is a means of maintaining one's credibility as a playwright of stature. Critical and academic interest remains high, he argues, only if one can deliver the occasional stage-piece (only Dennis Potter, it seems, was able to establish a major reputation almost entirely by writing for television). This is not to imply, however, that for Griffiths writing for the stage is merely a means to secure the next television contract, for he seems equally at home in both media and has been admirably prolific in his role as dramatist.

Two of his major early stage-plays debate the nature of socialist revolution: *Occupations*, which was first performed in Manchester in 1970 with Richard Wilson as Kabak, then in 1971 at The Place in London by the Royal Shakespeare Company under the directorship of Buzz Goodbody with Ben Kingsley as Gramsci. It was later toured by John McGrath's 7:84 Company; and *The Party*, which premiered at the National Theatre in 1973, directed by John Dexter, and later toured in a production by David Hare.

Occupations was Griffiths's first full-length play for the stage and 'is bedded in a lost moment of European socialist history – the occupation of the factories in Northern Italy in 1920'.[14] The title *Occupations* therefore refers literally to the take-over by the workers of the Fiat motor-car factories but also, in the sense of occupations as types of employment, points to the roles of the two leading protagonists, Gramsci and Kabak. Gramsci's occupation is to be a popular leader, to encourage proletarian revolution in a way that is coloured by dangerously optimistic idealism. Kabak's occupation is as the steely emissary from the Comintern to place a proto-Stalinist check on the workers' subversion. To Gramsci, Kabak's intervention seems like betrayal; to Kabak, his firmness is essential to prevent the workers sliding into dangerous anarchy and thus delaying the hoped-for national revolution, which has to be worked for in a painstakingly disciplined fashion: 'This isn't a revolution, it's a bloody Italian farce...Well, comrades, what do you think, eh? Shall we have a revolution, or shall we just play silly buggers for a bit and see what happens?'[15]

The political confrontation between the Italian and Russian leaders is reflected at a personal level. Kabak is caring for an unreformed Russian émigrée, Angelica, who is addicted to cocaine and is dying. Just after Gramsci has made a long impassioned speech about love ('There is nothing in the world more relevant than love'),[16] it is the ruthless politician Kabak who actually demonstrates love by swiftly crossing to the bed to cool and soothe the delirious Angelica. However, he is obliged to abandon her at the end of the play, because she, too, must not be allowed to stand in the way of working for the revolution. Griffiths reveals himself as firmly in the reflectionist camp in the way he uses individuals like Gramsci and Kabak to provide the focus for wider conflicts. Indeed, in an interview in 1982 he even refers to Lukács:

> I think my practice as realist is probably Lukácsian ... that whole idea of a character working as a confluence of important social and political and moral forces within society, in real historical time ... I didn't read Lukács and say 'Oh I want to write that way.' But reading Lukács offers some insight into the way one works.[17]

Griffiths admitted that he had written *Occupations* 'as a sort of Jacobinical response to the failure of the '68 revolution in France',[18] and his next major piece for the theatre, *The Party*, uses the events in Paris in 1968 as a backdrop to the play. While a television set reports on the street-fighting between students and police, a group of English left-wing intellectuals gather in a London living-room to respond to the developments across the Channel by discussing the setting up of a united party committed to revolutionary socialism.

One remarkable aspect of *The Party* is the fact that a thoughtful and unspectacular play about left-wing politics could be successfully staged at the National Theatre, employing a top director like John Dexter and stars like Ronald Pickup playing Joe Shawcross, Frank Finlay as Malcolm Sloman and Laurence Olivier in the role of John Tagg. Predictably the left-wing press was horrified at seeing a socialist play performed in the Establishment theatre temple, the National Theatre, with Lord Olivier acting a Marxist revolutionary, described in the stage-directions as a 'short, stocky, very powerful, about sixty, Scots, from Glasgow'.[19] As Griffiths admitted: 'I get tons of shit lowered on the plays quite regularly by *Workers Press* or *Socialist Worker* or *Tribune* or whatever.'[20] But again Griffiths could defend himself by reference to strategic penetration of the Establishment, and John McGrath in his comments on the production, while pointing to the risks Griffiths was running, generously admitted that 'it would be short-sighted to deny the value of trying'.[21]

As well as the surprise that a socialist playwright could penetrate the Establishment, it is remarkable that a play set in one room, virtually devoid of theatrical action and proceeding by means of often very lengthy speeches, could attract the interest of an actor like Olivier and hold the attention of the middle-class and tourist public that almost entirely constitute the audiences at the National.

The reason why Griffiths achieved considerable success with these two early plays rests on three achievements, all of which are well represented in *Comedians*: the intelligence of his dialectics, the quality of his writing and his theatrical exploitation of realistic style. John Bull subtitles his chapter on Griffiths 'Strategic dialectics', and begins with the following quotation by Griffiths: 'I'll probably never complete a play in the formal sense. It has to be open at the end: people have to make choices, because if you're not making choices, you're not actually living.'[22] More so than most of the political playwrights under discussion, Griffiths seems informed by Tom Stoppard's observation that part of the fun of writing plays is that you can contradict yourself in public (in this Griffiths is close in spirit to a piece like David Hare's *A Map of the World*, 1982). Again and again Griffiths examines issues from opposing viewpoints, often by embodying them in two people from the same background, typically a working-class brother in conflict with his sibling who has been educated out of the working class (as in *Sam, Sam*, premiered in 1972, in *Bill Brand*, in *The Party*, and in the two Murray brothers, one an insurance agent, the other a milkman, in *Comedians*). One never has the sense that Griffiths is preaching to his audience or peddling a particular political nostrum, but is inviting us to decide. In this way he continues the *agon* of classical theatre and the human conflicts of Shakespeare (he approvingly quotes Lukács: 'Shakespeare states every conflict, even those of English history with which he is most familiar, in terms of typical-human opposites').[23]

Primarily this dialectical approach is concerned with differing ways of initiating radical social change. So he asserted that his 'early plays were to some extent an attempt to explore the dialectical conflict that exists in the past, to see what energy could be released from it for the future'.[24] The debates about the way ahead that take place in *Occupations* and *The Party* are not intended to document socialist attitudes in 1920 or 1968 so much as to provide the opportunity for the present-day audience to consider how they would align themselves to the historical challenges faced by the characters in the play.

Moreover, Griffiths's willingness to articulate opposing viewpoints is not confined to debates about socialist alternatives. In *Occupations*, for example, Valletta, the factory-owner, speaks persuasively about the future of capitalism in a way that has indeed been realized much more convincingly than the socialist alternative:

> Marx ... underestimates our passion. He underestimates our intelligence and our discipline. Above all he underestimates our ability to adapt. (*Pause.*) Today, I was putting the final touches to our plans for a new social welfare programme ... I can see a day when Fiat workers will live in Fiat houses; when every Fiat worker will live Fiat, when every worker will *be* Fiat.[25]

As Griffiths said of Valletta:

> It seems to me pointless to present that man with horns and a tail as an irreducible, inescapable ugliness. Because that isn't the way capitalism presented itself to the working class, after the failure of the occupations in 1920. And I suspect it isn't the way capitalism presents itself now.[26]

Similarly, in the mouths of the middle-aged National Front supporter in *Oi! for England* or of the ex-Nazi in Ken Loach's *Fatherland*,

Griffiths has, ironically, become one of the finest right-wing apologists of recent decades. Griffiths does not intend, however, to fulfil some liberal notion of 'balance', but to provide a potent and discomfiting challenge to the quiescence of the typical middle-class audience. It is difficult not to take sides, and Griffiths leaves it to the intelligence of the audience to make the right choices.

The second key to Griffiths's success and stature is that – quite simply – he writes well. Gramsci's speech to the workers is a fine piece of rhetoric, moving from precise details like the papers in the director's safe at the Fiat Centre to lofty and inspirational generalizations: 'if you want revolution, you must take it for yourselves'.[27] Incremental repetition ('The army stands by. We wait. Italy waits. Europe waits')[28] and effective antithesis abound ('we are learning how to become producers, active, vital, controlling, instead of mere consumers, passive, inert, controlled').[29]

Even away from the rhetorical devices of public speaking, the seemingly interminable speeches of a play like *The Party* are carried along, as in Shaw, by the sheer force of their logic, peppered with memorable aphorisms: 'You can't build socialism on fatigue', 'You've contracted the disease you're trying to cure', 'You enjoy biting the hand that feeds you, but you'll never bite it off.'[30] Small wonder that Olivier enjoyed speaking these lines, however little they accorded with his lordship's own ideology.

The final key to Griffiths's success is his use of the stage. Superficially, his plays are almost entirely realistic, and he seems to accept this as a description of his style. For example, in defending *Occupations* from Tom Nairn's attack, Griffiths refers to Nairn's criticism that 'the play's naturalistic form tended to undermine, even devalue, the promise of its content and themes'.[31] Frustratingly, despite promising to do so, Griffiths does not answer Nairn's point. Nor, however, does he deny that the play is 'naturalistic'. The set of *Occupations*, while not prescribing a 'commitedly naturalistic design',[32] is essentially realistic – a hotel room, in which all the action of the play takes place. And yet, the room bursts open with images projected on to one of its walls. These images give a context for the action, reflecting the civil war in Russia, or establishing the factory setting for

Gramsci's speech to the workers or as an epilogue showing the eventual Fascist take-over of Italy and the signing of the non-aggression pact between Germany and the Soviet Union. In some ways the projections serve to illustrate and contextualize the action, as they did in Piscator's theatre or as used by writers like David Edgar; but they are more than this: they comment on the stage action in a Brechtian dialectical manner. So the threatened new Soviet regime of 1920 contrasts sharply with the administration of cocaine to the aristocrat on stage; the real physical danger encountered by the factory workers contrasts with the rhetoric of Gramsci; the final images provide a sobering commentary on the outcome of finding an accommodation with capitalism. In the same way, in *The Party*, the television images from Paris provide a continuous commentary on the intellectual games played by the left-wing theorists on stage. More recently, in *The Gulf Between Us* (1992), in which the tensions between the West and the Arab world are explored, Griffiths has the audacity to require that a wall be built on stage during the performance, even during the interval, a potent image of patient manual labour that may eventually come to threaten the pampered Western nations with their over-dependence on technology.

In a similar way, while the dialogue has the ring of naturalistic speech, it has already been noted how well-constructed some of the speeches are. As John Bull notes: 'His characters have an amazing facility for remembering and quoting long extracts of prose',[33] and this facility extends, too, to offering well-constructed, thought-out monologues, with no false starts, no redundancies, no hesitations. The attempt to reflect real life is willingly sacrificed in order to clarify the issues under discussion, and Griffiths's theatre is no poorer for that.

Another favourite means for Griffiths to break with naturalism and to present his material in a lively and entertaining way is to employ elements of popular culture in a way reminiscent of John Arden, but mercifully less folksy than is often the case with the older playwright. In *Oi! for England* he has a pop-group on stage. In the first half of *Sam, Sam* there is much comic business as characters struggle to gain possession of the bathroom on a Friday evening. In *The Party* the piece is introduced by a stand-up comic, in this case Groucho Marx, who admits that he is 'pretty nearly totally irrelevant to the rest of this play'.[34] It provides not only a jokey and arresting preparation for the serious discussions that follow; but also, by playing on the coincidence of the name Marx, Karl and Groucho, the potentially po-faced political debate is undercut by humour, in a way that Continental audiences would probably find trivial but English audiences regard as palatable.

It was not least this strain of popular humour that helped Griffiths to produce one of the best political plays of the decade, *Comedians*.

Comedians (1975)
Plot summary

In a night school, a Northern comedian, Eddie Waters, teaches a motley group of would-be comics how to perform stand-up comedy. In the first act Waters instructs his pupils in the need to perform acts that challenge rather than reinforce stereotypes. Unfortunately, it transpires that Challenor, the talent scout who has come to judge their performances and who is able to launch their careers, believes that comedy should merely entertain. In the second act the would-be comedians go through their sets with more or less success, culminating in a savage piece of performance art by the star pupil, Gethin Price, in which he stabs a female dummy and makes it bleed. The final act shows how those that followed Challenor's way of easy laughs get contracts, while the others have 'failed'. In a confrontation between Waters and Price, we see how Waters's gentle comedy is opposed to the violent, revolutionary attitude underlying Price's approach.

Comedians was first performed at the Nottingham Playhouse in February 1975, directed by Richard Eyre, with Jonathan Pryce as Gethin Price, and the aging comedian Jimmy Jewel as Eddie Waters. Stephen Rea and Tom Wilkinson played the two Irish characters, George McBrain and Mick Connor. It was subsequently performed in London, in an adapted version on Broadway and then on British television.

Despite the fact that alternative comedy has now become much better established and the traditional stand-up turns of working-men's clubs less popular since it was written, the play has lasted well. As Griffiths puts it:

> Comedians eschews political theory, professional ideologues and historically sourced discourse on political revolution – all the perceived hallmarks of those earlier pieces [Occupations and The Party] – in favour of a more or less unmediated address on a range of particular contemporary issues including class, gender, race and society in modern Britain.[35]

The adjective 'unmediated' is curious, since it would seem precisely the political discussions of Occupations and The Party which are in fact unmediated, whereas the socio-political issues raised in Comedians are mediated through comedy.

Once again, Griffiths shows himself capable of using realistic form to create strikingly theatrical moments. Indeed the piece is structured on very conventional lines. It has a three-act structure. The first act, set in the night school where a class in comedy takes place, is expositional and carefully prepares for the second act. In the second act the main action and dénouement take place, the actual performance of the pupils' turns and the surprise contribution by Gethin Price, which briefly launches the piece into a surrealist atmosphere. The third act is a kind of coda, reflecting on the second act, as contracts are awarded and the tutor tries to establish what lies behind Price's defiant performance.

The line-up of characters has also something of the formulaic quality that was seen in The Party, and indeed the night school pupils are six in number, the same as the main speaking parts in the earlier play. There is Phil Murray, the insurance agent, lower middle-class, clearly disillusioned with his life, if indeed he was ever illusioned by it; his brother Ged, a milkman, rough and extrovert, happy-go-lucky in contrast to his brother's sour pedantry; two very different Irishmen, George McBrain from the North, a burly, expansive docker, and Mick Connor from the South, a building worker, altogether more surly.

Then there is Sammy Samuels, a reasonably well-to-do club-owning Mancunian Jew; and finally, Gethin Price, the central character, a van driver, the only one who seems to possess an active political consciousness, signalled from his first appearance wearing a 'Lenin-like' hat. With workers, the Irish and a Jew all portrayed, several oppressed elements were represented: nowadays the line-up would include a woman and an Asian or Afro-Caribbean, but in the mid-seventies female comedians and those from ethnic minorities were a rarity on the stand-up circuit.

The theatrical style is also totally realistic, to the extent that the enacted time of the action exactly matches the time taken to perform the piece in the theatre. The opening stage-directions are so detailed that they include information, as much realist drama conventionally does, which cannot be apprehended by the audience in the theatre: 'A classroom in a secondary school in Manchester, *about three miles east of the centre, on the way to Ashton-under-Lyne and the hills of East Lancashire'*.[36] Once again, however, within the limits of a realistic framework both the action and dialogue rise above pure imitation. Clearly the performances of the second act transcend naturalism without actually breaking its rules by remaining plausibly framed in a realistic setting. Even in the night school setting the incongruous costumes and the curious large parcel of meat left by the Indian seeking his class lend a somewhat unreal appearance to the scene.

While most of the dialogue gives the impression of everyday speech, the cracking of jokes and the characteristically lengthy speech of Waters about his visit to a concentration camp again stretch the limits of naturalistic speech. Most striking in this regard is the use, as warm-up devices, of sexually toned limericks (reminiscent of Brenton's *Christie in Love*) and of a significantly worded tongue-twister, 'The traitor distrusts truth.'

Indeed, the piece is about accessing the truth and how easily it is betrayed. Eddie Waters, no longer a successful comedian but merely a teacher in a night school (and the only one of the group who never tells a joke) has condemned himself to an apparently failed existence, because he refuses to compromise the truth. He has stayed up north, in relative obscurity, because he refuses to peddle the racist and sexual stereotypes on which the prevalent humour of working-men's clubs depends:

> If all you're about is raising a laugh, OK, get on with it, good luck to you, but don't waste my time. There's plenty others as'll tek your money and do the necessary. Not Eddie Waters ...A real comedian – that's a daring man. He *dares* to see what his listeners shy away from, fear to express. And what he sees is a sort of truth, about people, about their situation, about what hurts or terrifies them, about what's hard, above all, about what they *want*. A joke releases the tension, says the unsayable, any joke pretty well. But a true joke, a comedian's joke, has to do more than release tension, it has to *liberate* the will and desire, it has to *change the situation* ... [W]hen a joke bases itself upon a distortion – ...a stereotype perhaps – and gives the lie to the truth so as to win a laugh and stay in favour, we've moved away from a comic art and into the world of 'entertainment' and slick success.[37]

As the men prepare for their final evening, which will include performing in front of a talent scout, two developments occur. First, Gethin Price, who has shaved his head, enigmatically announces that he has changed his act to something quite different, no longer 'finishing on a song'. Secondly, Waters announces that the talent scout, Challenor, who is coming up from London, is an old enemy and one whose ideas of comedy are diametrically opposed to Waters's own. Pointing to Max Bygraves as a model (one would have thought that Bernard Manning might have been a better choice, but perhaps Griffiths deliberately chose a Londoner), Challenor reveals his attitude towards comedy:

> A couple of ... hints. Don't try to be deep. Keep it simple. I'm not looking for philosophers, I'm looking for comics. I'm looking for someone who sees what the people want and knows how to give it them ... We're servants, that's all. They

demand, we supply. Any good comedian can lead an audience by the nose. But only in the direction they're going. And that direction is, quite simply . . . escape.[38]

The effect of Challenor's advice is to throw the men into confusion, some resolutely sticking to their planned act, others considering change, Price apparently already having altered his to accord with the ethic of 'escape'. Connor is the first to perform, offering a muted reflection on being an Irishman in England and on the nature of the Catholic faith. His act, while not very polished, contains one or two good jokes, but many of them are too concerned with Irish taboos to score a success with an English audience (both the presumed audience of the working-men's club and the actual audience in the theatre). At least he has remained true to the spirit of Waters's teaching and introduces an element of danger, as when he warns his audience not to keep slapping Irishmen on the back: 'One day he'll stick a pack of dynamite up his jacket and blow your bloody arm off.'[39] When it is Samuels's turn, he too begins to reflect on his Jewishness, but soon becomes aware of 'the stone-faced Challenor' and changes tack to bring forth a stream of racist and sexist jokes: the Irish are stupid, West Indians are cannibals and have big penises, feminists are aggressive and demanding, homosexuals catch diseases off each other. Phil and Ged also begin their act as rehearsed, reflecting working-class life in Manchester, but halfway through their act Phil changes direction without warning and insists that his brother tells a joke about a Pakistani rapist. The cruel stereotype does not succeed as a joke and it is apparent that the two have lost their way, to their own embarrassment and that of the audience.

Next up is McBrain, who has already reverted to what he knows will please Challenor. Apart from the obligatory racist remarks about blacks, Jews and the Irish, most of his act is at the expense of his wife (the kind of 'joke that hates women *and* sex', as Waters had observed earlier).[40] The irony is, as we learn in the final act, that McBrain is in fact utterly devoted to his wife:

MCBRAIN   . . . The wife's not bin too good lately . . . I'd best get off.
SAMUELS   She'll not begrudge you a celebration pint, surely to God?
MCBRAIN   (*steel suddenly*) She begrudges me nothing, Sammy.[41]

The fact is that, lovable as he is, McBrain displays 'bad faith'. He has no integrity as a comedian, and lies about his relationship with his wife for the sake of a few easy laughs.

Finally, it is Gethin Price's turn. He appears, 'half clown, half this year's version of bovver boy,' his whitened face suggesting the clown, his shaved head, denim jacket and Manchester United football scarf pointing to the soccer hooligan, the baggy trousers and big boots belonging to both personae: *'The effect is calculatedly eerie, funny and chill.'*[42] His act pursues this duality: a surreal gag with a violin, apparently derived from Grock, ends with Price crushing the violin under his boot, and then says that he wishes he could smash up a train – a not uncommon pastime of English football supporters. While he limbers up, two dummies appear, a well-dressed young man and his female companion, 'perhaps waiting for a cab to show after the theatre',[43] thus creating a link between the dummies and the middle-class public watching Griffiths's play in the theatre. We now see class war enacted, calculatedly, viciously ('There's people'd call this *envy*, you know, it's not, it's hate'):[44] Price's young thug taunts and threatens the couple of 'toffs' and finally stabs the young woman with a flower mounted on a sharp pin, so that her beautiful white dress is slowly discoloured by a spreading dark red stain of blood. The act ends with Price playing 'The Red Flag' on a magically restored violin. It has been an angry display, calculated to embarrass and provoke the audience, both Price's one in the club and the real audience in the theatre.

Griffiths has here employed a strategy of confrontation. The audience will have lent Price considerable empathy, as indeed Waters does, because he stands out from the others as being very much his own man, as being more sensitive and aware than his classmates. In the event, his act is almost totally unfunny (apart possibly from the clown sequence with the violin at the start), and frankly the audience, despite their better judgment, will have enjoyed the racist and sexist jokes of McBrain and the others much more than it is possible to like Price's act. In this way the audience are forced to reflect on and reconsider the value they place on 'entertainment'.

Griffiths, however, does not seek to imply that Price has got it right. His defiant gesture is not embraced as a model. While, predictably, the second half of Samuels's act, and all of McBrain's, reap praise from Challenor and are rewarded with contracts, Price is rebuked by his fellows, by Challenor, and eventually by Waters too: 'No compassion, no truth. You threw it all out, Gethin. Love, care, concern, call it what you like, you junked it over the side... It was ugly. It was drowning in hate. You can't change tomorrow into today on that basis. You forget a thing called... the truth.'[45] Price responds by accusing Waters of having lost his capacity for anger: 'Truth was a fist you hit with. Now it's like... now it's like cowflop, a day old, hard until it's underfoot and then it's... green, soft. Shitten.'[46] Waters confesses that he changed after visiting a concentration camp in Germany – a place that contained a hideously grotesque joke, that in the middle of this factory of death there was actually a place called the 'Punishment Block' – he decided that 'there were no jokes left'.[47]

This does not mean that Waters has abandoned humour or comedy, but simply jokes as they are normally told, because most jokes, except harmless puns, depend on a stereotype, on reducing the dignity of the individual subject to a laughable object. From regarding a Jew as a figure of fun, it is a small step to seeing him or her as an *Untermensch* and so to the gas chamber, where society can 'cleanse' itself of these dehumanized beings.

Price goes off to an empty and uncertain future, raging but ineffectual ('I stand in no line. I refuse my consent'),[48] resisting compromise but lacking compassion. On the other hand Waters's prospects are also bleak: he will continue to teach the art of being a comedian, while dissuading his pupils from telling jokes, his only successes those, like Samuels and McBrain, who ignore his advice.

The only glimpse of hope is offered at the end, when the Hindu, Mr Patel, reappears to reclaim his parcel of meat. Waters listens to Patel's old and gentle Jewish joke of the starving Jew about to kill a pig, which reminds him that he may not eat pork, to which the Jew responds: 'My God, a talking horse!' Patel has adapted the joke to refer to killing a cow, and it is a joke that derives from a background of exploitation as an Asian and of the hunger of his fellow Indians, and the gentle self-mockery is legitimized by the fact that a Hindu is telling the story about a Hindu. Waters suggests that Patel might join his next class: perhaps in the innocence of the Asian's humour, comedy and revolt may be reconciled after all.

Once again there is no clear resolution of the dialectics of the play. Griffiths refuses to choose between the uncompromising revolutionary posture of Price (like that of Kabak and Tagg) and the more humane approach of Waters (like that of Gramsci and Sloman). All we are told is that, if we commit ourselves to revolution, it will not be fun: there will be no jokes, and people will get hurt.

By facing the truth about the way a fairer socialist society would have to be called into being, Griffiths carries out the inestimably valuable task of warning his largely middle-class audiences about the dangers of playing at revolutionary politics from the comfort of a theatre seat. They, too, might find bloodstains gradually spreading across their chests.

5 Appropriating middle-class comedy: Howard Barker's *Stripwell* (1975)

A lot of my work is quite clearly pessimistic and I think the reason for that is that it is very difficult to be an optimistic socialist in England.[1]

Where Howard Barker is concerned it is arguably more perverse than with any of the other writers considered in this volume to focus on one of his earliest pieces, which is cast in the form of a realistic comedy. While all playwrights of any significance develop, mature and reassess in the course of their careers, Barker has been engaged in a constant process of reinvention. This may well be one of the major reasons why interest in his work remains high in academic circles, while theatre journalists and the wider theatre-going public have frequently approached his later work with dismissive incomprehension. Indeed, one of the major motives for Barker to have established his own company to perform his works, the Wrestling School, was to ensure that he can maintain some control over the way in which his writing is translated to the stage, a process which requires an understanding and familiarity with his methods.

The early Barker play, *Stripwell*, is a particularly problematic choice for discussion, since Barker freely admits that this was a piece he 'planned coldly to be a commercially successful play for a particular management',[2] and significantly it does not even appear in the list of twenty-five works by Barker which prefaces his *Arguments for a Theatre* (1989). However, *Stripwell* has been chosen here for analysis for a number of reasons. It falls most obviously into the period of the 1970s when a belief in the potential efficacy of political theatre remained strong, before the disillusionment of the Thatcher years.

While original and provocative, *Stripwell* debates political issues in a transparent and realistic manner. Barker employs a reflectionist strategy by appropriating the form of middle-class comedy: the play has a story, rounded characters, and proceeds by sequential dialogue and conflict. In addition, *Stripwell* contains many elements that were to become refined in the mature Barker. In Barker's later work, which is more imaginatively poetic (and some would say obscure), the same political conviction remains present but it is revealed (and some would say obscured) through action which does not follow a clear story-line and is presented by figures and dialogue which reflect all the ambiguities and complexities of postmodernist deconstruction. While this later work has a significance which perhaps only distance in time will accord its justified place in our assessment of contemporary British drama and which undoubtedly provokes political thought, a piece like *Stripwell* still speaks with the brash and confident voice of a generation of playwrights who wrote in the hope of effecting a change in the society in which they lived. Barker's later work offers metaphor in place of manifesto.

Even in the 1970s, however, a number of factors set Barker aside from his contemporary political playwrights. Unlike so many of them, he did not become a darling of the Royal Court; nor, at the other extreme, did he join Brenton and Hare in their unsophisticated touring work in the Portable Theatre. His political perceptions also differed considerably from the other writers considered in this volume.

For one thing he did not share the prevailing view, which Wesker's work implied, that the working classes suffered from being inarticulate. While impressed with Bond's *Saved* (1965), he had been dismayed by the limited expression of the dialogue: 'The monosyllabic responses didn't do much justice to working-class dialogue which I rather fancied I could write.'[3] This perception – and the aspiration to draw on the articulacy of the working classes – was due in no little measure to the fact that Barker had grown up in a very politicized working-class home, his father being 'an active trades unionist, an old hard-line Stalinist. I was brought up to be interested in politics.'[4] Since *Stripwell* contains mainly well-educated upper-middle-class figures, the level of expression, as we shall see, remains high. But the articulacy of those lower on the social ladder is acknowledged too: for example, Noel Biledew's father in *Claw* (1975), clearly modelled on Barker's own father, has pushed himself into an understanding of Marx's writings and can now expound on them with clarity. Articulate communication and a sense of poetic rhythm become the dominant register in Barker's later work for all his characters, now allying him closer to Arden than to Bond or Wesker.

Another notable feature of Barker's writing which sets him apart from his contemporaries may similarly have its roots in his Stalinist upbringing: the unwillingness to compromise. Traditionally a characteristic of British politics and supposedly a source of the nation's stability, compromise is something which Barker despises. Sandy Craig speaks of Barker's 'tendency to attack the waverer and the compromiser as much and even more than the hated extremist',[5] and still with a recent work, *(Uncle) Vanya* (1996), it is the atrophied will of Vanya that drove Barker to rewrite Chekhov:

> Its charm lies in its appeal to the death-wish in ourselves. In its melancholy celebration of paralysis and spiritual vacuity it makes theatre an art of consolation, a funerary chant for unlived life... It is therefore necessary to demonstrate the existence of will in a world where will is relegated to the comic or inept.[6]

Barker differs also from many of his contemporary political playwrights in that he does not place much faith in the efficacy of the stage as a political tool; he believes merely, to repeat Lessing's phrase, that theatre cannot cure the sick but merely confirm the healthy in their health.[7] As Barker put it in an interview in 1984:

> [theatre] is not a good propaganda art, but it is very good for loosening the matrix of received wisdom, unpicking habits and responses, setting up healthy confusions, and above all, giving a form to the lurking popular will, the thing that the public believes but can't articulate, which is repressed under so much news and propaganda, or just as sinister, theory.[8]

This is not to undermine the power of theatre, however, only realistically to assess its function. Describing himself 'as a playwright first and a socialist second',[9] Barker does not regard the stage as 'a place for reconciliation or relief',[10] but rather, as Brenton does, acknowledges the power of theatre to generate excitement and interest far greater than that which might be expected from the few who attend a piece of political theatre. Comparing television with the power of the theatre to stimulate, Barker said:

> So there are 10 million people watching – it's an audience to the power of n. But it may as well be 15 people from the point of view of reaction; there is no contact . . . I feel happier working on the stage – the occasion is bigger even if the audience is infinitesimal, there is electricity – not just from the author's nerves.[11]

Humour is a constant and welcome element in Barker's work and offers a strategy for ambushing British audiences with political ideas: 'Arguably a play is a lecture, but it must come at them [the audience] obliquely; they are trained in suspicion.'[12] It is this electricity or passion that makes him special. Especially in a piece like *Stripwell*, he comes close to easy satire, but it is a 'reflex' that he dismisses in search of a more intense form of communication with his audience: 'the satirical element in my work . . . has always been an easy reflex for me . . . I am for passion in the theatre and satire is at the opposite pole.'[13] One is here reminded of the German writer Jean-Paul Richter's distinction between the satirist and the humorist: the satirist stands aside from the person he is ridiculing, pointing the finger at the absurdity of another; the humorist includes him/herself in the laughter, recognizing that absurdity is part of the human condition. In political terms this means that no-one, certainly no political action, is pure or wholly rational; all is tinged with absurdity and subject to chaos, a viewpoint that is hardly likely to endear Barker to the socialist faithful nor to the middle-class audiences, who will inevitably feel uncomfortable in the presence of his passion.

So, predictably, Barker is deeply pessimistic about the future of Britain and offers no programme for change ('I have nothing to teach anyone').[14] Small wonder then that he could move so easily from the more obviously political theatre of the seventies into the doubts and ambiguities of post-modernism revealed in his later work, in what he now terms 'Theatre of Catastrophe'. By 1986 he was mourning 'the extinction of official socialism', and proclaimed: 'when the opposition loses its politics, it must root in art'.[15]

Stripwell (1975)

Plot summary

When Graham Stripwell, a judge, sentences Cargill to prison, Cargill swears that he will murder Stripwell. Stripwell lives with his wife, Dodie, and his cantankerous father-in-law, Jarrow Houghton, a former Labour politician. He also has a relationship with a young go-go dancer, Babs. His son, Tim, is intending to smuggle drugs into the country hidden inside elephants. When Tim meets Babs, she switches her affections to Tim and refuses to leave with Stripwell as planned. Stripwell informs the police about Tim's drug smuggling. Dodie walks out on him in disgust. Finally, Cargill reapppears as threatened and shoots Stripwell.

In *Stripwell* Barker explores one of his favourite themes, which he described as 'the ambiguous state of power, its mediation, the complicity of victims and so on'.[16] He does this by presenting the story of a weak and philandering judge who has practised law for thirty years, and who is now threatened and finally shot by a criminal whom he has condemned to prison.

This wittily told story might seem on the surface the stuff of a standard West End play with little political import, a suitable vehicle for the talents of Michael Hordern, who played Stripwell in the 1975 premiere at the Royal Court Theatre. In fact, the piece is full of unexpected surprises. Within a realistic framework Barker employs many distancing devices; he explores interesting contradictions in the lives of his characters; his humour, while at times safely congenial, ranges into the disturbingly grotesque; his political statement is ambiguous and challenging; above all, the piece is eminently theatrical, reinforcing his assertion that he is 'a playwright first and a socialist second', an order of priorities refreshing in the world of political theatre.

Even before the play begins, we are aware that we shall hardly be offered an attempt to tell the story in a conventionally realistic manner. The name Stripwell, presumably indicative of the central figure's hypocrisy, is improbable and reminiscent of Restoration comedy (just as Jarrow, the name of his father-in-law, is a suitably symbolic name for a Labour politician, recalling the Jarrow March of unemployed protesters in 1933).

The play begins with a lengthy burst of rock music before, inappropriately, a spotlight isolates Stripwell sitting as judge under the royal coat of arms. Without exposition or any attempt to provide a context, Stripwell delivers, in artificially rhetorical style, judgment on an anarchic individual, Cargill. Cargill utters his threat of revenge in one bald statement, the court is adjourned, and the music resumes to become the music that Babs, the go-go dancer, is gyrating to in her pub. The main motor of the action and its dénouement is therefore established in one brief scene without any preparation. Stripwell is isolated both by the din of popular music and by the single spotlight, suggesting already that he is remote from real life.

The piece goes beyond naturalism by using various devices, for example direct address to the audience: 'Me and my judge. We do our circuit together. While he does the Southern Assize, I do Watneys Gaytime Bars.'[17] Babs is also writing her autobiography, and will sometimes speak her own stage-directions: 'And I came in, and he was there, looking at me with those eyes that seemed to consume me, melting my defences like twin laser beams, as I was to write later. Chapter 14.'[18] There are also metatheatrical moments, when one character comments on the performance of another, as in the following exchange between Stripwell and his son Tim:

TIM ...I'm in the final stage of what they call youth.
STRIPWELL (*Acknowledging with a finger*) Good one.

TIM   Greed, lust and spitefulness. And tiny outbursts of pure insensitivity.

STRIPWELL   (*smiling, nodding*) Oh yes... oh yes, very good...[19]

Some of the incidents of the piece are also so improbable as to seem more properly to belong to an absurdist play. So, with as little hope of doing good trade as the blind match-seller in Pinter's *A Slight Ache* (1961), an ice-cream van twice appears in the play, driven by a moralistic voyeur, whom Babs ironically addresses as 'Godot'.

It would be a mistake, however, to conclude from this that *Stripwell* operates purely on a cartoon-like or absurdist plane. For example, Stripwell's revelation at the end of Act One of his affair with Babs to his wife Dodie, who in turn confesses a past infidelity of her own, is a fine example of psychological realism. Barker typically will not box himself into a single style and fills his piece with rich contradictions.

These contradictions and surprises occur not only in shifts of style but also in plausible but arresting moments of theatre. So at the beginning of Act Two we encounter Tim in his full jungle kit, but when the lights go up, he is revealed as standing in his parent's home, 'a traditional middle-class environment'.[20] Later, in Act Two, Scene Seven, as a mirror image to this, Babs, at the end of her tether in the actual jungle, begins to dance her go-go routine.

Characters, too, reveal convincing contradictions: Stripwell, the powerful figure of the Establishment, is meek and clumsy with the young dancer Babs, cannot open a bottle of wine without a corkscrew, fails miserably in his confrontation with the ice-cream salesman and cannot even command respect from a waitress in a tea room. Jarrow, a senile politician, has a collection of pornographic magazines. Tim, a brilliant young Marxist, deals in drugs. Babs, the youngest and brightest character in the play, is weary of life and subscribes wholly to Samuel Beckett's pessimistic view of existence.

Contradiction is of course at the basis of all humour, the juxtaposition of two apparently unrelated ideas, most obviously in wordplay ('Stop baiting him. Stop waiting on him').[21] Comedy, in what is a very amusing play in performance, operates here on many different levels. There is simple visual humour, as with Stripwell's entrance in 1,6, sporting two black eyes. There are running jokes, as in Jarrow being offered a choice and his decision being promptly ignored, and there are old gags, as in someone being asked to speak louder and then overdoing it:

STRIPWELL   I've received a death threat.

BABS   (*Straining forward*) What?

STRIPWELL   (*... still inaudible*) I've received a death threat.

BABS   (*Straining more*) I can't hear you –

STRIPWELL   (*Loudly*) I've received a death threat!

BABS   All right![22]

Barker even permits himself some satire, despite his discomfort with it. So, when asked about his collection of hard-core pornography, Jarrow responds: 'Best in the Labour party. Mediocre for the Tories.'[23]

Most interesting, however, are Barker's ventures into the grotesque, a kind of humour that is at once funny and disturbing, where the contradictions are felt most strongly. The most extravagant and grotesque example is the way in which Tim intends to smuggle a large quantity of drugs into Britain, namely by concealing them in the vaginas of two female elephants. This is a wildly improbable idea, and yet it could be a very effective means of concealment. The need to hide drugs contrasts with the blatantly obvious presence of two huge animals. The high value of drugs is totally at odds with being stashed in the internal organ of a beast.

One of the central grotesque and contradictory elements of the play is in the figure of Stripwell himself, the representative of justice, who is presented as weak and immoral and an abuser of power, no better than a dealer in drugs or the criminals he condemns to imprisonment, 'The sort of person who ends up running concentration camps',[24] as Dodie describes him. Apart from his peccadilloes in deceiving his wife and in his wavering commitment to Babs, Stripwell is revealed as having no moral fibre, certainly no real sense of justice. His role as judge is presented as dishonourable, derided by Babs as 'a man who stuck his fellow creatures in dark holes!'[25] He himself admits that in court it is obvious who represents Justice: 'Justice is the one with shifty eyes.'[26] Early in the second act he admits that his job is 'grotesque', but that he is now 'sick of sarcasm, and cynicism and belittling', and he resolves 'to be moral'.[27] In the event, Stripwell succeeds only in cutting his hand after the futile gesture of knocking a glass out of Tim's hand, and his only decisive moral act in the play is to betray his own son to the police. Even here when, after 'Thirty years of legal poncing, like a monkey on a stick',[28] Stripwell declares: 'This is the first just thing I've ever done',[29] it is easy to recognize that his sudden conversion to justice is hardly pure. As his wife quickly points out, it can all too easily be construed as revenge on his son for taking his mistress from him. He has not even the determination to stand by his decision, for he phones the police again, presumably in order to withdraw his allegation, were it not for the fact that he is interrupted by the arrival of his awaited assailant.

We also look in vain to the left-wing political figure, Jarrow Haughton, for any representative of social justice. Personally he is totally ineffectual, an old man locked in reminiscences about past struggles. One of these, a rambling account of Harold Wilson dealing with the Unilateral Declaration of Independence by the Rhodesian government in 1965, is interrupted by an apparently chance event, but in fact a deliberately cynical theatrical comment by Barker:

DODIE (*Seeing the record she is holding*) Oh, look! We must hear this! *She winds up the gramophone.*
JARROW ...I have only one word of advice, I said. (*Pause*)... I have just one word of advice, I said. (... DODIE *puts the needle on the record.*) Talk. (*Pause*) Talk. (*Pause*) More talk.
Suddenly the music of 'The Laughing Policeman' bursts out.[30]

Even where the policies of the Labour Party are treated less cynically, they are seen at best as a way of preventing a genuine social revolution. So Dodie says of her father: 'They loved Jarrow. They thrived on him. If it hadn't been for Jarrow I think they might have... risen up.'[31] Stripwell sums up the gradualist nature of British politics, when he is threatened by his avenger's shotgun:

We only have a reasonable society because – [*Pause, then he forces himself on*] We aren't attempting the impossible. That's how we do things in this country. We keep our grievances down to a manageable size... [*Pause*] It isn't perfect, obviously...[32]

One looks in vain, too, to the Marxist intellectual for a genuine confrontation with social injustice. Tim, who has been predicted a double first at Cambridge for his studies of Marx, merely uses Marx's economic theories to explain his growing involvement in the drugs trade: 'The iron laws of capital, which [Marx] described, accorded perfectly with my experience. The narcotics market has been saturated as far as Cambridge is concerned.'[33]

Disturbingly, the only figure who refuses to compromise with the status quo is Cargill, the violent criminal whom Stripwell sentences to one year in prison. As Barker said in an interview with Catherine Itzin:

> If you're working class and you have a real resentment, crime is one of the ways in which you operate it. Political knowledge is another, but because political knowledge is not widespread in the working class, crime is a very natural and legitimate outlet. That's why my characters more often drift into crime than politics. After all, there are more juvenile delinquents than there are Young Socialists.[34]

Cargill's initial crime, 'an orgy of malicious damage', was prompted, in Stripwell's words, by 'some ill-defined sense of grievance and social injustice'.[35] When he returns to fulfil his threat to murder Stripwell, Stripwell pleads with him, begging him to compromise: 'We have to make adjustments, do you see... make do with less', to which Cargill responds: 'Shall I just cut your leg off, then?'[36]

Finally, in a brilliantly tense theatrical climax, after a 'long, agonizing silence', Cargill slowly leaves, Stripwell shakily pours himself a drink, and suddenly Cargill reappears letting out '*a defiant yell: No!*'[37] The gun is fired, and Stripwell collapses.

Paradoxically Cargill's violent refusal to compromise is the most positive image of the play, an unsettling challenge to the middle-class Stripwells and Dodies, who would have been mirrored by the Royal Court audience, happily applauding this attack on the comfortable compromises by which they lived their lives.

As harsh as Stalinism, but rejecting its orthodoxy, as revolutionary as Marxism, but rejecting its theorizing, as caring as traditional socialism, but rejecting its gradualism, Barker's political position is outrageous, disturbing and extreme. Seducing us with the fun of theatre, which he handles with astonishing skill, he leads us into a quite uncompromising area. One can be glad only that the Barker of the seventies chose to resort to a pen rather than a machine-gun.

6 Staging the future: Howard Brenton's *The Churchill Play* (1974)

> I dream of a play acting like a bushfire, smouldering into
> public consciousness. Or – like hammering on the pipes being
> heard all through a tenement.[1]

The majority of playwrights in this volume began writing for the fringe theatre, and all went on to become established writers for mainstream theatre. Brenton stands out as a writer who preserved much of the outrageousness of the fringe in his later work. As John Bull writes: 'More than any of the writers in this book [Hare, Griffiths and Edgar], his roots were firmly in the fringe, and more than any of them he has brought the shock tactics of the fringe into mainstream theatre.'[2] Brenton's ability to shock is notorious, especially since the *Romans in Britain* trial in 1982, in which Mary Whitehouse mounted a prosecution against Michael Bogdanov, the play's director, for 'having procured the commission, and been party to, an act of gross indecency'. What had upset Mrs Whitehouse and other guardians of British morality was a scene in which a Roman soldier attempts to rape a young male Celt. Significantly, it would appear that the depiction of attempted, or even actual, heterosexual rape on stage would have caused far less fuss, not to mention the acceptance of other horrific crimes performed by actors – as one correspondent to a national newspaper pondered, could Macbeth be charged with murder?[3]

More importantly still, although the one prosecution witness sitting 90 feet (27 metres) from the stage erroneously assumed 'that an actor's thumb was his penis',[4] no rape was in fact enacted, but merely threatened and then abandoned. This is characteristic of the

way Brenton does shock his audiences – through the suggestion of
violence rather than through its actual representation.

The shocks in Brenton's plays occur in his use of provocative
content and unexpected juxtapositions rather than in an aggressively
interventionist style of theatre. The attempted rape of the Celt takes
place in a realistically written scene (indeed a symbolic representation
would no doubt have been more acceptable). Brenton may therefore
be regarded as inherently a reflectionist writer: we seldom encounter
the explicit 'aggro-effects' of Edward Bond (an exception is the ado-
lescent image of corpses being turned into jam in the play on which
he collaborated with six other writers, *Lay-By*, 1971). The real shock
of even as unrealistic a piece as his *Christie in Love* (1969) derives
not so much from the symbolic portrayal of Christie's crimes as from
the attitude of the police, the Constable's smutty limericks and the
Inspector's brandishing of a sample of Christie's semen.

The desire to shock, to toss 'petrol bombs through the proscenium arch', as the title of a 1975 interview put it,[5] was not mere
defiance but a considered strategy. As he said in this same interview:
'I think the theatre's a real bear-pit. It's not the place for reasoned
discussion. It is the place for really savage insights.'[6] Rejecting the
humanism of Wesker, the pacifism of the early Arden and Bond and
the idealistic hippy culture of the sixties, Brenton committed himself
to revolutionary socialism:

> I think the fringe has failed. Its failure was that of the whole
> dream of an 'alternative culture' – the notion that within
> society as it exists you can grow another way of life, which,
> like a beneficent and desirable cancer, will in the end grow
> throughout the western world, and change it ... The truth is
> that there is only one society – that you can't escape the world
> you live in. Reality is remorseless. No one can leave. If you're
> going to change the world, well there's only one set of tools,
> and they're bloody and stained but realistic. I mean
> communist tools. Not pleasant. If only the gentle, dreamy,
> alternative society *had* worked.[7]

Brenton's political philosophy is not clearly defined ('When it comes to agit-prop, I like the agit, the prop I'm very bad at'),[8] but by his own admission, one major influence on his thinking was that of 'situationism'. This form of political analysis, which had had profound importance for the rioting students in Paris in May 1968, is described with admirable clarity by Richard Boon:

> Broadly speaking, the situationists offered a reassessment of the traditional Marxist view of the relationship between the individual and his society. The need to change society remained, of course, paramount; but conventional political struggle – not only parliamentary democracy, industrial relations and so on, but Marxist revolution itself – was rejected as no more than the deployment of tactics within an existing system that would remain fundamentally unchanged. That system was defined as 'the society of the spectacle'. The situationist analysis argued that the main agent of capitalist repression had ceased to be located at the point of production – on the factory floor – and had transferred to a point of consumption: the consumption of bourgeois ideology as transmitted through culture generally and the mass media in particular. The relationship between the individual and society was thus analogous to that between the spectator and the events on a screen: both were passive consumers of a two-dimensional charade. It was by shattering the hegemony of received images that individuals had of society that the ground-work of revolutionary change could be established; smashing the screen of *public* life could expose the realities of *private* and *daily* life beneath.[9]

One way in which Brenton attempted to smash 'the screen of public life' was to reassess major figures whose stature in the public mind was legendary, whether for their evil (Hitler, Stalin, Reginald Christie) or for their heroism (John Wesley, Scott of the Antarctic, Winston Churchill). Thus in *The Churchill Play* Brenton undertook a task not dissimilar from Bond in his treatment of Lear; but while

Bond reassessed a mythical past, Brenton also set out to reassess the future.

The Churchill Play (1974)

Plot summary

Four servicemen are guarding the coffin containing the body of Winston Churchill at his lying in state in 1965. Suddenly Churchill rises out of his catafalque, and it is soon revealed that this is a rehearsal for a play in a British internment camp in 1984. As an extension of the army's role in Northern Ireland, all political dissidents are now imprisoned and face punishment or death. The second half of the play shows the performance of the prisoners' play, a retrospect of the Churchill years, plotting the move towards ever greater oppression. The planned breakout from the camp fails, but it was pointless anyway, since there is no longer anywhere to escape to.

The Churchill Play, as originally performed,[10] was set in 1984, ten years after the premiere, and an ominous date to those familiar with George Orwell's bleak vision of the future in his novel *1984*. It is set in an English internment camp, 'Churchill Camp', in which various types of subversives are incarcerated as an effective means of maintaining law and order in the realm.

But none of this is immediately apparent to the audience in the theatre. For, apart from the 'savage insights' which Brenton brought with him from the fringe, he had also learnt from his work with fringe groups like the Brighton Combination, Bradford University Drama Group and Portable Theatre how to create striking theatrical effects with minimal and essentially realistic means. Unlike Wesker, Arden and Bond, whose practical involvement with the theatrical process came only after they had established themselves as writers, Brenton had already worked 'as stage manager and bit actor in reps all over the country',[11] and one of his early pieces *Gum and Goo* (1969), written for a teachers' conference, had to manage on a budget of thirty shillings (£1.50). It is also significant that Brenton originally intended to become a painter and had been offered a place at an art college in Bath – further testimony to his strong visual sense.

As a consequence of all this, Brenton's work is characterized by a strong theatrical awareness that is achieved with deceptive simplicity. So *The Churchill Play* opens with a tableau, which the audience takes to be set in 1965: before a huge stained glass window stands a sombre catafalque, a serviceman at each corner. There is a long silence. One of the servicemen, an army private, begins 'roaring his lines. Choked, awkwardly'.[12] More extreme even than Arden's minimal sentences, the communication is now stripped to single phrases: 'Body! (*A pause.*) Body a! (*A pause.*) Body a Sir Winston! Churchill! (*A pause.*) Laid in State! (*A pause.*)'.[13] The effect is surreal, dream-like, the motionless sentinels surrounding the catafalque, words shouted into the semi-darkness, ominous pauses, and, in the 1974 version, wind gusting mysteriously across the scene, curling newspapers and 'blowing tiny little Union Jacks'.[14] The audience is misled into believing it is witnessing an imaginative reconstruction of Churchill's actual lying in state. Then, after mysterious knocks being heard from the coffin, Churchill suddenly bursts forth. It is a profound shock, providing an exciting moment of theatre, reminiscent of the sudden appearance of Christie from beneath piles of old newspapers in *Christie in Love*. However, we still imagine we are in 1965, seeing Churchill risen from the dead, for the actor representing Churchill 'must assume an exact replica'.[15] Provocatively, Brenton is basing a subversive piece of theatre on the man whom many British would regard as the greatest figure of the twentieth century.

The Marine has voiced criticism of Churchill for sending troops against the miners in 1910, and Churchill reveals himself as a disillusioned ninety-year-old. The bubble of Churchill's heroic legend is, however, truly pricked when he begs the Sailor to kiss him. It is precisely at this moment that the second striking *coup de théâtre* takes place, when the lights are ordered to be switched on and we suddenly understand that we have been watching a rehearsal in some sort of military camp. From an apparently surreal moment we are plunged into stark realism. Brenton has still got surprises in store for us, however. As the nature of the camp is slowly revealed and we discover that, far from being in the past, we are in fact in the future, another figure suddenly emerges from the catafalque. We can see this time that he is a self-consciously theatrical figure, because he is blacked up, but 'His left arm is fearfully wounded, hanging by a sliver of flesh,' and he speaks in the character of a dervish, whom Churchill had encountered as a 'young sightseer'.[16]

Just as the audience has begun to find its bearings, it is thrust briefly back into the surreal world of the dream, soon to discover that the 'dervish' is yet another actor, and that the action is still firmly set in the camp. In fact, *The Churchill Play* may be accounted a realistic piece, because all the action is plausible, and the characters all behave in an acceptably coherent manner. But by using the time-honoured device of the play-within-a-play, Brenton creates an opportunity to introduce powerfully theatrical moments and make sharp political points in true agit-prop fashion.

Saying that *The Churchill Play* is realistic, and indeed possibly the most realistic piece Brenton has written as a solo author (only *Pravda*, 1985, written with David Hare, would otherwise qualify), does not imply that it retains all the characteristics of realism. In particular, like Arden before him, Brenton has little interest in the personal psychology of his characters ('I've always been against psychology in my plays').[17] All of the figures in *The Churchill Play* are defined by their social attitudes rather than by personal biography, e.g. the ineffectual liberal, Captain Thompson, or the anarchistic neo-Luddite, Jimmy Umpleby. As Brenton rather defensively argues: 'Through Ibsenite glasses, the glasses worn by our bourgeois theatre critics, the characters often look like cartoons or fanatics because the way they are written has nothing to do with the finely expressed peeling of the onion toward a fine, hidden centre of "true feeling"'.[18] Rather than peeling the layers of some psychological onion, Brenton creates characters with whom we establish a certain empathy through sharing the pain of their situation and sensing the passion of their response to it. For the actor the need is to plunge headlong into the role without the crutch of Stanislavskian motivation. As Julie Covington, who played Janice in *Weapons of Happiness* (1976), said: 'it was like opening a furnace door – your time comes, you open the door and blaze, then shut it. There is no "edging up" to a revelation of character as there is in, say, Ibsen.'[19]

Brenton compared this kind of characterization to a two-dimensional 'Kodak camera girl outside a chemist's shop'. As you walk past it, 'suddenly you realize that the hand is real, and it grabs you'.[20] So neither the actor nor the audience will gain much from a 'character study' of, for example, George Lamacraft, the young man who suddenly appears as the dervish and is later beaten to death by the camp guards. As Boon says: 'Nothing is known of his background; no explanations are given for the recklessness of his action, nor for the degree of obsessive, suicidal anger that drives him to quote Churchill's prose, from memory, even as he dies... it is more a *role* than a conventional "character".'[21] When Lamacraft rises up out of the catafalque, it is realistically plausible, although it would not be very helpful to consider why he has remained hidden for so long in what must have been some discomfort. It is a brilliant theatrical moment, which makes a strong political point, and does not need any psychological explanation to justify it.

It is difficult to discuss such characterization without reference to Brecht. Yet Brenton vehemently rejected any influence:

> I'm an anti-Brechtian, a Left anti-Brechtian. I think his plays
> are museum pieces now and are messing up a lot of young
> theatre workers. Brecht's plays don't work, and are about the
> thirties and not about the seventies, and are now cocooned
> and unperformable... I think Brecht's influence is wholly to
> the bad.[22]

It is a polemical statement, uttered in 1975, only a few years before he completed a commission to translate Brecht's *Galileo* for the National Theatre. Even so it contains a certain amount of truth, since the misunderstandings that have grown up around Brecht, especially through mis-application of the concept of *Verfremdung* (usually unhappily translated as 'alienation'), have indeed led to theatre work that is derivative or downright turgid. Nevertheless, in terms of political commitment, of his views of characterization, and of the occasional 'epic' form of his plays (e.g. in *Magnificence* (1973) and *Weapons of*

Happiness, less so in *The Churchill Play*), Brenton, while still pursuing an essentially reflectionist strategy, is clearly also an heir to Brecht's legacy. However, he prefers, like Arden, to point back to the Jacobeans for his inspiration. What he certainly does share with Brecht is a strong visual sense and an awareness of the importance of *Gestus*. To take two examples from *The Churchill Play*:

> *The* PRIVATE *makes a farting noise. The* CORPORAL *steps smartly forward and slaps him on the face and points at him. All stock still. Then slowly they change into their prisoner clothes.*[23]

> THOMPSON *puts his hand on* BALL's *arm, to turn him back to the argument.* BALL *stares at the hand.* THOMPSON *removes it and steps back.*[24]

In the first example, a playwright with less theatrical sense would have merely indicated that the Corporal should hit the Private in the face for his insolence. Brenton reinforces the moment by following it with a tableau of the Corporal pointing at the 'guilty party' and the shocked silence as the prisoners react, motionless and unspeaking. This 'beat' intensifies the first piece of physical aggression in the play.

In the second example, we are dealing not with a full-stage tableau but a close-up gesture. Thompson, the liberal-minded doctor, reaches out to touch his superior, Colonel Ball, in a way that might be acceptable between close friends but is inappropriate physical contact with a senior officer. Ball's silent stare at the hand on his arm and Thompson's withdrawal say more about their relationship than many lines of dialogue would be able to communicate. In accordance with Brecht's famous dictum that even a deaf member of the audience should be able to follow the action of his plays, Brenton consistently establishes the 'gest' of the scene by strong visual signals.

Where Brenton succeeds, therefore, in *The Churchill Play* is not so much in conveying any specific political message but in creating an imaginative theatrical world, which is itself the statement of the play. Little that is actually said is of great significance. We have, as noted, the Marine's attack on Churchill for sending troops against the

Welsh miners in 1910. There is also a rewriting of the famous words, supposedly shouted at Churchill by an old woman standing in the bombed ruins of her London slum in 1940: 'We can take it, Guv. Give it 'em back.' Convinced that the working classes were in fact alienated from their upper-class war leaders from his reading of Angus Calder's book, *The People's War*,[25] Brenton now gives the words to a worker as: 'We can take it ... But we might just give it back to you one day.'[26] Perhaps most effectively, he allows Churchill to condemn himself by using his own words: 'You ask, what is our aim? I can answer that in one word – Victory, victory at all costs, ... however long and hard the road may be; for without victory, there is no survival. Let that be realized; no survival for the British Empire ...'[27] The aim is victory, not peace; it does not matter what this costs in terms of human suffering, and the primary aim is to preserve the subsequently much discredited British Empire. If one were to substitute the German *Volk* for the British Empire, then it is exactly the sort of sentiment that Adolf Hitler was uttering.

However, political debate is not at the centre of *The Churchill Play*. What it achieves is to create a plausible negative image of the way British society is moving. Brenton had reason enough to be pessimistic about the erosion of civil liberties in the United Kingdom at the time he wrote the play. On 9 August 1971 three hundred citizens of Northern Ireland were arrested in dawn raids and held without charge in internment camps. Many were suspected terrorists; others were simply prominent civil rights activists. Meanwhile, in Britain the trade unions were squaring up to a confrontation with the Heath government, culminating in the miners' strike of January and February 1972. This led to the declaration of a State of Emergency on February 9. A year later, in February 1973, the so-called Diplock courts were introduced in Northern Ireland, permitting judges to try and to sentence defendants without a jury being present, thereby dislodging a centuries-long keystone of British justice. After 1974, when the play was written, the policy of internment was abandoned in Northern Ireland, but more because of Britain's poor international image and because the effects of internment were counter-productive in suppressing terrorism than because of concern over preserving civil liberties. Moreover, no internment camps have yet been created in Britain; however, the threat of terrorism has allowed many civil liberties to be eroded (e.g. the legislation in the wake of the terrorist action of 11 September 2001, allowing detention without trial for up to six months). Therefore, Brenton's gloomy prediction of subversive elements in the population being locked away without charge may not have been fully realized, but the potential danger is possibly greater than at the time of writing. Indeed, the 1988 revival at the RSC was due to an awareness that 'the play's time had come'.[28] As Boon writes:

> In the light of the Conservative government's anti-Trade Union legislation, its smashing of the miners' strike of 1985, the banning of interviews with Sinn Fein and the withdrawal of the right to silence in Northern Irish courts, one wonders if the writer allowed himself a bitter smile of satisfaction in recalling the accusations of paranoia levelled against him in 1974.[29]

Brenton's image of the future, therefore, like all convincing futuristic essays, reflects much that is already in the present. Probably the character that middle-class audiences will find it easiest to identify with is the naive, non-political Peter Reese. He has been arrested on arrival at work for some undefined act of 'petty vandalism', and, in the rehearsal of the parodistic agit-prop scene of the Yalta Conference, is asked to represent truth. His plight is shared by the many who fear or have been subjected to arbitrary arrest: 'I know I am in a camp. I am detained. Please, let my family know where I am. That I'm well. I have three children. Let my wife know. Can you help me?'[30]

Apart from Reese, we are not invited to identify strongly with any of the inmates. Indeed the young thug, Jimmy Umpleby, would probably be locked away even in a very liberal society, and the inmates' failed breakout provides an ending to the play without engaging the audience strongly in disappointment over their failure. Our engagement is on a more general level of recognition: recognition of the unfair plight of the prisoners, recognition that it could, as with Peter Reese, affect our own lives, recognition that something must be done before it is too late. Brenton suggests that there is little hope in party politics: the Labour MP, Gerald Morn, is 'caught in some vast conspiracy of obedience',[31] just as the British Labour Party consistently supported Conservative-initiated anti-terrorist legislation and subsequently introduced even more draconian measures of their own. Morn now has to assuage his guilty conscience through drink.

The conclusion of the piece is that action is needed, but, as ever, Brenton is not precise about the course this must take. Certainly the violent mini-revolt of the attempted camp breakout is not much of a model. The actual ending of the play is different in all three versions: in 1974 the Colonel's wife, Glenda Ball, appeals vaguely for some resolution: 'Don't let the future...'[32] In the 1978 version the final words are cataclysmic and frankly quite crass: to Glenda's 'I don't want the future to be...,' Joby Peake responds: 'The Third World War'.[33] The 1988 version has a much less militant ending, something of 'a requiem', as Barry Kyle the director called it.[34] The final line is again spoken by Joby Peake, the former journalist, who had in the second act asked: 'When did freedom go?... Wun ev'nin'. Y'were in 'pub. Or local Odeon. Or in 'bed w' your Mrs. Or watchin' telly. An' freedom went. Ay, y'look back and y'ask... When did freedom go?'[35] Now the final lines of Joby are: 'I never noticed.'[36]

Eschewing political debate, which he feels has little place in the theatre, Brenton provides us with two powerful theatrical worlds, that of Winston Churchill and that of the Churchill internment camp. By encouraging us, in a situationist manner, to revise our thinking about the received notions of the heroic figure of Churchill, he is also exhorting us to greater clarity in our perception of the world about us. In this respect he has compared himself to Chekhov, a writer who, in taking his scalpel to the society in which he lived, showed the origins of its own overthrow that took place in the October Revolution of 1917: 'In a way I think we're all a bit like Chekhov. He didn't *know* what was only a few years away, but he felt it in his bones.'[37]

While not possessing the poetic strengths of Arden or Bond, Brenton displays an exciting theatricality and a startlingly plausible vision of the future in *The Churchill Play*. Perhaps more than any of the plays discussed in this book, this piece most immediately and most urgently demands us to reconsider the nature of the society we live in. Brenton's strategy is not to preach revolution but to harness the impulse for change, which he believes is common to everyone:

> [People] are not satisfied, they do not lie down, they do not celebrate suffering. They do everything they can to stop it. And if they're oppressed, they don't say – 'this is the nature of the world, this is how we're born' – they try and change it. Our plays should help them by succouring their instinct for change.[38]

Part 4: The interventionist strain

7   Agit-prop revisited: John McGrath's *The Cheviot, the Stag and the Black, Black Oil* (1973)

To tell the truth is revolutionary.[1]

Political theatre can take many forms, and, as the Introduction makes clear, the focus of this volume is on political playwrights and not on the many groups who have made political theatre from devised and documentary material. There is one group, however, whose work, uniquely,[2] has been consistently linked with the work of a major playwright. The group is 7:84, and the playwright John McGrath. Their varied output will be considered primarily in one example, a supremely interventionist piece of theatre, *The Cheviot, the Stag and the Black, Black Oil.*

The 7:84 Theatre Company was founded in 1971 by McGrath and like-minded theatre-workers, including his wife Elizabeth MacLennan. It was named after the disturbing statistic, revealed by *The Economist* in 1966, that a mere 7 per cent of the population of Britain owns 84 per cent of its capital wealth.[3] The founding of the company was based on the recognition that 'there has to be a struggle, there has to be a political organisation, there has to be a very hard, bitter, disciplined fight against the powerful forces of capitalism'.[4]

Unlike Edgar, Hare and Brenton, who began with small-scale touring and then went on to write for major playhouses, McGrath started as a well-paid provider of scripts for theatres, television and the cinema, and then turned towards more modest venues. Born in 1935, he attended grammar school and, after completing National Service as a gunner, studied English at Oxford University, where his first plays were performed. Although trained as a teacher, his first job was as a play reader and writer at the Royal Court. In 1965 he began working

109

at the BBC, where he co-founded *Z Cars*, a police series: 'It seemed to me perfectly obvious that all the people I knew and cared about at that time were watching television, so I thought, well, fuck it, I'll go and write for television, and try to use the medium in my own way, and contribute through that to people's lives.'[5]

Until this time, police television series had been particularly anodyne, as in the popular *Dixon of Dock Green*, which presented a lovable English bobby dealing with minor criminal acts that would not upset the sensibilities of a middle-class viewer. By contrast, *Z Cars*, influenced by American models, showed crime that resulted from social problems and a police force that was less than perfect. In words that accord with Griffiths's agenda of 'strategic penetration', McGrath stated: 'What we wanted to do was to use a Highway Patrol format. But to use the cops as a key or a way of getting into a whole society ... to use a popular form and try and bang into it some reality.'[6]

In the theatre, McGrath had his first major success with *Events while Guarding the Bofors Gun*, which was premiered at the Hampstead Theatre Club in April 1966. This was an essentially realistic piece, based on McGrath's own experiences during his two years' National Service in the army, and is reminiscent of Arnold Wesker's *Chips with Everything* (1962). The setting, a gun-park with guard hut, is naturalistic, and the characters are introduced with detailed Shavian biographies. There is little that is overtly political about the play. The anarchic figure of Gunner O'Rourke, whose death ends the play, does indeed address the audience about the futility of guarding an obsolete weapon like the Bofors gun, but the device of direct address is crude and inappropriate to the representational style of the rest of the piece. Since, too, O'Rourke is off stage for much of the action, his suicide neither engages the audience nor seems to contain any clear implications. It appears as arbitrary as the suicide of the Actor with which Gorky's *The Lower Depths* (1902) ends. The main interest is in fact in the situation of the liberal but weak Lance-Bombardier Evans, in whom no doubt McGrath reflected much of his own experience in the army as a university entrant attempting to be 'one of the men'. Evans faces the dilemma of trying to be popular and relaxed but at the same time not endangering his prospects of becoming an officer. He is challenged by Flynn, the oldest of the soldiers, to make a choice:

> One thing or the other. I want you to say either God's curse on those two black bastards [O'Rourke and Featherstone], I'll put them away for a lifetime, or bugger the lot of it, rot all the Bofors, I'm off to the NAAFI to join them. One or the other. Life's too short.[7]

This is the closest the play gets to a political statement: that between vigorously supporting the status quo or rejecting it defiantly there can be no compromise.

After a favourable reception in the theatre, *Events while Guarding the Bofors Gun* was adapted by McGrath as a film two years later. This led to further film-script commissions, including the very successful *Billion Dollar Brain* (1967) and *The Virgin Soldiers* (1969), and to two *Plays for Today* for BBC Television. Even a 'blockbuster movie' like *Billion Dollar Brain*, directed by Ken Russell in 1967, was not without its political implications: a fanatical anti-Communist Western capitalist, General Midwinter, is defeated in his harebrained scheme to invade Latvia by a likeable and committed Russian, Colonel Stok, played by the former Brechtian actor, Oskar Homolka. Indeed, McGrath never regretted his apprenticeship writing for television and cinema:

> I learnt a great deal about popular entertainment I would never have learnt if I had stayed in the Royal Court mode of writers, which is the exact opposite of popular entertainment...If you work in popular media like television and then subsequently film, you learn the very very hard rules of how quickly people turn off their television sets or walk out of a cinema. You begin to learn the basic rules of popular entertainment.[8]

Apparently on the brink of a highly successful career in the media, McGrath accepted the much more humble post of Writer in Residence at the Everyman Theatre in Liverpool, where he worked from 1970 to 1973:

I finally came to the conclusion that the mass media, at the
moment, are so penetrated by the ruling-class ideology, that to
try to dedicate your whole life – as distinct from occasional
forays and skirmishes – to fighting within them is going to
drive you mad.[9]

The major turning point, however, came with the founding of
7:84 in 1971. Rejecting the glitter and financial rewards offered by
writing for film and television (just as Elizabeth MacLennan gave up
her promising career as a West End actress), McGrath decided to devote himself to touring socialist plays mainly to non-theatre venues.
While some have derided both Mr and Mrs McGrath's decision as an
assuaging of middle-class guilt, it was based on the clear recognition
that this would be the only way McGrath's work might be seen by
audiences who would not normally attend the theatre. Personally,
he also found the experience of playing to unsophisticated, largely
working-class audiences much more stimulating than was possible at
the National Theatre or even the Royal Court: 'I just don't know about
National Theatre audiences...I'd rather have a bad night in Bootle.
You get more from it if somebody's going to come up at the end and
say, do you know what's happening in Bootle?'[10]
    Two years after the founding of 7:84, the company decided
to split into two sections, 7:84 (Scotland) and 7:84 (England). Gavin
Richards, a member of the original 7:84, went off to found Belt and
Braces, another successful activist theatre group. McGrath moved to
Scotland to work with the northern company and, until his resignation in 1988, directed seventeen shows with them (including work by
Griffiths and Arden). He also wrote twelve shows for the company. He
continued to maintain close links with 7:84 (England), and they too
performed a dozen of his plays.
    The decision to work in a touring political theatre affected
McGrath's style of writing. Up to this point, despite a shift towards
clearer political analysis, his plays had remained essentially naturalistic. Thus *Random Happenings in the Hebrides*, written 1968 to 1969
and performed at the Lyceum Theatre in Edinburgh in 1970, shows
how the Labour government betrays the Hebridean fishermen in their

fight with a big corporation. It also reveals the powerlessness of the idealistic politician, Jimmy Litherland, whose character, like that of Lance-Bombardier Evans, contains autobiographical elements. Indeed, the personal situation of Litherland, especially his sexual philandering, is given a prominence which distracts from the central political issues. Even after the founding of 7:84, McGrath still did not immediately embrace the lively forms of popular theatre for which he was to become renowned. *Trees in the Wind*, with which 7:84 began its life at the 1971 Edinburgh Festival, while not wholly realistic, proceeds mainly by verbal debate.

It was the move to Scotland that caused a decisive shift in McGrath's playwriting. No doubt influenced by working on John Arden's *Serjeant Musgrave's Dance* (in an updated version renamed *Serjeant Musgrave Dances On* (1972)) and on John Arden and Margaretta D'Arcy's *The Ballygombeen Bequest* in 1972, McGrath abandoned realism and turned to a more agit-prop style. This aggressively interventionist form of performance was especially popular in Germany and Russia in the 1920s but has since been regarded as too unsubtle by most political playwrights.

In his two books, *A Good Night Out* (1981) and *The Bone Won't Break* (1990), and in his article, 'The theory and practice of political theatre' (1980), McGrath undertakes to explore theatrical forms that will engage with working-class culture and thus, it is hoped, offer entertainment that relates more directly to the lives of his target audience. In this he parts company with both Arnold Wesker, whose Centre 42 was concerned with bringing middle-class culture to the masses, and also with David Edgar, who considered British popular culture as being irredeemably reactionary.[11] Influenced by the writings of the Italian Marxist Antonio Gramsci and, more immediately, by the work of Raymond Williams, McGrath believed that the struggle for a revolution in the economic structure of the nation must be accompanied by a change in its cultural consciousness. McGrath did not insist that his approach was the only effective means of communicating political ideas, but it was the one he regarded as viable for penetrating to the working classes and helping to undermine the hegemony of middle-class culture:

> If David Hare is best at writing passionate plays about the corruption of the middle classes and the way the class structure affects the upper and middle classes, then that's what he should write. I just don't think that it's of any help in creating a counter-culture within the working class, which is what I'm interested in.[12]

McGrath admitted that much popular culture is tawdry: 'It bears all the marks of the suffering of the urban industrial working class... – the brutality, the violence, the drunkenness, the sexism, the authoritarianism that have been part of its life since the Industrial Revolution.'[13] Nevertheless, he maintained a respect for the working class and their values:

> We're interested in telling the people who are being exploited *first of all* that they are, and *secondly* that their values and their ways of living are good, worthwhile, and something that we like, something that's got a richness, and a depth, and a fruitfulness, which is of more value in the ultimate than the values of the middle class and the upper middle class who're actually doing the exploiting.[14]

In working-class culture McGrath recognized elements that could be incorporated successfully into progressive work in the theatre. The popular theatre that he envisaged must contain the following:[15]

1. *Directness.* 'A working-class audience likes to know exactly what you are trying to do or say to it. A middle-class audience prefers obliqueness and innuendo.'
2. *Comedy.* 'On comedy working-class audiences are rather more sophisticated.'
3. *Music.* 'Working-class audiences like music in shows, live and lively, popular, tuneful, and well-played.'
4. *Emotion.* 'In our experience a working-class audience is more open to emotion on the stage than a middle-class audience, who get embarrassed by it.'
5. *Variety.* '[The working-class audiences] seem to be able to switch from a singer to a comedian, to a juggler, to a band,

to a chorus number, to a conjurer, to a sing-along, to bingo, to wrestling, to striptease, and then back again to a singer ... with great ease.'

6. *Effect.* 'Middle-class audiences have been trained to sit still in the theatre for long periods, not talk, and bear with a slow build-up ... working-class audiences have come to expect a high standard of success in gaining effects.'

7. *Immediacy.* '... my experience of working-class entertainment is that it is in subject matter much closer to the audience's lives than, say, plays at the Royal Shakespeare Company are to middle-class audiences.'

8. *Localism.* '... the best response in working-class audiences comes from character and events with a local feel.' '[Localism] not only of material, but also deriving from a sense of identity with the performer.'

On this last point, one is reminded of Richard Schechner's observation on folk-theatre: that one of the major effects is achieved by seeing someone known from daily life *transformed* into a character on stage. In the same vein, McGrath suggested that the performer should be like a plumber, someone who comes into the house, relates naturally to the householder, then performs a task with special skills, and returns to being an ordinary visitor on finishing his job. Thus, on 7:84 tours it was the practice for the performers to socialize with the audience both before and after performances. This not only helped to demystify the role of the actor and remove any potential 'pedestals'; it also increased the pleasure of the entertainment to see the 'wee lassie' one had been chatting with a few moments ago now playing a serious part in the action on stage.

With these elements McGrath hoped to create 'a new, genuinely oppositional theatre', one that avoided the danger that threatened mainstream writers like Bond, Edgar, Hare and Griffiths 'of being appropriated in production by the very ideology they set out to oppose'.[16] In order to achieve this, 7:84 mounted a considerable number of shows (a term McGrath prefers to 'plays'), which incorporated music, song, comedy and an energetic mode of performance, which interspersed enacted episodes with comment and factual information, spoken directly to the audience. The material was usually derived from history, and related to the experience of the intended Scots working-class audiences:

> Nearly all our shows have got a rather long historical
> perspective. It's why naturalism doesn't work in our terms,
> because naturalism is incapable of making long historical
> connections, and is usually an examination of relationships
> between people on a stage internally, looking in. I'm
> interested in a kind of theatre which makes longer
> connections, where you can see where you come from, and
> you can see how it can affect where you go to.[17]

In rejecting naturalism, the company sought for a performance style that was derived from Brecht's proposals for demonstrational acting, what the Germans call *plakativ*, i.e. like a wall-poster. As Elizabeth MacLennan writes in her account of 7:84, *The Moon Belongs to Everyone: Making Theatre with 7:84*: 'I have found it pretty disastrous to employ anything other than the epic acting style. By epic I mean larger than life, but fiercely true to it. The performer must engage the audience's attention by music, gesture, speech or action.'[18] It is significant that MacLennan insists that the performances, while 'larger than life', should be 'fiercely true to it'. In rejecting naturalism, McGrath and 7:84 never turned to the surreal or the abstract. When he wrote a 'comic strip play about capitalism', *The Trembling Giant*, he was obliged to admit that it had not fully succeeded:

> It didn't work with working-class audiences, because they
> thought it was a bit tittish. They thought it was a bit silly, you
> know. It was basically that thing about directness. If you want
> to say something about capitalism, fucking say something
> about capitalism. Don't dress it up in all this paraphernalia.
> Because you dress it up as an allegory, ... it makes it
> impossible to check against reality. Or against history.[19]

By embracing popular culture and making working-class audiences the arbiters of quality, McGrath frustrates the middle-class critic in his or her attempt to apply standard theatrical criteria to his work. As Colin Chambers states the problem:

> Given that 7:84 is a touring company with the emphasis on the where and how of a performance, the critic has to take on board the totality before being able to comment. The familiar put-down response to the critic is that 'you missed the really wonderful performance in front of 800 miners in their club hall' and therefore cannot comment.[20]

For most playwrights, the aesthetic success of their work is primary; any political message that is communicated to an audience is a bonus. With McGrath, these priorities were reversed. This is not to say that his writing was slapdash, merely that conventional concerns about plot, characterization and layers of meaning are not particularly relevant to his work. The immediacy of audience response is the barometer of quality. However 'good' the play, if it has bored an audience in, say, a working-men's club, then it has failed. Thus, McGrath reported proudly that after the television screening of *The Cheviot, the Stag and the Black, Black Oil*, generally acknowledged not to have succeeded well within the confines of the small screen, 'the mail and feedback that came from it was [sic] fantastic'.[21] Even more compelling are the post-performance comments recorded by Elizabeth MacLennan, e.g. 'If I said what I thought about the landlords, I'd lose my job. You have said it for me'; 'If I die tonight I'll be a happy man. I'll have seen the history of my people.'[22]

Undoubtedly the work of 7:84 has often had considerable impact on certain audiences, and has brought theatre to communities who would otherwise have no access to it, so it seems almost mean-spirited to challenge McGrath's strategy of political theatre. However, one is obliged to question elements of his work. First, while he insisted on the importance of working-class audiences, it is a well-known fact, encountered by most touring political theatre groups, that their audiences comprise mainly left-wing intellectuals. Some of these may come from a working-class background but they will have mainly lost this identity through their education. I, as an undeniably middle-class academic, have sat in community centres, schools and clubs to watch political theatre and have been surrounded by students, school-teachers, social workers and the occasional trade unionist. True, 7:84 (Scotland) succeeded better than most by touring to remote venues and playing in places where there is still an identifiable community. It is also true that their work has been warmly hailed by genuine working-class audiences at times of acute industrial conflict, for example, during the miners' strike in the mid-1980s.

Here, however, one must recognize that the theatrical offering in such contexts is virtually interchangeable with any other expression of political solidarity. As the German director Peter Stein commented after reviewing the success of a performance in front of two thousand students holding a sit-in the Technical University in former West Berlin in 1971: 'It was a tremendous get-together...It wasn't us who were performing, but the students – they were the most important actors...It really had nothing to do with theatre...I might just as well have put up posters or strummed a guitar, I could simply have read out a text.'[23] In similar vein, McGrath admits that during the student uprising in Paris in 1968, an experience which helped to politicize the young McGrath, the real theatre was taking place on the streets: 'It wasn't a theatrical expression, but it was an expression in the theatre. The theatrical expression was happening night after night with flames in the streets...That was a real theatre of revolution.'[24]

If the success of McGrath's work with 7:84 depends on the composition of the audience and the context in which it is seen, then it is not necessarily reproducible. All theatre that is conventionally regarded as 'great' is reproducible. Thus, tragedies written for a clearly defined homogeneous Athenian audience can still have considerable impact on an audience over two millennia later. McGrath would have countered that he was not concerned with writing for posterity or entering a canon of drama approved by critics. However, it is noteworthy that, when in *A Good Night Out* McGrath praises 'the miraculous flowering of Kurt Weill and Brect [sic] in the late 20s and early 30s', he speaks of 'their *enduringly* popular songs'.[25] But to be enduring the songs have, of course, to have a quality not confined to a specific audience or specific context. As Colin Chambers eloquently sums it up:

For someone who has done so much to present history on the stage, McGrath has a curiously unhistorical view; present context overwhelms text, therefore one judges a play by where it is performed and not for what it says and how it says it. But where does that leave 'our' theatre and the 'good night out' recipe? It denies the possibility of learning from or using 'their' theatre even in the individual way that McGrath himself learnt. In a complex society there are many channels for presenting a vision of the future or an understanding of the present.[26]

The Cheviot, the Stag and the Black, Black Oil (1973)
Plot summary

After a song telling of the love of the Scottish Highlands, a series of historical episodes reveals different phases of exploitation by the rich. The 'Clearances' in Sutherland from 1813: the absentee landlord arranges for the removal of the Highland crofters to make way for the Cheviot, a hardy breed of sheep; all resistance is brutally suppressed. Enforced emigration: Highland families are displaced to the British colonies, where they in turn oppress the native populations. A revolt initiated by the people of Skye, 1882: a small victory is achieved by remaining tenants who force their landlords to treat them better. The Highlands become the playground of the nobility: emulating Queen Victoria at Balmoral, the rich and powerful come hunting the stag in the Highlands. This continues into the twentieth century, with the Highlands becoming a holiday theme park. The discovery of oil, 1962: with the construction of oil rigs off the Scottish coast, the lives of the Highlanders are further disrupted, and in a grotesque conclusion the tourists now come to see the polluting oil refineries.

In a letter to the Scottish Arts Council, pleading for the necessary funding to make the next tour of 7:84 viable, John McGrath wrote: 'I have always felt that a serious writer today has to re-invent the theatre every time he sits down to write a play.'[27] The 're-invention' to which he was referring resulted in arguably his most successful touring play,

The Cheviot, the Stag and the Black, Black Oil. It was, as McGrath admits, perhaps not so much 'a new contribution to theatrical form' as 'a new version of a very old tradition'.[28]

McGrath's enterprising innovation was to adopt the ceilidh form of the Scottish Highlands and to provide it with historical and political content. The traditional ceilidh is much more than just a party; it is a parade of local talent. Most of this consists of music, usually played on the fiddle, sung or danced to, but there are also recitations, mainly of comic or sentimental ballads. In appropriate regions, some of the entertainment, especially the songs, is in Gaelic. The offerings are spontaneous, normally called forward by those present, and do not therefore follow any particular pattern. Thus a mournful air may be followed by a rumbustious song to be followed in turn by a tear-jerking recitation, all lubricated by a plentiful supply of alcohol. Aesthetic considerations are secondary. A fine fiddle-player will be duly acknowledged, but someone who sings horribly off-key or another who dances a few drunken steps will be generously applauded. The overriding feeling is of warmth and togetherness. If the ceilidh is in any way a political act, it is because it serves to lend solidarity to a community of the otherwise underprivileged.

The ceilidh fulfilled all McGrath's criteria for good popular entertainment: Directness, Comedy, Music, Emotion, Variety, Effect and Localism, although one may question whether it achieves Immediacy in the sense in which he uses it: of immediate concern to the participants. Most of the material of the ceilidh is either traditional (e.g. ballads about emigration) or imported (e.g. recitations about gold-mining in the United States) and so not directly related to the contemporary problems of those present.

McGrath, while embracing the ceilidh format of music, song and use of Gaelic, and above all retaining its sense of fun and spontaneity, attempted to find the Immediacy that was lacking. In assessing the merits of *The Cheviot, the Stag and the Black, Black Oil,* there is therefore no point in complaining about the episodic and disjointed structure nor the superficial cartoon-like characterization nor the unsophisticated dialogue. All that matters is that information and political awareness are communicated in an entertaining way.

The show starts as soon as the first members of the audience arrive, establishing the feeling that this is a party, which begins with the first guests, and not a conventional theatre performance, at which the audience have to wait patiently until the curtain rises. To reinforce this feeling, the music has already started, and the performers chat with the audience:

> The evening begins with THE FIDDLER playing Scottish and Irish fiddle tunes among the audience, in the bar, foyer, etc., as the audience are coming in. The Company are preparing their props, costumes, etc. at the side of the platform, talking to friends in the audience, playing drum, whistle, etc. to accompany the fiddle; the audience stamp their feet, clap, etc. to the music, if they want to.[29]

Importantly, too, there is no raised stage. Scenes are performed on a platform, and the performers sit on the same chairs as the audience either side of the platform, all of which reduces the separation of actors from audience. The stage that is commonly found in village halls and community centres is normally used for the scenery, created simply but effectively by a large pop-up book lying on its back, designed by John Byrne, later to become a noted playwright himself.

The evening begins with a simple song about love of the Highlands, in which all the audience are invited to join. There then follows a scene of dialogue, which introduces the theme of the Clearances, the forcible removal of the Highland crofters to make way for the Cheviot, a hardy breed of sheep. So the action proceeds, from the Clearances up to the present-day exploitation of Scottish oil, alternating songs and dialogue, with the occasional section in which the performers address the audience directly with historical facts and quotations. This is the least dramatic device in the show and potentially the most harmful and sententious way of spoiling the ceildih atmosphere. However, the intention is to communicate information as well as to entertain, and at least it is an honest device. Rather than attempting to impart facts by clumsy use of dialogue or by otherwise disguising the educational nature of the performance, the actors, here called 'readers', openly declare their intentions by apparently quoting from the books they are holding.

The comedy of the piece is generally unsubtle, hardly fulfilling McGrath's assertion that 'On comedy working-class audiences are rather more sophisticated.'[30] Thus we have a brief music-hall-type act with two Highlanders, pantomime farce, weak puns ('Thank heaven for little Gaels!')[31] and silly satire of the aristocracy:

LADY PHOSPHATE   Oh Archie...Capital, capital, capital...
LORD CRASK   Oh yes I've got bags of that too – 200,000 shares in Argentine beef, half a million tied up in shipping, and a mile or two of docks in Wapping.
LADY PHOSPHATE   Topping –
LORD CRASK   No Wapping –[32]

Lord Crask also repeatedly fails to get the name of his ghillie right in a predictable sequence of less than hilarious incremental humour.

While the villainous upper classes have about as much complexity as the pop-up book, and the Minister indulges in a predictable rant rather than appealing to Christian patience, McGrath does at least suggest that the common Highlanders themselves are not models of perfection. It is admitted that 'There is no doubt that a change had to come to the Highlands: the population was growing too fast for the old, inefficient methods of agriculture to keep everyone fed.'[33] When forced into emigration, the Highlanders hardly behaved in an exemplary fashion: 'The highland exploitation chain-reacted around the world; in Australia the aborigines were hunted like animals; in Tasmania not one aborigine was left alive; all over Africa, black men were massacred and brought to heel.'[34] Nevertheless, there is little subtlety and therefore little truth in the conflicts referred to in the piece. It is also doubtful whether the piece will serve to energize an audience into trying to take control of their own lives. After witnessing a long history of exploitation, it is all too easy to feel that one's political duty has been done. By the time one has shaken one's head resignedly over the plight of the poor, a final rallying cry to action probably has little effect:

At the time of the Clearances, the resistance failed because it
was not organised. The victories came as a result of militant
organisation... We too must organise, and fight – not with
stones, but politically, with the help of the working class in
the towns, for a government that will control the oil
development for the benefit of everybody.[35]

One wonders whether the Hollywood film with Mel Gibson as
William 'Braveheart' Wallace would not win as many converts for
fairer distribution of power as did McGrath's play.

One also has to acknowledge that, with the advent of television, the ceilidh in the kitchen has almost entirely been relegated to
the past, unless revived by enthusiastic visitors. The ordinary High-
lander is more likely to be watching *EastEnders* than playing the fiddle
to his neighbours. As Bernard Sharratt points out, there is in this attempt to employ a traditional form 'a sense of cultural nostalgia', 'the
utilisation of a largely *superseded* sub-text, model or medium'.[36]

Admittedly, McGrath's claims for the piece were modest
enough:

The theatre can never *cause* a social change. It can articulate
the pressures towards one, help people to celebrate their
strengths and maybe build their self-confidence. It can be a
public emblem of inner, and outer, events, and occasionally a
reminder, an elbow-jogger, a perspective-bringer. Above all, it
can be the way people can find their voice, their solidarity and
their collective determination. If we achieved any of these, it
was enough.[37]

The celebratory nature of the ceilidh performance and the re-
counting of their own history certainly helped audiences to discover
solidarity and to reinforce a sense of identity, as MacLennan's record-
ing of post-performance comments shows. Rick Rylance offers a fair
and generous assessment of McGrath's achievement, when he writes:

This work does not lend itself to the kinds of formal analysis
usually practised on canonical texts. It is low in ambiguity,
irony and ambition to turn metaphysical. Its language is

demotic, its imagery often sparse and unoriginal, its forms
come from a history barely visible from our usual studies...
The emphasis this work places on the use of communal,
shared language and forms, and on the human, emotional and
social contexts and relationships of the business of making
meanings, provides a model of communication which – to
make the very minimal case – is closer to that envisaged by
both the best education and the best democratic practice, than
that envisaged by the theoretical *avant-garde*.[38]

8 Brecht revisited: David Hare's *Fanshen* (1975)

The theatre is the best way of showing the gap between what is said and what is seen to be done, and that is why, ragged and gap-toothed as it is, it has still a far healthier potential than some of the other, poorer, abandoned arts.[1]

David Hare's *Fanshen* is notable for two reasons: first, it was one of the earliest theatre pieces that was created by an author working with a group of actors on a non-dramatic text; secondly, it was one of the few examples of British political theatre that, instead of portraying the problems inherent in Western capitalism, looked towards the East for a positive alternative, in a manner and style reminiscent of the Prologue to Brecht's *Caucasian Chalk Circle* (1948).

Fanshen is not characteristic of David Hare's work. As a Cambridge graduate, something he shares with his frequent collaborator Howard Brenton, he tends to write about the milieu that he knows best: the world of privilege which has betrayed the hopes of progressive elements in society. Most of his early plays are set in middle-class or upper-middle-class settings. *Slag* (1970) is located in an exclusive girls' school, which is in steep decline and where the staff are unexpectedly radical but wholly ineffectual. In *The Great Exhibition* (1972) we find ourselves in the Hampstead home of a nominally Labour politician who cannot bear to travel to his grimy constituency in the North of England. The action of *Knuckle* (1974) takes place in the commuter land of Guildford in Surrey, where a son rejects the ruthless and corrupt capitalistic City trading of his father by getting involved in the equally ruthless international arms trade. *Teeth 'n' Smiles* (1975) is set in a location particularly familiar to Hare, a Cambridge college during the May Ball, when an anarchic punk band signally fails to make any real impact on the world of privileged education. The setting for the television play, *Licking Hitler* (1978), is an English country house, although admittedly there is now the distance of time, since the action is based on a wartime anti-German propaganda exercise, and the protagonist is no longer English middle-class but a working-class Scot. In *Plenty* (1978), probably Hare's best-known work, not least because of the film version with Meryl Streep as the heroine Susan, the two elements of wartime sacrifice and post-war 'plenty' (and with it the betrayal of the aspirations of those who bravely fought in the war) are brought into sharp relief.

By the 1980s Hare had begun to paint on a broader canvas, with plays like *A Map of the World* (1982), set at an international conference, *Saigon: Year of the Cat* (1983), a television play dealing with the United States withdrawal from Vietnam, and in his collaboration with Brenton, *Pravda* (1985), a play based on the British press. But characteristic of Hare's earlier work is the concentration on an enclosed, self-absorbed English middle class. As he admitted in an interview for *Plays and Players*: 'I'm fascinated by self-enclosed societies – a very middle-class obsession. There has to be a degree of parody about plays with that theme. My plays are intended as puzzles – the solution of which is up to the audience.'[2] Because Hare has written several well-made plays (John Bull tells us that in this respect his name has been 'linked with that of Osborne and even Rattigan'),[3] because he can create witty acerbic dialogue and offer an amused view of the English middle classes, the political impact of his plays can easily be underestimated or misconstrued. For instance, in the case of *Plenty*, the piece can all too easily be seen merely as a contrast between the heroism of Susan working with the French resistance and the self-indulgence of post-war society. But this is not the puzzle Hare has set his audience; for Susan's wartime escapades are themselves a form of self-indulgence. John Bull again:

> It looks as though, on a narrative level, there is only a choice between the cynical manipulation of the establishment and romantic idealism. The more subversive suggestion can be

drawn from the sub-text of the play, that interaction between play and audience that Hare talks of, that there was a possibility of something else happening, that the presentation of English history is not only that of a pessimistic procession towards decline, but also there to be learned from.[4]

Fanshen is, in both style and content, a totally different form of theatre from most of Hare's other work and is usually described as such, an anomalous excursion into interventionist Brechtian territory.[5] Nevertheless, it will be seen that *Fanshen*, although the only one of his plays not to be set in Britain, is not so very far removed from the self-enclosed quality of Hare's middle-class plays and the ambiguity of response generated by them.

The process of creating *Fanshen* was quite different from the work Hare had been engaged in before. The conventional method of theatre production consists of a playwright writing a text in isolation, then passing it on to a director, who in turn hires a cast to perform the text according to his or her ideas. Only occasionally, perhaps, will authors direct their own work, as Hare has also done, or sit in at rehearsals and then possibly make minor changes to the original script in the light of practical work on the text.

Since the early seventies, however, in line with democratic aspirations which led to attempts to set up greater worker participation in industry, there have been challenges to the authority of the single author and to the role of the director (with the ominously authoritarian ring that this name carries). If a more participational form of management could be considered in industry, so ran the argument, then surely those involved in promoting political change through theatre must reconsider their own hierarchical practices. Across Britain, theatre groups based on a collective ethos were created: Welfare State, Red Ladder, 7:84, Belt and Braces, to name but a few. Notionally at least, the concept of the director as the artistic mind behind a production was replaced by a group creative process with performers taking turns to 'direct' or by nominating one of the group to filter suggestions from the group and to act as an outside eye but without establishing that individual as a figure of authority. Indeed, much of the mediocre

quality of political theatre of the sixties and seventies was a result of
this political idealism, leading to productions that frequently lacked
coherence and clarity of intention – 'theatre designed by a committee,'
as it was sometimes dismissively described. John McGrath described
one such production by 7:84 (England):

> There was this dreadful democracy within the structure of the
> play, that everybody had a large, long monologue; that all the
> parts were almost to within a syllable identically the same
> size; and that nobody actually was more interesting than
> anybody else. In fact they were all equally boring... I think it
> could almost stand as a classic example of the reason that
> May '68 failed in Britain. The whole movement failed as it
> sort of epitomised... [the] crushing of individualism.
> Crushing of difference between people, trying to make
> everyone the same. Crushing of... or rather frightened
> democracy, in the sense that one felt all the parts were equal
> almost out of a sense of fear rather than out of a sense of
> celebrating everybody's equality.[6]

Eventually most theatre groups recognized that performing and
directing require different and equally valid skills, and that a director
could, in the best traditions of democracy, assume power with the
consent of his or her constituency. This search for a more democratic
foundation for the role of the director has had its effects even in the
mainstream theatre. In Britain today it would be a bold (and possibly
quite foolish) director who would attempt to impose his or her will
on actors without their agreement.

The same democratization of the creative process can hardly
be said of playwrights. While Hare and Caryl Churchill have achieved
striking results by working in close collaboration with actors, they are
very much the exception. Howard Barker, who is notable for now always directing his own work, is remarkable also in the fact that, even
after rehearsal, he hardly makes any changes to his original script.
John McGrath may work in close association with his 7:84 group,
but the process of writing is an independent precursor to the production process. Even Hare and Churchill, while responding to the ideas

offered by the performers with whom they are working, will withdraw to complete the business of writing in their own time and space. In fact, it is not the writing that is a collaborative process but the research that precedes it. The process of shaping the material, of writing and refining the dialogue and of defining the characters remains the work of the playwright. Only with certain contemporary groups who entirely devise their own pieces or in the work of Mike Leigh, where actors' improvisations form the basis for the script, has the author been, if not entirely banished from the theatrical process, at least reduced to being a recorder of the performers' discoveries.

Fanshen (1975)
Plot summary
In a Chinese village after the defeat of the Kuomintang, the peasants undertake the arduous process of *fanshen*, a total restructuring of their society. The first task is to overcome their timidity and to denounce former collaborators with the Japanese. A Peasants' Association is established, which has the difficult task of overseeing the redistribution of the landlords' property and of assessing the needs of the community. Decisions are reversed, open criticism is invited, a Communist ideology is propagated. While *fanshen* promises a better future for the formerly oppressed peasants, there is still much to be done to ensure that the revolution is successful.

David Hare's work on *Fanshen* provided the second production for the Joint Stock Company,[7] which he had recently founded together with the directors William Gaskill and Max Stafford-Clark. William Gaskill in particular, after working for years at the Royal Court Theatre and at the National Theatre, had become aware of the difficulties of stimulating political enquiry in his work: 'You can have democracy with a group of eight people, but it's very difficult with a group of sixteen...I have better working conditions in Joint Stock than I've ever had in any other theatre.'[8] For Gaskill, the possibility of working with thinking actors in a genuinely collaborative situation was worth more than large subsidies and sophisticated technical support. As one of the original Joint Stock actors, Robert Hamilton, put it: 'It's quite simply that Joint Stock directors assume you have a mind and demand that you use it.'[9]

The minds of the members of the Joint Stock Company were exercised in this instance by spending five weeks reading, discussing and exploring in workshops a heavy tome of over 600 pages by William Hinton, *Fanshen: A Documentary of Revolution in a Chinese Village*.[10] Hinton, himself a farmer from the United States, had observed at first hand the impact of the Communist revolution on a Chinese village after its liberation from Japanese occupation in 1948. The word *fanshen* literally means 'to turn over' and was used to describe the radical new thought adopted in the Chinese revolution. In Hinton's words:

> the peasants, under the guidance of the Communist Party, had
> moved step by step from partial knowledge to general
> knowledge, from spontaneous action to directed action, from
> limited success to over-all success. And through this process
> they had transformed themselves from passive victims of
> natural and social forces into active builders of a new world.
> This, as I understood it, was the essence of *Fanshen*.[11]

For Hare work on *Fanshen* provided relief from 'writing about England –...writing about this decadent corner of the globe'.[12] In what might be taken as a commentary on the political playwrights of whom he was a prominent member, the Preface to the published text of *Fanshen* points to the need, occasionally at least, to propose a positive model for political and social change:

> In 1948 George Orwell wrote: 'When you are on a sinking
> ship, your thoughts will be about sinking ships.' No one has
> put the writer's difficulty better. European literature of the
> last seventy years annotates the decline of the West, both in
> theory and in practice. Nearly every outstanding piece of
> writing since 1900 belongs to a culture of dissent. Writers
> have been trapped in negatives, forced back into sniping and
> objection, or into the lurid colours of their private

imaginations. At some stage they will have to offer positive
models for change, or their function will decay as irrevocably
as the society they seek to describe.[13]

For Hare, and for the members of the Joint Stock Company,
work on *Fanshen* was to prove a profoundly politicizing influence. As
Gaskill recorded: 'When we were working on *Fanshen* we were part
of a political process... you couldn't really do it in any other way,
because that is the way the political meaning is made clear... The
aesthetic clarity came as a consequence of getting the political line.'[14]
Through group discussion and analysis of Hinton's text, and even by
evaluating themselves as 'class animals' and employing methods of
self-criticism like those portrayed in the play, the cast sought *fanshen*
in their own working practices.[15] Whether Hare's strategy succeeded
in similarly politicizing his audience is a more problematic question.

In terms of conventional dramaturgy, *Fanshen* does not appear
to contain much promising theatrical material. The plot, which describes historical events, does not have a compelling beginning, middle and end. It does indeed begin with the defeat of the Japanese in
China, but, with civil war taking place between the Communists and
the Kuomintang, even this is not a very clear-cut opening. Events in
the play are repetitious, and sometimes their order could be inter-
changed. There is no dramatic conclusion.

There is also little opportunity for identification with particular characters. There are over twenty speaking roles, which were originally played by only nine Joint Stock actors, thus reinforcing their
lack of individual identity. Most of these characters are minimally
sketched in, identified more by their economic status than by individual characteristics. The dialogue is matter-of-fact and frequently
deals with political ideas. Apart from one or two moments of violence, there is no dramatic on-stage action. The set is deliberately
minimal, allowing for the fluent staging of several different locations.
Despite all this, the Joint Stock performance was a clear and compelling theatrical event, described by John Bull as 'one of the most
peculiarly gripping evenings that [he had] spent in a theatre in the
entire decade'.[16]

Fanshen opens in a typically Brechtian manner. Each of the nine actors steps forward in turn to introduce the major character they will play, to define their economic status and to offer an introductory description of the village of Long Bow. Most of these descriptions are appropriate to the role that is being presented; thus the landlord figure speaks of the Catholic church which also operated as a bank. Two moments of Brechtian 'distancing' are significant: first, one actor holds up a copy of William Hinton's book, giving the publisher and the current price. This is not only an acknowledgment of the group's debt to Hinton, but also a device to jolt the audience out of the world of theatrical illusion and remind them that the piece is a documentary, its events based on factual account. In the same vein, the final words of the scene are: 'Many of the characters are still alive.'[17] Thus, the audience were encouraged not so much to settle down to watch a play as to become aware, sitting in their theatre in Britain, of the political struggle vigorously being engaged in at that moment by real people on the other side of the globe.

The first stage in this struggle is a public meeting, the first to be held in the village for twenty years. In a process of empowerment, the peasants are encouraged to denounce those who collaborated with the Japanese in oppressing them. This process is not idealized: the peasants are at first fearful, and one, the ex-bandit Yu-Lai, immediately becomes violent, striking the accused viciously before beginning to name his crimes. Even after the traitors have been publicly tried and shot, the peasants scatter at the sight of the landlord, Shen Ching-Ho.

The next stage is for this empowerment of the peasants to achieve something more than acts of retribution. The Communist Party secretary Liu arrives to oversee the formation of the Peasants' Association. The villagers talk for three days, indicated by a banner that is unfurled. Significantly Liu and his local supporter T'ien-Ming ask as many questions as they make statements, encouraging the peasants for the first time in their lives to think for themselves: 'You must work it out for yourself. If you want to serve the people you need to think.'[18] By the end of their discussions, the peasants resolve to stop paying rent, and a red banner bearing the word *Fanshen* is raised.

The next round of confrontations now takes place, that between peasants and landlords. When the peasants refuse to pay rent, the landlords are at first threatening, but are soon forced to give up their hidden gold and hoarded flour and salt (which they have allowed to go rotten). One, in an attitude which parallels the welfare state system of capitalism, freely offers a bag of flour and appeals to their sense of 'community': 'I know your life is hard. On this soil. The valuable work you are doing. Service to the community. But we are all ... citizens of one village.'[19] Once again, the reaction of the peasants is not idealized; their brutality towards the landlords is considerable: 'Of the seven landlords in Long Bow, three died after being beaten to death by the Peasants' Association. Two more died of starvation when they had been driven from their land.'[20]

The next stage is one of great optimism, 'moving from hell to heaven':[21] the division amongst the peasants of the wealth accumulated from the landlords. Already, in this upbeat phase, however, Hare is honest enough to plot moments that may cause us to question the totally honourable nature of *fanshen*. First, there is the rule that goods are allocated not only according to need but are also dependent on the amount that individuals have spoken out their grievances at landlords. This penalizes those who are naturally shy, like Hsueh-chen, and it sounds the first warning note that political orthodoxy will be paramount in the new order. Secondly, the leaders, while granting smaller shares to themselves, make the pragmatic decision to take over the inn without consulting the people. Even though the inn is to be managed for the benefit of the Peasants' Association, this represents a first if modest step in the tendency in the history of Communist states to replace a system where the rich are powerful by one where the powerful become rich. Thirdly, when choosing how to spend their allocation, some near-starving peasants show themselves unfit to make sensible decisions: thus one proudly bears away a landlord's coat, another a huge pot, far bigger than he will ever need.

Until now the progress of *fanshen* has been a matter of the restitution of wrongs and as such would win the approval of most audiences. The next step is towards discovering a coherent political ideology to inform *fanshen*, specifically that of Communism.

This is where many, especially with the hindsight of the collapse of Communism in Eastern Europe and after Mao's disastrous Cultural Revolution, would become more critical of developments described in the play. T'ien-Ming, revealing himself to be a Party member, argues that, 'Without the party the village is a bowl of loose sand.'[22]

One effect of Communist education, recorded by Hinton as the liberation of 'half of China',[23] is the freeing of women from the traditional tyranny of their menfolk and is described in Section Four, Scene Two of the play. That this process was not universally achieved is shown in the following scene, where Yu-Lai exercises brutal and abusive authority over his daughter-in-law. Perhaps more disturbing than this example of individual exploitation is the fact that the Party workers present do not comment on or intervene in this reprehensible behaviour by Yu-Lai.

Yu-Lai also features in the next major episode in the village. It is now 1948, and the village is visited by a 'work team', sent to the village to acquaint the peasants with the new Draft Agrarian Law. Within hours of their arrival the youngest member of the work team is attacked and left for dead. Suspicion, supported by some circumstantial evidence, immediately falls on the unpopular Yu-Lai and his son. The towel stuffed down the victim's throat is identical to others in Yu-Lai's household, although it is revealed later that nearly all the towels in the village are the same. Not only are Yu-Lai and his son arrested on very flimsy evidence, but more disturbingly, Hou, the leader of the work party, uses the incident to impose absolute rule over the village. *Fanshen*, it seems, is already in danger of abandoning its revolutionary and democratic ideals.

Not without humour the work party's attempts to get the peasants to classify themselves under the Draft Agrarian Law are portrayed in Section Seven of the play. Although the declared intention is that allocation should no longer be dependent on merit, the peasants find it difficult to disregard this in the two cases of a blacksmith who carries out shoddy work and of a man, now poor, who lost his wealth and sold his wife to feed his heroin addiction. In a wider context, the ideals of *fanshen* are being undermined now by bureaucracy, the attempt to force living individuals into rigid classifications, which, according to the officials, will determine 'how they are to live for the rest of their lives',[24] even though we have seen how the previous redistribution of wealth has lasted only two years. With bureaucratic intervention comes also the misleading attempt to solve economic problems with doctrine. What is really needed are raw materials and economic growth (something of which the political leadership of China has now, half a century later, become fully aware).

The second half of the play begins with a re-enactment of 'The Gate', the result of a courageous decision by the Communist Party to reveal its membership and to invite elected delegates of the peasants to listen to the self-criticism of Party members and to decide on their fate. The forty-six pages of William Hinton's book devoted to the six days of The Gate are rendered succinctly and sometimes amusingly in Hare's script, and the outcome, that twenty-two of the twenty-six who undergo investigation pass the Gate, represents a laudable achievement for the Communist Party. As Hinton recorded:

> I lay awake for a long time thinking over the events of the last few days. The power of the Revolution to inspire and remold people had stirred me. It seemed to me then that no decent person could fail to be touched by the challenge of the new society and that this was what gave the movement such confidence and momentum.[25]

This process of self-criticism is continued, as, once again a new classification has to be embarked on, one that it is hoped will not alienate the middle peasants in the way that earlier classifications had done. More meetings have to be held, revised classifications undertaken. Meanwhile Yu-Lai and his son return to the village, and are required to appear before The Gate. Both fail ignominiously, but the decision is taken to re-educate Yu-Lai: 'There is no "just do this one thing and we will be there". There is only the patient, daily work of re-making people. Over each hill, another hill. Over that hill, a mountain.'[26] If the brutal and devious Yu-Lai can be *fanshen*-ed, then there is indeed hope for the success of the revolution. As Hare summed it up:

In the play *Fanshen* [the dialectic] is dynamic. Political practice answers to political theory and yet modifies it; the party answers to the people and is modified by it. The fight is for political structures which answer people's needs; and people themselves are changed by living out theoretical ideas. It is a story of change and progress.[27]

With the recognition that the new Agrarian Land Reform went too far in unfairly dispossessing middle peasants, the Party now changes direction again and begins speaking of collectivization, not equal shares of land but land held in common. The long-suffering work team returns to the village to begin to explain and debate the new policy with the peasants. The ending is ambiguous: with a 'superb massive groundswell of music',[28] the unfurling of red banners all round the stage and the eager questions of the work team, asking what the villagers themselves think, the conclusion is one of triumphant progress. This is undercut, however, especially in the way it was performed by the Joint Stock Company, by the image of a solitary peasant trying to get on with tilling his soil, interrupted by the demand to attend yet another meeting, and grudgingly abandoning his hoeing to comply.

In this ambiguous ending Hare offers a positive image of the Chinese revolution but does not glamorize it. The laudable seizing of control by the oppressed peasants leads to some negative outcomes: the denunciations do not permit the proper filing of evidence, adequate defence of the accused or reference to established law. Moreover, they are frequently accompanied by torture. The intervention of the Communist Party leads to centralized control and the dead hand of bureaucracy. Perhaps for the sake of clarity, some of the more sinister elements thrown up by the revolution do not feature in Hare's script: for example, there is no reference to the role of the militia men in the early violent attacks on landlords' property, described by Hinton.[29]

But on the whole, Hare is scrupulously fair in his portrayal of *fanshen*, not least in admitting the time and energy required to attend the repeated meetings: '"Under the Nationalists too many taxes. Under the Communists, too many meetings"',[30] as one of the villagers cynically quotes. By acknowledging the problematic aspects of revolution, Hare is not painting a utopia but is inviting his audience into a debate about how their society should be structured:

> I write about politics because the challenge of communism, in however debased and ugly a form, is to ask whether the criteria by which we have been brought up are right; whether what each of us experiences uniquely really is what makes us valuable; whether every man should really be his own cocktail; or whether our criteria could and should be collective, and if they were, whether we would be any happier. However absolute the sufferings of men in the totalitarian Soviet countries, however decadent the current life of the West, the fact is that this question has only just been asked, and we have not even the first hundredth of an answer. To give up now would be death.[31]

Hare's strategy is the essentially Brechtian one: to face us with a choice. We cannot simply indulge in some radical chic and play at being revolutionaries for as long as the play lasts, only then to climb into our cars to return to our middle-class homes, which is the risk run by the reflectionist strategy. *Fanshen* engages us in a genuine dialectic, prompting us to consider alternatives to the social and economic ordering of our world. As Hare said with reference to his play *The Great Exhibition* (1972), the audience 'imagine that they're there to find out what this man on the stage thinks. They're not: they're there to find out what *they* think.'[32] In similar vein he said in his Cambridge lecture: 'if a play is to be a weapon in the class struggle, then that weapon is not going to be the things you are saying; it is the interaction of what you are saying and what the audience is thinking'.[33]

9 Rewriting Shakespeare: Edward Bond's *Lear* (1971)

> Critics annoy me. If a house is on fire and I shout 'Fire! Fire!' I
> don't want people to commend my shouting ability, I want
> them to join in the firefighting.[1]

Edward Bond calls his brand of playwriting 'Rational Theatre'. More
than any other contemporary British political dramatist, in fact more
than any English-language dramatist since Shaw, Bond has theorized
about his work and its intentions, about society and its problems, in
numerous prefaces, interviews, essays and letters.

The focus of his concern is human suffering, especially the violence perpetrated by man against man. The argument runs as follows:
we live in a world characterized by violent aggression, but humankind
is not naturally aggressive. The aggression stems from the unnatural
conditions in which an exploitative society forces us to live:

> We have a *capacity* for violence and, like many animals, are
> violent when we are afraid or frustrated. This is as natural as
> when a drowning man fights for his life. But it is not natural
> for him to keep falling in the water... Violence is like pain,
> not a normal condition but a sign that something is wrong.[2]

We are like caged animals, but, instead of turning on our keepers, we
fawn on them because they bring us sufficient food; so we vent our
frustration and animosity on our fellow captives.

The traditional response, a Christian attitude embraced glee-
fully and understandably by the Establishment, is that things have
always been like this and that the way to rise above such suffering is
through resignation and acceptance of the status quo. If the cage-door

were left open, we would fear to step into freedom, because we would not know what lay beyond. So we acquiesce in our imprisonment, 'the fascism of lazy men',[3] as Bond calls it; or, worse, we actively support the system in order to oppress others and so feel slightly freer ourselves.

The alternative – proposed in the 'Rational Theatre' – is to create a new existence for ourselves by breaking out of our cage. How this is to be achieved is never exactly clarified by Bond. It appears that he generally subscribes to a benevolent version of Marxism, one that decries violence as a means of pursuing a social ideal. Admittedly, Bond has, only rarely, suggested that violence *may* have to be employed in the pursuit of liberation, e.g. in one of the critical comments in *The Activists Papers* of 1980, where he writes: 'The struggle for rationalism ... may have to be violent.'[4] But in the early seventies he still appeared to be seeking a peaceful path towards his utopian ideal.

This lack of clarity is not necessarily a failure; it is not the task of a political playwright to supply answers so much as to raise questions, and as a political thinker, Bond presents a convincing argument for his vagueness: 'I have not tried to say what the future should be like, because that is a mistake. If your plan of the future is too rigid you start to coerce people to fit into it. We do not need a plan of the future, we need a *method* of change.'[5] Wherever the future lies, Bond fears there is not much time left to steer towards it. Given the achievements of modern technology, whereby humankind faces imminent self-annihilation from nuclear weapons or through destruction of the environment, we are, in Bond's view, teetering on the edge of an abyss. Only immediate and radical change can save us; hence, his description of himself as a man shouting 'Fire!'

This is one reason Bond gives for writing plays rather than novels: 'when I write, the rhythm – the whole concentration of the writing – requires action. Finally, somebody has to get up and do something – mere words on paper are not expressive enough.'[6] Only the theatre, which offers the immediacy of enactment in a public context, would seem to answer Bond's sense of urgency.

This perceived need for immediate action is also the source of Bond's major quarrel with Shakespeare. Again like Shaw, Bond often reveals his irritation with 'bardolatry'. However, while annoyed at the uncritical reception of Shakespeare, especially by those bogey-men, 'university professors', Bond acknowledges a colossal debt to Shakespeare. Indeed, his first encounter with Shakespeare in the form of Donald Wolfit's *Macbeth* in 1948 was decisive: 'for the very first time in my life – I remember this quite distinctly – I met somebody who was actually talking about my problems, about the life I'd been living, the political society around me'.[7] Then in 1969, while working on a translation of Brecht's *Roundheads and Peakheads*, Bond went back to its major source, *Measure for Measure*, where he discovered the theme of the demands of law and order opposed to those of justice, a concern that was to resurface in his *Lear*. But despite his interest in Shakespeare and his 'enormous admiration'[8] for *King Lear*, Bond felt that it suffered from one major if excusable flaw, the preaching of resignation:

> the social moral of Shakespeare's *Lear* is this: endure till in time the world will be made right. That's a dangerous moral for us. We have less time than Shakespeare.[9]

> Shakespeare does arrive at an answer to the problems of his particular society, and that was the idea of total resignation, accepting what comes . . . What I want to say is that this model is inadequate now: that it just does not work. Acceptance is not enough. Anybody can accept. You can go quietly into your gas chamber . . . you can sit quietly at home and have an H-bomb dropped on you. Shakespeare had time . . . But . . . for us, time is running out.[10]

In his rejection of 'acceptance', it was clearly insufficient for Bond to reflect reality; he wished to intervene in it. Considering Shake-speare 'too much a part of his own time to fully understand [the government of his day]',[11] Bond felt impelled to undertake a radical reassessment of Shakespeare's greatest play for our own time: 'as a so-ciety we use the play in a wrong way. And it's for that reason I would like to rewrite it so that we now have to use the play for ourselves, for our society, for our time, for our problems.'[12] There is here more than a hint of Bond, the former 11-plus failure, wanting to show the academics and the theatrical establishment what all their learning and talent had failed to reveal. It was a brave undertaking and one that seemingly had to be confronted by Bond: 'Lear was standing in my path and I had to get him out of the way.'[13]

Lear (1971)

Plot summary

Lear is a tyrannical King of England and has built a huge wall to keep out his enemies. His daughters, Bodice and Fontanelle, grow weary of his despotism and lead armies against him. Lear, now mad, seeks refuge with a gravedigger's boy. Soldiers arrive, kill the boy and rape his wife, who is called Cordelia. Cordelia leads the fight against Bodice and Fontanelle, proving herself to be as ruthless as her opponents. Lear is captured and blinded, but gains in wisdom. He rejects the temptations offered by the ghost of the gravedigger's boy to live his life in peaceful isolation. Instead, he returns to the Wall, makes a brave gesture by beginning to dismantle it and is shot.

One reason why Bond's *Lear* is successful in its own right is because his intervention is so decisive that his version has little to do with the original. Most adaptations at least preserve the characters from the original and present them in new situations, perhaps prior to the start of Shakespeare's play (as in Gordon Bottomley's *King Lear's Wife*, 1915) or in an entire rewriting of the ending (as in Nahum Tate's version of *King Lear*, 1681) or in a foregrounding of minor characters from the original (as in Tom Stoppard's reworking of *Hamlet* in *Rosencrantz and Guildenstern Are Dead*, 1966).[14] Bond, however, creates an almost entirely new situation out of elements of the original, the effect being to alert us by the freedoms he takes to his new treatment of the Lear theme. His *Lear* is, to use Gerd Stratmann's term, an 'anti-Lear'.[15]

The major shift of emphasis is hinted at in the title: the dropping of 'King' immediately implies that Bond is not interested in the royal nature of the king but in his function as an individual in an oppressive state, the character of which Lear gradually discerns in the course of the play. As Richard Scharine points out: 'To Bond, whether Lear gave up his control over society or had it wrested from him is beside the point.'[16] Indeed, whereas Shakespeare's Lear retains 'the name and all th' addition to a king' and in the fifth act is still referred to as 'King Lear', Bond's Lear is king for only the first two scenes. Similarly, the most prominent lord no longer bears the name of an English shire (Gloucester, Kent), but is named after a nondescript northern town, Warrington. The division of the kingdom also does not proceed from King Lear's concern for the future but is an already established fact, although the carving up of territory 'that future strife may be prevented now' (1, 1) finds echoes in Lear's: 'I built this wall to keep our enemies out. My people will live behind this wall when I'm dead. You may be governed by fools but you'll always live in peace. My wall will make you free.'[17] What Bond does is to posit what kind of state would have emerged in the Britain of Shakespeare's *King Lear*, had Goneril and Regan been victorious and then been violently repulsed by Cordelia, who restored Lear to his throne. In place of Albany's hope that Kent and Edgar will 'Rule in this realm, and the gor'd state sustain' (5, 3), Bond predicts that any rule, however well-intentioned, will maintain the cycle of oppression initiated by Lear.

In Bond's play Goneril and Regan appear as Fontanelle and Bodice, the first name perhaps suggesting the rather infantile quality of her character, the second possibly indicating her sense of being constrained: 'I don't decide anything. My decisions are forced on me. . . I must move them here and there . . . – because the map's my straitjacket and that's all I can do. I'm trapped.'[18] Cordelia retains her name but in Bond's play is not one of Lear's daughters. Instead, she becomes an eventually victorious rebel-leader after her husband has been murdered and she herself has been raped by soldiers loyal to Fontanelle and Bodice.

Otherwise, there are echoes of Shakespeare's play, but little that immediately derives from it. The torture of Warrington and the blinding of Lear have their parallels with the blinding of Gloucester; the figure of the Gravedigger's Boy and his relationship with Lear are similar to the Fool and also to 'Mad Tom's' relationship with Gloucester. The bloody autopsy of Fontanelle, in which Lear participates, seems to be an enactment of Shakespeare's 'let them anatomize Regan, see what breeds about her heart' (3, 6). However, Bond has declared to Katharine Worth that he had not been thinking of this passage when he wrote the scene.[19] Other verbal echoes may have been fortuitous too; for example Lear, just before his death, says: 'I have only one more wish – to... become as cunning as the fox';[20] King Lear, just before his death, says: 'He that parts us shall bring a brand from heaven / And fire us hence like foxes' (5, 3).

It is the differences from the original that are more striking than the similarities. This may be observed in the structure of the two pieces. While Shakespeare's play has a certain 'epic' quality, ranging as it does over several months and right across Britain, Bond's *Lear* is a more truly epic piece, in the Brechtian sense that 'each scene stands on its own' rather than leading from one to the next. Within reasonable limits it would be possible to change the order of many of Bond's scenes without destroying the narrative thrust of the play; it would be far harder to do so in *King Lear*.

Another 'Brechtian' approach is a much greater awareness of the role of the common people in the events of the play. Apart from the three servants who witness the blinding of Gloucester, the only 'common people' we encounter in Shakespeare's play are two noblemen in disguise, Kent and Edgar. Even in the storm scene, when King Lear awakens to some sense of social responsibility, the poor are apostrophized as a distant generality: 'Poor naked wretches, *whereso'er you are...*' (3, 4).

In Bond's treatment of the common people one is reminded of Brecht's observations on Goneril's steward, Oswald, and on King Lear's followers:

> [*King Lear*] contains an account of the social life of people in the distant past; it is up to you to complete this account... It is wrong for an audience, especially for the servants amongst them, to be so much on Lear's side that they applaud when, as in the fourth scene of the first act, a servant is beaten for carrying out his mistress's orders... One can show the king's

servants, after he has been turned away everywhere, as a pathetic band who have to go hungry and who hound him with their silent reproach.[21]

In contrast with *King Lear*, only three short scenes of the eighteen in Bond's play have no lines for workers, soldiers or prisoners (1, 2; 1,3; 1,4). However, although the common people form a constant presence throughout *Lear*, the concentration remains on the central character and his own progress towards enlightenment, while the mass upheavals form a backdrop to this individual concern, in a way not far removed from the way the events of the Thirty Years' War serve as a background to Mother Courage's experiences. Indeed, few of the 'proletariat' even receive a name, being referred to by number (Prisoner 1), letter (Soldier H), or occupation (Gravedigger's Boy, Carpenter). Presumably comparing himself to the Brecht of the *Lehrstücke* rather than to the Brecht of the later plays, Bond commented: 'Brecht wrote in the time of the "masses". I write in the time of the "individuals" – yet this must be seen not as a reactionary retreat but as a further concretization of socialism.'[22]

Consistent with Brechtian method though, Bond perceives the social function of 'individuals' rather than their psychology as important. As William Gaskill, the director of the premiere of *Lear*, advised his cast: 'Never play the character, always play the situation.'[23] It has often proved difficult for British actors, generally trained according to Stanislavskian methods, to respond to the demands of Bond's writing, and this may be one of the reasons that he has been performed with greater success in German-speaking countries than at home. Bond himself – in a very Brechtian poem, 'Advice to actors' – begins:

> Actors
> Don't try to make your character possible
> Men do things that ought not to be possible
> Don't say 'he'd never do this'
> Men don't behave in expected ways[24]

Similarly, Gaskill had to warn his actors not to tread a naturalistic path in the playing of group scenes: 'Don't try to relate to everything that happens on stage',[25] advice that runs counter to the usual requirements of realistic performance. Such need to establish the autonomy of each role is seen most obviously in the asides given to Fontanelle and Bodice in Act One, Scene Three, where the two daughters comment on their husbands and their future plans, while clearly not being overheard by the others on stage. Gaskill was again obliged to offer some help in coping with this Brechtian device: 'Bill explained to the girls [sic] that in an aside you have to explain your emotion and communicate directly with the audience. You can hide nothing, keep nothing back.'[26]

Bond's technique, therefore, is to write dialogue that is explicit, devoid of subtext. His sentences are short, and abstract nouns are seldom used. Subordinate clauses are a rarity, most of these being simple temporal clauses introduced by 'when', 'before' or 'after'. This is not to exclude poetry, however. Some of the minimal sentences have all the force and richness of poetic expression. So, for example, as Lear looks down at the dissected corpse of Fontanelle, he observes: 'The blood is as still as a lake.'[27] The simile is striking and multi-layered: it suggests the calm of death in contrast with the 'beast' which drove Fontanelle to evil, and the large expanse suggested by the word 'lake' (compared, say, with 'pool' or 'pond') reflects not only the shocking amount of blood revealed in the autopsy but also the elemental quality of Lear's feelings in the presence of death. As Bond has said of his writing: 'we have to restore the theatrical vitality of language by relating it again to image, by giving it a conceptual sharpness and a poetic hardness or concreteness – otherwise the "story" lies'.[28]

It is in fact through such concrete images that Bond creates his most powerful theatrical effects. Few theatre-goers will remember a single line from *Saved*; all will recall the scene where the baby is stoned in the pram. His shocking images of violence have lent Bond a certain notoriety and have set him apart from many of his contemporaries. In the case of *Lear* he was fortunate that Shakespeare's portrayal of the blinding of Gloucester had established a precedent for on-stage violence associated with this play. But what is profoundly disturbing in Bond's depiction of violence is not so much the brutal act itself as the relationship of the perpetrators to it. When the youths stone the baby to death in the pram, it is just a game; they have no more relationship with the baby as a victim than they have with the pram itself. An element of deliberate cruelty might be healthier; at least the baby would be something other than an object.

Similarly, in the two most horrific episodes of *Lear*, the torture of Warrington (1, 4) and the blinding of Lear (2, 6), it is the attitude of the participants that makes the experience so disturbing. In the first case Fontanelle behaves with sadistic excitement, the Soldier operates as a detached professional, and Bodice continues to knit for most of the scene, until she uses her needles to pierce Warrington's ear-drums: 'I'll just jog these in and out a little. Doodee, doodee, doodee, doo.'[29] The word 'jog', more normally associated with an involuntary movement, coupled with the hideously playful baby-talk, makes the torture not only brutal but extremely grotesque. Equally grotesque is the blinding of Lear. Whereas Gloucester's blinding in Shakespeare is motivated by personal revenge for his supposed treachery, in Bond's play it is a surgical act: 'Understand, this isn't an instrument of torture, but a scientific device.'[30]

In portraying violence not only with clarity but also as casual and emotionless, Bond is making a comment on the world we inhabit. The disturbing detachment of the torturers reflects Bond's vision of modern society, in Hubert Zapf's formulation, as 'abstract and anthropofugal'.[31] It is reminiscent of another post-war playwright concerned with the problem of violence, Peter Weiss, in whose *Marat/Sade* the Marquis de Sade complains:

> Our murders lack fire
> because they are part of a daily routine
> We judge without passion
> no longer encountering
> a fine and individual death
> merely an anonymous worthless dying
> to which we send whole peoples
> in cold calculation[32]

Both Weiss and Bond have felt the need to go further than Brecht in their portrayal of violence on stage. The aim of Brechtian 'distanciation' was to make the spectator see the familiar with fresh eyes. So, in order to avoid giving the audience an emotional thrill, which would obscure the critical contemplation urged by Brecht, any moments of brutality were underplayed in his theatre. The closest we get to on-stage violence in Brecht is the shooting of Kattrin in *Mother Courage*, and even here the perpetrator is reluctant to have to kill her. The risk of such underplaying is that the violence can become almost comfortable. So we can sing along happily with the 'Ballad of Mack the Knife' with its references to murder and child-rape.

In order to shock his audience into awareness, to achieve an 'alienation effect' in a world considerably desensitized to violence, Bond felt it necessary to be much more explicit in his representation of violence. He employed what he called 'aggro-effects', which, in their ability to make the spectator see things with fresh eyes, come paradoxically very close to the intentions of Brecht: 'Sometimes it is necessary to emotionally commit the audience – which is why I have aggro-effects. Without this the V-effect can deteriorate into an aesthetic style.'[33]

While images of violence most obviously distinguish Bond as a playwright, and *Lear* is arguably his most violent piece, other less horrific images are equally powerful. The wall offers a potent central image, even though it is physically present only in the last scene of the play. It stands as a symbol of oppression derived from fear. The wall is supposedly needed to keep enemies out, but in order to build and maintain the wall, people have to be deprived and their labour exploited. Its most obvious parallel at the time of composition was the so-called nuclear deterrent, and one may recall that Bond wrote *Passion*, his occasional piece for the Campaign for Nuclear Disarmament's Festival of Life on Easter Sunday, 1971, in the middle of his work on *Lear*. Like the wall, the nuclear armaments stockpiled by both Western and Eastern nations were a response to fear of an unpredictable enemy, for as Bond has said, 'fear has always been a more potent force than violence in human affairs'.[34] While millions of dollars, pounds and roubles have been spent on weapons which it would be suicidal ever to use, the social fabric of the United States, Britain and the Soviet Union has been weakened by poverty, unemployment

and underfunded social services, to the point where one of these participants in the arms race collapsed entirely. So in Bond's *Lear* the
wall comes to represent the perverse logic of an oppressive regime
that considers that it must defend its 'stability' and 'freedom' by sac-
rificing both to the policy of national defence. The most disturbing
revelation for Lear is that Cordelia, having won her revolution, intends to maintain and even extend the wall:

LEAR   Don't build the wall.
CORDELIA   We must.
LEAR   Then nothing's changed! A revolution must at least reform!
CORDELIA   Everything *else* is changed!
LEAR   Not if you keep the wall! Pull it down!
CORDELIA   We'd be attacked by our enemies!
LEAR   The wall will destroy you. It's already doing it. How can I
make you see?[35]

Cordelia's betrayal of the revolution by adopting the same
repressive measures that Lear and his daughters had done represents Bond's view of Stalinism. 'Cordelia represents Stalin, it's as
simple as that',[36] wrote Bond in 1977, and explained in an earlier
interview:

> The simple fact is that if you behave violently, you create an
> atmosphere of violence, which generates more violence. If you
> create a violent revolution, you always create a reaction ...
> Lenin thinks for example that he can use violence for specific
> ends. He does not understand that he will produce Stalin, and
> indeed must produce a Stalin ... So a violent revolution
> always destroys itself.[37]

Bond declared that his confrontation with Stalinism was one of the
major reasons for writing the play: 'The play was a preparation for what
would follow. I needed to distance myself from Stalinism because that
was a propaganda-block to socialism in the West.'[38]

Here we encounter one of the first attempts amongst British
political authors to come to terms with the recognition that so-called
socialist revolutions, most notably in Russia, had tended to create

states more repressive than the capitalist countries of the West, a fact also confronted by Howard Brenton in his *Weapons of Happiness* of 1976. Since the 1990s we have become even more aware of the iniquities of Stalinism in Eastern Europe than Bond can have been in 1971. But even then it was a familiar argument amongst right-wing apologists to point to the USSR as an example of the failure of socialist thinking; equally, it was a familiar argument of left-wing apologists to dismiss the model of Soviet Russia and its satellites and to insist that Marxism–Leninism was nevertheless the way towards a more just and humane society, however difficult it seemed to achieve in practice. In creating the figure of the self-righteous Cordelia (who shares a certain priggishness with her Shakespearian prototype), Bond therefore wished to forestall the expected critique of the Establishment. It is a negative strategy to warn against a mistaken application of a socialist philosophy.

What positive strategies does Bond adopt? In contrast with Shakespeare there are no wholly positive characters in *Lear*. There is no good daughter, no Kent, no Edgar, no Gloucester, not even an Albany. What we have instead is Lear's own gradual enlightenment, not by being cast out in the storm, but through his own suffering and his insight into the suffering he has caused others. In a cliché stage-metaphor, Lear's physical blindness is the beginning of his seeing the truth.

By the third act Lear sees clearly but is still uncertain how to use this understanding. He is tempted by the Ghost of the Gravedigger's Boy into withdrawing into his own world and pledging silence to the authorities:

GHOST   ... That's the world you have to live in. Learn it! Let me poison the well.
LEAR   Why?
GHOST   Then no one can live here, they'll have to leave you alone. There's a spring hidden in the wood. I'll take you there every day to drink. Lie down. Look how tired you are. Lie down. *Lear lies down.* Cordelia will come tomorrow and you can tell her you know how to keep silent at last.[39]

However, after his confrontation with Cordelia, Lear rejects this temptation to withdraw into himself. Instead of becoming a 'hippy', he resolves to become an activist, or in the more elegant phrasing of James C. Bulman: 'Cordelia and the Gravedigger's Boy represent the Scylla and Charybdis, married in opposition, of political defensiveness and private retreat between which Lear must sail if he is to become a genuinely moral man.'[40] But here Bond encounters a difficulty: if Lear's final gesture were to be the start of a major revolt by the oppressed, it would be seen to be foolishly optimistic, part of a socialist fairy-tale; if, however, his action has no consequences, it would seem at best ineffectual, at worst absurdist.

What in fact happens is that Lear climbs to the top of the wall and begins to shovel the earth down. Presumably summoned by a passing boy, several workers arrive and stare at Lear. A junior officer enters and kills Lear with one shot from his pistol. He then ushers the workers off, but 'One of them looks back.'[41] Much of the effect of this scene will depend on how it is performed in the theatre. The possibility that Lear's act will inspire others will appear stronger if the workers are given some time to watch Lear digging before the junior officer joins them, and especially if something is made of the 'look back' as the workers are shepherded off. But even then the symbolic act offers a very slender hope of change, and it is small wonder that some critics, to Bond's great annoyance, considered the ending a piece of absurd theatre, an individual gesture that could have no political or social consequence.

Clearly, despite embracing a so-called Rational Theatre, Bond's belief in revolution involves no small measure of faith, an irrational hope that somehow, without the use of violence, the natural goodness of humankind will one day win through, an aspiration that has been described as 'pessimistic optimism'.[42] It is a political standpoint more closely associated with religion than with reason. In the same way *Lear* does not portray a rational and tangible world. While it would be impossible to date the period of Shakespeare's play with any precision, since it is set in ancient Britain but has elements of Jacobean society, Bond's *Lear* deliberately thwarts any attempt to place it historically by frequent use of anachronisms. While apparently also set in

pre-Christian Britain, there are guns, photographs, knitting, a chauf-
feur and an aerosol can. Bond explained to Gaskill that such anachronisms are

> rather important and part of my style ... The play isn't ... a
> period piece. Any creation of any age on the stage is
> arbitrary ... So I'm allowed to bend the arbitrariness in a
> direction I choose. The anachronisms are for the horrible
> moments in a dream when you know it's a dream but can't
> help being afraid.[43]

It is a nonsense to claim that 'Any creation of any age on the stage is arbitrary'; for many historical plays, not least many of Shakespeare's, depend on a precise and anything but arbitrary historical setting. Brecht
insisted on such accuracy and maintained a clear sense of period in
pieces like *The Life of Galileo* and *Mother Courage,* for he felt that
any vagueness about the age of the setting would reinforce a sloppy
Romantic view that the problems portrayed were 'timeless and universal' and did not proceed from a specific historical and economic
situation.

Lear also reveals a similar vagueness about its geographical setting. We may accept a lack of precision about location, because it
frankly does not matter where headquarters or prisons are situated in
the context of the piece, and to give them locations like London or
Winchester *would* be arbitrary. However, given that the wall is such
a central image in the play, one might expect a certain geographical
logic to reinforce its meaning. In the opening scene we learn that the
wall has been erected to protect the nation from 'the enemies on our
borders – the Duke of Cornwall and the Duke of North'.[44] The plu-
ral use of 'borders' and the geographical suggestion of the two names,
North and the southernmost county of Britain (not to mention the
Shakespearian precedent of dividing the country into three), all imply that Lear has to defend his territory on two fronts. Yet there is
apparently only one wall, and North and Cornwall seemingly combine their forces with ease to launch a joint attack from one location.
Even if we let this pass, there remains a far greater vagueness about
the function of the wall after Cordelia's victory. Clearly, North and

Cornwall are now defeated and their territories are presumably under Cordelia's control. In other words, there can be no threat from these former enemies, unless we allow that others have taken the place of North and Cornwall. But there is no suggestion that this is the case, and it is far more likely that Bond permits such vagueness to be a part of what he confessed he cherished in his comments about his anachronisms, that the play should have the quality of a dream. By contrast with *Lear*, Shakespeare's *King Lear* is in fact a far more *rational* piece of theatre. As Benjamin Henrichs, reviewing a German production of *Lear* commented: 'Whatever... has changed through revolution – is of no interest to either Lear or Bond. Thus the play avoids any definitions and settles itself comfortably on its one great and portentous symbol.'[45]

By embracing both historical and geographical vagueness, by avoiding any definitions, Bond creates a political theatre which dispenses with facts, and a theatre that dispenses with facts cannot be challenged on grounds of authenticity. William Gaskill recognized the tension in *Lear* between 'the poet and the political thinker':

> Bond makes a dream world in which the reality of rifles jostles a Shakespearian myth. The poet and the political thinker are trying to co-exist, a struggle that has gone on in Bond ever since. But the play, as far as it is polemical at all, is pacifist, against violence, and sceptical of political change by the masses. It is finally the action of one man that counts.[46]

What we are offered here in *Lear* is Bond's vision, a vision it is impossible to test against our own experience, a major characteristic of interventionist writing, as John Peter has pointed out.[47] The political unrest in *Lear* is never coherently explained, any more than the efficacy of any solution is argued. As John Peter observes, Bond seems to regard such unrest as inevitable, like the weather.[48] And, as with the weather, it would be pointless to seek rational means for changing it.

Bond's political theatre is therefore not a 'Rational Theatre', whatever he may claim in order to gain credibility as a political thinker. On the contrary, his great strength is as a myth-maker. More powerfully than any contemporary dramatist except Beckett, he has managed to create images for our age: a baby stoned to death in a pram, the cannibalism of *Early Morning* (1968), the murder of the children in *Narrow Road to the Deep North* (1968), or the blind old man standing atop a wall, vigorously digging into the earth for the few moments of life left to him.

This ability to create arresting images, through the use of compassionate characterization and minimal, poetic dialogue has made Bond one of the most important political playwrights of the second half of the twentieth century; not by the exercise of reason but by the painstaking construction of pictures: 'Suppose there's a mosaic and I just move one piece. As a result of that every piece of the mosaic has to readjust itself. You can do that and end up with a different picture.'[49] That different picture refers not only to the new shape of a play like *Lear* but also to the possibility of transforming the whole of society into a new composition.

10   The strategy of play: Caryl Churchill's *Cloud Nine* (1979)

> Playwrights don't give answers, they ask questions. We need to find new questions, which may help us to answer the old ones or make them unimportant, and this means new subjects and new forms.[1]

A recurrent theme of this book is that the revolutionary aspirations of the socialist playwrights in Britain of the 1970s and 1980s ultimately failed to bring about any clearly discernible social or political restructuring. Indeed, political opinion has generally swung to the right over the succeeding years. However, there was one radical political movement that has had an obvious and immediate effect on the laws, economy and social attitudes of the British nation, namely the women's movement. While there is undoubtedly much that remains to be done before a wholly successful revolution may be proclaimed, the achievements of feminism are nevertheless considerable: revision of laws affecting women, decisive moves towards equal pay and conditions in the workplace, and generally the acknowledgment of the rights of women, right down to the avoidance of gender-based terminology.

The simple but ultimately effective message of the feminist movement was summed up in the oft-repeated phrase, 'The personal is political.' In place of – or often alongside – the demand for a total restructuring of society along socialist lines, feminism in the 1960s sought to establish more immediately attainable principles of equality and justice by organizing a fairer share of labour in the home and by rewarding women equally in the workplace. In some versions of feminism this resulted in women having 'to imitate men to succeed'.[2]

The most dramatic manifestation of this so-called 'bourgeois feminism' was the forceful leadership of Margaret Thatcher, whose political style showed little of the supposedly 'caring' side of women
and instead revealed itself as more domineering and ruthless than
most of the male prime ministers who had preceded her. By contrast,
some women wished to break away entirely from the patriarchal structures imitated by 'successful' career women. In 'radical feminism' they
sought a total rejection of all things male, even to the point of living
in single-sex communities, having contact with men only to become
impregnated by them when they decided to bear children. Other feminists again perceived in such isolationism a dangerous splitting of
radical thinkers, allowing capitalism to thrive while progressive men
and women exhausted their energies in gender conflict.

A third approach, which attempted to combine change on a
personal level with revolution on a social level, is known as 'socialist
feminism' or 'materialist feminism' and has arguably been the most
effective in bringing about social change. Unlike America, 'where feminism is strongly based in the middle class', the feminist movement
in England 'is at once largely working-class and heavily socialist'.[3]
In the theatre, this approach was summed up by the two banners unfurled at the end of the Red Ladder production *Strike While the Iron Is
Hot* (published 1980): 'Workers will never be free while women are in
chains' and 'Women will never be free while workers are in chains.'[4]

Like all political movements, feminism has had its propagan-
dists, its street demonstrations and writers championing its cause.
Writing in 1984, Helene Keyssar noted that 'since the early sixties
approximately 300 plays by women have been published in Britain
and the United States', over half of which might be described as feminist, and adds: 'At least another 100 feminist plays have been produced but remain unpublished.'[5] This was a remarkable development,
since the history of the theatre is not noted for the number of women
playwrights. While women have excelled in poetry and especially the
novel, they have until the latter half of the twentieth century been
very poorly represented in writing for the stage. There were some isolated pioneers, like the German nun Hrotsvita and Aphra Behn, by
no means the only significant woman playwright of the Restoration.

Then, in the first half of the twentieth century, there were Lady Gregory in Ireland, Christopher St John in Britain, Marieluise Fleisser in Germany, and amongst American dramatists, Gertrude Stein, Susan Glaspell and Lillian Hellman.[6] They are few in number, and none are likely to feature strongly if at all in conventional (i.e. male-edited) surveys of world drama.

Various reasons could be sought to explain this phenomenon. One particularly unsatisfactory explanation points to a supposed biological difference between men and women. It has been established experimentally that men's spatial awareness is superior to that of women. So, runs the argument, women are not good at visualizing the three dimensions of a stage and writing effectively for it (just as there have been very few successful women chess players, whereas women have competed very successfully in other mind games like contract bridge). There are three reasons why this explanation is nonsense: first, this spatial awareness may not be genetically determined but rather the result of training (so boys spending more time playing ball games than girls might enhance their sense of space); second, women novelists have never had difficulty in creating wonderfully plastic scenes for the imagination (attested, for example, by the ease with which Jane Austen's novels can be adapted for screen or television); finally, the male superiority in spatial awareness was estimated at 10 per cent, which would hardly account for the overwhelming number of male dramatists.

A more reasonable explanation is the economic one. The theatre has been, and remains, like most public institutions, dominated by men. Moreover, it is an essentially public art-form. Women could write poetry and novels at home and, often by employing the subterfuge of adopting a male persona like Currer Bell (Charlotte Brontë) or George Eliot (Mary Anne Evans), get their works read merely by sending them to a publisher. Even so, one must not underestimate the colossal difficulties women had in order to find the time and leisure to write fiction and to get it published.[7] The female dramatist, in addition, would, in order to have published and perfected her art, probably have had to travel to theatres and to associate with male producers and performers in a manner that would have appeared compromising for the day. Virginia Woolf speculated about an imagined sister of Shakespeare, possessing as much genius as her brother, but who would no doubt never have had the opportunity to join the theatre and would have ended instead by committing suicide and being buried at the crossroads.[8]

It was also Virginia Woolf who suggested that one reason why women turned to the novel was because the aesthetics of the form were more flexible: 'all the older forms of literature were hardened and set by the time she became a writer. The novel alone was young enough to be soft in her hands – another reason, perhaps, why she wrote novels.'[9] This brings us to the third reason for questioning the criteria by which women dramatists have been dismissed as minor talents, summed up by Susan Koppelman's syllogism: 'I have never encountered these good women writers, therefore they do not exist.'[10] It is notable how conventional dramaturgy embraces a male ethos, reflected in clichés like 'All drama is based on conflict'. Indeed, it is asserted that the traditional dramatic structure, which consists of a struggle leading to a climax followed by a cathartic release, exactly mirrors the male orgasm. As Caryl Churchill remarked: 'Women are traditionally expected not to initiate action, and plays are action, in a way that words are not. So perhaps that's one reason why comparatively few women have written plays.'[11] In a similar vein, Gillian Hanna of the women's theatre group Monstrous Regiment related the structure of plays to women's experience of life: '[Men] are born into a world where they can map out life... it has to do with a career... Now for a woman, life is not like that. It doesn't have that pattern. For a woman life and experience is broken-backed.'[12] Feminist critics who reject the insistence on external action and challenge 'phallic' dramaturgy have not only encouraged the growing number of contemporary women playwrights to find their own voice; they have also recognized the quality of former women writers all too easily dismissed by applying conventional criteria.

Of course, the whole tendency of modernist and post-modernist writing for the stage has been to question Aristotelian precepts, challenging the need for a linear plot development and rejecting the dependence on external action. Thus Brecht's montage techniques and

Beckett's *Waiting for Godot* (1952), in which famously 'nothing happens, twice', do not conform to received notions of dramaturgy. Yet neither writer was noted for his feminist tendencies. The danger is that by appearing to evaluate women's writing in its own terms, one may be 'ghettoizing' it, risking the implication that it cannot be judged on equal terms with male products. In fact, it is arguable that in the twentieth century dramatic structure has become more feminine by eschewing vigorous 'male' action and by allowing a series of minor climaxes rather than by building inexorably to a major climax towards the end of the play. It would seem then that women are now able to write within a more congenial dramatic environment. Certainly, they have reinforced this development, but it was hardly the result of a programmatic act by feminists. As with all successful change, it could only take place when the ground was ready for it.

The subject of this chapter, Caryl Churchill, has enjoyed a success that is definitely not dependent on a revision of dramatic criteria, having been hailed as a major playwright without reference to her sex ('the most profound and theatrical writer of her generation', as Ruby Cohn describes her).[13] Nevertheless, in terms of both her ideology and her dramatic style, Churchill has shown herself to be identifiably a feminist writer. She, too, has recognized 'the "maleness" of the traditional structure of plays, with conflict and building in a certain way to a climax',[14] and both the content and structure of her plays, as Frances Gray points out, 'reflect the "broken-backed" experience of women'.[15]

Churchill acknowledges that she is a socialist feminist: 'If pushed to labels, I would be prepared to take on both socialist and feminist, but I always feel very wary.'[16] She had only gradually become politicized: coming from a reasonably prosperous background, it was not until her late teens that she 'began to see how things worked, and why things were the way they were...I was made unhappy by things being unjust.'[17] Her years at Oxford University gave her clearer insights, but she has admitted that she 'started personally and emotionally' and later confessed that she was 'still groping towards what that means in political terms'.[18] Her eventual move towards political commitment was prompted by her personal situation as a woman: 'What politicised me was being discontented with my own way of life – of being a barrister's wife and just being at home with small children.'[19]

One way forward that Churchill rejected was to use her intelligence and education to compete with men on their own ground. Indeed, she warns against successful 'bourgeois feminists' in *Top Girls* (1982), a play in which Churchill wanted 'to be celebrating the extraordinary achievements of women' but in which she also wished to recognize that 'this sort of movement is useless if you don't have a socialist perspective on it...there's no such thing as right-wing feminism'.[20] Instead, she found herself 'broadly groping towards anti-capitalist plays',[21] and after working on her play *Vinegar Tom* with Monstrous Regiment in 1976, declared that she had at last managed to get beyond her 'own personal pain and anger' to embrace 'a more objective and analytical way of looking at things'.[22]

It might be thought inappropriate that Churchill appears in this monograph on political theatre, since she has written very few plays that are 'political' in a narrow sense. The only obvious candidate is *The Legion Hall Bombing*, a ninety-minute television play, broadcast by the BBC in 1978. This piece documented the actual trial of a boy in the infamous Northern Irish Diplock Courts, which sat without jury. The lad was convicted and sentenced to sixteen years' imprisonment for planting a bomb, even though the only evidence against him was the uncorroborated claim by the police that he had confessed, and despite the fact that an eye-witness had declared that it was a case of mistaken identity. The BBC refused to broadcast Churchill's mild and objective commentary on the Diplock Courts that accompanied the broadcast, and she and her producer withdrew their names in protest.

Both the immediate content of the piece and the associated protest reflected a clear political commitment. However, it stands alone in Churchill's work as 'the only documentary play I've done'.[23] For the rest, she has focused more on general social questions, and in particular the role of women in society. That this is as genuinely political as male concerns with party politics and revolution will be clear from the following discussion. To quote from Virginia Woolf again, this time in ironical mood: 'This is an important book, the critic assumes, because it deals with war. This is an insignificant book because it deals with the feelings of women in a drawing-room.'[24]

Churchill's approach to theatre is perhaps best summed up by her words in an interview with John F. O'Malley in the early seventies: 'I desperately wanted to see if I could make things happen.'[25] Churchill wanted to make things happen politically by encouraging a radical change in society, and she wanted to make things happen on the stage by using theatre in a joyfully playful manner to challenge our perception of reality. The Swiss playwright Friedrich Dürrenmatt spoke of the fun and freedom he enjoyed as a playwright at being able to have his characters enter the stage, for example, through a grandfather-clock,[26] and the same element of play permeates Churchill's work. Explaining why she preferred writing for the theatre to writing for television, she said: 'I don't find [television] anything like as exciting myself. I do like things that actually happen.'[27] So, while not wholly rejecting a realistic style, her theatrical playfulness represents a decisively interventionist stance. In *Vinegar Tom* she turns a treatise on witchcraft into a music-hall act, in *Fen* (1983) she introduces ghosts and a strange figure on stilts into the dreary landscape of the fens, and in *Top Girls* gathers together a group of women from different historical periods to celebrate the promotion of a female executive.

One of her favourite devices is to manipulate traditional forms of exposition and plot. In one of her earliest full-length plays, *Traps*, which she began writing in 1976, the first act is set in a town flat. Syl's baby cries a great deal; Christie comes to the flat in an attempt to escape from her husband. Act Two, which presents an identical stage set to Act One, is now in the country. Syl has not yet given birth to the baby, and Christie is attempting a reconciliation with her husband. Meanwhile, doors that were locked are mysteriously opened, and broken pots curiously become whole again. Even Pinter, whose characters are frequently enigmatic and contradictory, had never gone this far. 'It is', wrote Churchill in her preface to the piece, 'like an impossible object, or a painting by Escher, where the objects can exist like that on paper, but would be impossible in life.'[28]

By freeing the action – and the audience – from the normal constraints of a coherent and linear structure, Churchill may, as Kritzer asserts, be promoting 'non-patriarchal subjectivity';[29] she is certainly suggesting that there are alternative paths of action and response to those that appear to be laid down for us. Linear thinking is replaced by lateral thinking, and the inevitability of a predetermined outcome, familiar from classical drama, is replaced by a range of possibilities, reminiscent of the choices implied in Brecht's dialectic theatre. Yet the optimism of the piece is tempered by the fact that choices are limited. The play ends with the characters taking it in turns to have a bath naked on stage and finally sharing a communal meal. For the present, the characters remain trapped, but the final image holds out the possibility of a way forward through gentle communality, a domestic version of Hare's *Fanshen*.

We shall encounter the same playing with time, and the same muted optimism, in *Cloud Nine*. We shall also find here Churchill's readiness to play with casting, particularly with regard to gender. Another of the joyous freedoms of theatre is that the same individual (actor) can appear with several different personae (roles), merely by offering some semiotic clue to the audience, possibly a change of costume or even a simple alteration of posture and vocal delivery. The Shared Experience Theatre Company under Mike Alfreds were pioneers in this field, dramatizing complex novels with half a dozen performers. Given the economic stringency faced by the theatre today, such 'doubling' may proceed partly from necessity; but it can also lend significance as well as fun to the drama. As Churchill stipulated in her 'Note on the Production' of *Light Shining in Buckinghamshire* (1976):

> The characters are not played by the same actors each time they appear. The audience should not have to worry exactly which character they are seeing. Each scene can be taken as a separate event rather than part of a story. This seems to reflect better the reality of large events like war and revolution where many people share the same kind of experience ... When different actors play the parts what comes over is a large event involving many people, whose characters resonate in a way they wouldn't if they were more clearly defined.[30]

Such a fluid approach to casting, which challenges the conventional identification of actor with role, is not only playful and expedient; it also focuses attention, in a Brechtian manner, on collective events rather than individual fates. In *Cloud Nine*, as we shall see, the casting is even more adventurous, deliberately challenging presumptions about gender.

The third way in which Churchill has determinedly eschewed traditional dramatic modes lies in the ambiguity of ideas revealed in her plays. While clearly espousing the feminist cause, Churchill refuses to idealize women, recognizing that many have sold out to patriarchal values. Thus figures like Marion in *Owners* (1972) and Marlene in *Top Girls* are shown to be as ruthless as men, a theme repeated in *Serious Money* (1987), Churchill's play set in the City of London's financial market. Similarly, the main supporter of the cruel Witchfinder in *Vinegar Tom* is a woman, as is one of the main accusers of the defenceless 'witches'; and one of the most vicious episodes in *Fen* shows a woman forcing her step-daughter to drink scalding hot water. Churchill opens up possibilities rather than urging a particular viewpoint on her audience. By playing with ideas, frequently with a strong element of humour, Churchill has run the risk of appearing too frivolous to be accounted either a dedicated feminist or a committed political playwright, but it is in fact precisely this playful quality in Churchill's work which makes her such a major figure in the political theatre of the 1970s and 1980s.

Cloud Nine (1979)

Plot summary

Clive is a British colonial administrator in Africa in Victorian times. With him live his wife, Betty, his mother-in-law, Maud, his two children, Edward and Victoria, the governess, Ellen, and his African servant, Joshua. The native populace is rioting, and Mrs Saunders, a widow, comes to them to seek safety. Her arrival is soon followed by that of Harry Bagley, an explorer. Clive makes passionate advances to Mrs Saunders, Betty fancies Harry, who is, however, a homosexual who has sex with Joshua and the young Edward, and then, mistakenly, assumes Clive to be offering him sex. Ellen, who reveals herself to be a lesbian, is forced into

marriage with Harry. The first act ends with the wedding cele-
brations, the final tableau being of Clive giving a speech, while
Joshua points a gun at him. The second act is set in a London park
in 1979, but the characters from the first half are only twenty-
five years older. Betty has left Clive, Victoria is now married to
Martin and has a son, and Edward lives with a promiscuous gay,
Gerry. Victoria decides to leave Martin and begin a lesbian relationship with Lin, who has a young daughter, Cathy. When Gerry
leaves him, Edward moves in with Lin and Victoria. After suggesting that she too might come and live with them, Betty begins
a relationship with Gerry.

Cloud Nine was the second play, after *Light Shining in Buckinghamshire*, which Churchill worked on with the Joint Stock Theatre
Company in 1978/9. She had decided that she would like to work on
a piece immediately concerned with sexual politics, and so, with Max
Stafford-Clark, the director, she assembled a cast which represented
different sexual orientations. Thus workshops were concerned not so
much with establishing character or creating a story-line as in exploring the relationships between the different participants:

> People talked about themselves and their own lives. They talked
> about their sexuality, and we did improvisations about stereo-
> types. One person would have a stereotype they would lay on
> another, and the first person would find themselves becoming
> like that – how people would expect them to be. A wife expects
> her husband to be dominating and he expects her to be hysterical.
> We made those things happen.[31]

Although it has been asserted that *Cloud Nine* was the result of 'a collective scripting process',[32] Churchill in fact followed her usual proce-
dure, which is to work with the director and cast, not on the writing,
but on workshops around a theme. She then goes away and writes the
play, presenting it later to the cast to be rehearsed 'like any other play',
as Antony Sher, the actor who played the original Clive, reported.[33]
Churchill herself admitted the tenuous link between the preparatory
period and the play itself: 'During the workshop itself I didn't think at
all what the play would be like...I can't actually trace back...It was

much more attitudes and values',[34] and Sher stated: 'Eventually, the play didn't relate that much... specifically to [the workshop period]. It had the spirit of the workshop.'[35] In this way Churchill maintains her autonomy as an author but draws on the 'attitudes and values' of the people she will be working with, thus offering them on the whole the opportunity to identify with roles and situations that they have provided themselves. This represents a reasonable and practicable compromise between a democratic working method and the need for the writer to confront her creation in isolation. This dual approach is especially welcomed by Churchill: 'If you're working by yourself, then you're not accountable to anyone but yourself while you're doing it. You don't get forced in quite the same way into seeing how your own inner feelings connect up with larger things that happen to other people.'[36]

It was during the workshop period that a title was found for the piece: it happened when the woman caretaker of the rehearsal rooms spoke of an orgasm as like being on 'cloud nine'. The workshops also suggested the major theme of *Cloud Nine*, namely 'the connection between colonialism and the male colonialism of women',[37] or, as Churchill puts it in the Introduction to her first volume of plays, 'the parallel between colonial and sexual oppression'.[38] When she came to write the play, she therefore decided that the first act should be set in British colonial Africa in Victorian times, whereas the second act would take place in London in the present. In order to provide continuity between the two periods, *Cloud Nine* retains many of the same characters as in the first half. Since, in real time as opposed to theatrical time, they would all be dead some hundred years later, Churchill stipulates that the characters have aged by only twenty-five years – a typical and impressive example of her willingness to experiment with time in her plays.

Apart from being set in Africa, with Queen Victoria on the throne, the first act is 'deliberately historically imprecise'.[39] This disjunction is reminiscent of the vague colonial setting of Brecht's *Man Equals Man* (1926), which is supposedly set in India in 1925 but includes a pagoda and has a queen on the British throne. The action of the first half of *Cloud Nine* focuses on the home and surroundings belonging to Clive, a colonial administrator, and the threat to the family comes mainly from the discontented African populace outside. By contrast, the second act takes place in the public setting of a London park in 1979, and the threat to the characters comes mainly from an interior struggle to discover sexual fulfilment. A further link is that, to the male colonial mind, both Africa and woman share the inherent threat that they are dangerous, dark and unpredictable.

Perhaps the most adventurous decision taken by Churchill was in the casting. Unlike the casting decisions forced on her by the composition of the cast for *Light Shining in Buckinghamshire* and *Vinegar Tom*, the cross-gender casting of the first act of *Cloud Nine* was a provocatively theatrical device. Betty, Clive's wife, is played by a male actor, and Edward, his son, is performed by a woman. On the most basic level, this provides simple theatrical fun, especially when Harry, who anyway is a homosexual, receives passionate advances from the man/woman Betty. Indeed, Loren Kruger has rightly pointed out that these are 'old panto tricks and not, as fondly supposed, Brechtian innovation'.[40] However, Churchill's intentions go beyond mere fun: in the case of Betty, the woman has had to deny her self and take on male values and so is appropriately represented by a man. As John Peter has pointed out, Churchill's strategy is, by having a female character played by a male actor, to show how femininity is an artificial and imposed construct, which, all too easily, can become the determining feature of behaviour.[41]

Edward is played by a young girl, because he is having difficulty assuming the masculine identity his father is trying to force on him and prefers playing with a doll. By the second half Betty and Edward, who have now both discovered their own sexuality, are played by performers of their own sex. Only the four-year-old Cathy is played by a man (the same actor that played Clive), 'partly because the size and presence of a man on stage seemed appropriate to the emotional force of young children, and partly, as with Edward, to show more clearly the issues involved in learning what is considered correct behaviour for a girl.'[42]

The other bold casting decisions taken by Churchill were to have Victoria, Clive's daughter, played by a dummy, and thus incapable of speech or independent action; and for Joshua, the black manservant, to be performed by a white actor, since, like Betty's assumption of patriarchal values, he has become so conditioned by his white master that he even disowns his parents: 'I had the image of a black man aspiring to white values and literally being a white negro. And the idea of a woman who has taken men's values, a sort of man-made woman who has no sense of herself as a woman',[43] explained Churchill, and spoke in another interview of 'those characters [that] had no sense of their own identity but were trying to be what the white man wanted them to be'.[44]

Other aspects of the casting produced interesting outcomes. Thus, as Anne Herrmann has pointed out, the fact that Ellen and Mrs Saunders, although they are so well suited to each other, are played by the same actress, means that 'they can literally never meet'.[45] By contrast, Churchill can provide the ending with a powerful image of reconciliation, as the two Bettys, one Victorian and repressed, the other contemporary and on the way to liberation, are able to meet in a final embrace.

This playful treatment of the stage, with its underlying seriousness, is reinforced by the overall theatricality of the piece. The play opens with a song, which in truly Brechtian manner allows the characters to introduce themselves. Thus conventional exposition is dispensed with, and the action can begin at once with the imminent arrival of Harold Bagley. Because of the external theatricality of the first act and, of course, owing to the inevitable distance between contemporary actors and these figures from the past, there is a great danger that the first half of the play degenerates into farce. Caryl Churchill recognized this. In a lengthy letter to the San Francisco director of *Cloud Nine* she insisted:

> What is important ... is that the feelings and characters of the
> first act should be played for real, so that we do care about
> them as people ... if the first act does just go as farce it's for
> one thing not a very good farce and for another sets up
> expectations of a kind of entertainment that aren't met in the
> second act ... The first act obviously isn't naturalistic but

should be played for real; the second act clearly gets played for real but mustn't get naturalistic.[46]

The second act with its recognizably contemporary figures in a familiar setting is indeed more realistic, but even here Churchill introduces a ghost, and all the characters join together for the 'Cloud Nine' song.

Similarly, Churchill's diction is provocatively playful. Her dialogue is amongst the finest written for the British theatre today, and she has explored innovative ways of writing for the stage. In *Top Girls*, for example, she prescribes points at which characters should talk over each other, one beginning a line before another has finished speaking. This offers a more effective imitation of everyday speech than has been attempted by playwrights heretofore, where, implausibly, everyone waits for the other to finish before responding. This device might therefore seem to be extremely naturalistic. In fact, the precise orchestration of these moments, like the carefully laid pauses in Pinter, represents an artistically conceived rhetoric. In *Serious Money* Churchill has the less than poetic figures of the London Stock Exchange speak in verse, not the heavily ornate verse that Steven Berkoff uses in his London plays (*East*, 1975, and *West*, 1980), but a witty, light, fluid verse, slightly reminiscent of T. S. Eliot.

In *Cloud Nine* most of the dialogue is simple and direct. Abrupt sentences reinforce the sense of minimal communication between the characters of the first act:

CLIVE   ...And what has my little dove done today?
BETTY   I've read a little.
CLIVE   Good. Is it good?
BETTY   It's poetry.
CLIVE   You're so delicate and sensitive.
BETTY   And I played the piano. Shall I send for the children?
CLIVE   Yes, in a minute.[47]

Even where Clive becomes positively verbose, as in his excitement at the arrival of Mrs Saunders, the staccato sentences, the proliferation of abstract nouns, and the hyperbole, for example a 'duty' to 'seek... help', make Clive's attempts to communicate seem absurd:

It is a pleasure. It is an honour. It is positively your duty
to seek my help. I would be hurt, I would be insulted by
any show of independence. Your husband would have been
one of my dearest friends if he had lived. Betty, look who has
come, Mrs Saunders. She has ridden here all alone, amazing
spirit. What will you have? Tea or something stronger? Let
her lie down, she is overcome. Betty, you will know what
to do.[48]

Of the eighty-one words used, only the fact that Mrs Saunders 'has
ridden here all alone' conveys any information; the other seventy-five
are redundant, and very funny. The effusiveness of Clive's welcome
and his use of high-sounding words like 'honour' and 'duty' stand in
comic contrast to his ineptitude and his reliance on Betty to 'know
what to do'.

In the second act there is obviously less sense of pastiche, but
the language is similarly cropped. Here the effect is one of immediacy,
and the lack of ornamentation suggests sincerity in the speaker. Thus,
Betty's famous speech about masturbation, so effective that the New
York production inadvisably ended with it, is written with such open-
ness and clarity and with such a childish piling up of main clauses
that it reflects the innocence and lack of prurience of the speaker. An
extract:

I used to touch myself when I was very little, I thought I'd
invented something wonderful. I used to do it to go to sleep
with or to cheer myself up, and one day it was raining and I
was under the kitchen table, and my mother saw me rubbing
away, and she dragged me out so quickly I hit my head and it
bled and I was sick, and nothing was said, and I never did it
again till this year... Sometimes I do it three times in one
night and it really is great fun.[49]

Occasionally Churchill uses the ambiguity of simple language
to great effect. For example, Clive reprimands Edward for playing with
his sister's doll in the following words: 'we had you with Victoria's doll

once before, Edward'.[50] On one level, 'had you' simply means 'found you', but the word 'had' in colloquial English can imply both violence and sexual possession, and so makes Clive's reprimand unpleasantly aggressive and threatening.

As stated earlier, Caryl Churchill is not a political playwright in the way that writers like Bond, Brenton or Hare clearly are. The major political statement of *Cloud Nine* is that colonialism was oppressive, hardly a profound or new insight in the last quarter of the twentieth century. The only potentially political commentary in the second act is provided by the ghost of Lin's brother, a soldier who has lost his life in the Northern Irish conflict. But here there is no attempt to suggest that Britain's colonial rule in Africa is replicated in its modern role in Northern Ireland. It is characteristic of Churchill to avoid such glib historical parallels and not to attempt a political analysis of the Irish problem in a play. Instead the Soldier is concerned only with his personal situation, using the word 'fuck' as both a violent adjective and as the pleasure he seeks to release him from his misery:

> That was the worst thing in the fucking army. Never fucking let out. Can't fucking talk to Irish girls . . . Man's fucking life in the fucking army? No fun when the fucking kids hate you. I got so I fucking wanted to kill someone and I got fucking killed myself and I want a fuck.[51]

Here again the personal is the political. In place of the broad canvas of revolutionary socialism, Churchill shows how individuals are oppressed: the wife and son bent to the will of the Victorian patriarch, the working-class man brutalized by armed conflict. Thus she provides a political statement as valid and indeed more relevant than those of many male playwrights.

The analysis of sexual politics in the first act of the play holds few surprises. Apart from a certain independence of mind shown by Maud, Clive's mother-in-law, there is little awareness of the power women manage to retain even in extreme patriarchal situations like that of Victorian Britain. Betty is wholly dominated by her husband. Revealing the totalitarian colonizing of her life, she sings:

> I live for Clive. The whole aim of my life
> Is to be what he looks for in a wife.
> I am a man's creation as you see,
> And what men want is what I want to be.[52]

When she gets Clive to reprimand his manservant for being offensive to her, Clive complies but then '*winks at* JOSHUA, *unseen by* BETTY'.[53] Male solidarity takes precedence over support for his wife. Sex is also something for men alone to enjoy:

ELLEN   Betty, what happens with a man? I don't know what to do.
BETTY   You just keep still.
ELLEN   And what does he do?
BETTY   Harry will know what to do.
ELLEN   And is it enjoyable?
BETTY   Ellen, you're not getting married to enjoy yourself.[54]

Undoubtedly the first act offers a great deal of fun, with its cross-gender casting and the irony of the strong adventurer, Harry Bagley, turning out to be a homosexual who is obliged to marry a lesbian in order to follow a code of 'compulsory heterosexuality'.[55] But the first act does not offer much more than feminist platitudes, lending some justification to Loren Kruger's comment: '*Cloud Nine* titillates its audience with the display of a "concern for gender" rather than offering dramatic interaction of these concerns that might challenge us to think about them differently.'[56]

However, the second act is considerably more subtle. At first sight, it seems that conditions have improved greatly. The first act had taken place in constant sunshine without seasonal change or night-time scenes, reflecting the stasis in the lives of the characters. By contrast, the second act moves from winter through spring to late summer, suggesting the flux in the lives of the contemporary figures. The young girl, Cathy, is not oppressed but able to express herself freely. Victoria is transformed from a dummy to a woman who is married to a progressive husband. Edward has discovered his own sexuality; he is openly gay and so willing to challenge sexual stereotypes that he even wonders whether he is a lesbian. Most significantly, Betty has been brave enough to leave Clive, and, while missing his presence, has started to discover herself as an individual, something that is reinforced in performance by the fact that Betty is now played by a woman:

> I thought if Clive wasn't looking at me there wasn't a person there. And one night in bed in my flat I was so frightened I started touching myself. I thought my hand might go through space. I touched my face, it was there, my arm, my breast, and my hand went down where it shouldn't, and I thought well there is somebody there . . . I felt triumphant because I was a separate person.[57]

As Frances Gray observes, 'recognition of her own sexuality enables her to move from object to subject'.[58]

Despite these advances on the oppressive rigidity of the Victorian family, Churchill does not present us with some sort of contemporary utopia. The child Cathy may be freer than a Victorian child like Edward, but she uses her freedom to chant obscene rhymes, play aggressively with a toy gun and to behave in an utterly selfish manner. Victoria's marriage to Martin notionally offers her the freedom to discover herself and become independent. In fact, however, Martin's attitude as a 'new man' is as oppressive as Clive's had been, but in a much more subtle and in some ways more pernicious manner. Thus, while urging Victoria to be free in both her career and in bed by encouraging her to take a job away from home and by trying to organize orgasms for her, Martin shows that, despite his good intentions, he still plays the dominant male role:

> You take the job, you go to Manchester. You turn it down, you stay in London . . . I don't want to put any pressure on you . . . Whatever you want to do, I'll be delighted . . . Don't cry again, Vicky, I'm not the sort of man who makes women cry . . . Do you think you're well enough to do this job? You don't have to do it. No one's going to think any the less of you if you stay here with me. There's no point being so liberated you make yourself cry all the time. You stay and we'll get everything

sorted out. What it is about sex, when we talk while it's happening I get to feel it's like a driving lesson. Left, right, a little faster, carry on, slow down – ... I'm not like whatever percentage of American men have become impotent as a direct result of women's liberation, which I am totally in favour of, more I sometimes think than you are yourself. Nor am I one of your villains who sticks it in, bangs away, and falls asleep. My one aim is to give you pleasure ... I'm not putting any pressure on you but I don't think you're being a whole person. God knows I do everything I can to make you stand on your own two feet. Just be yourself. You don't seem to realise how insulting it is to me that you can't get yourself together.[59]

It is small wonder that, to escape the new oppression of the well-meaning male, Victoria leaves Martin to begin a lesbian relationship with Lin, a working-class woman and the most positive character in the play. Edward too may be freer, but his relationship with the promiscuous Gerry is anything but ideal: they endure all the tensions of a traditional unsatisfactory marriage. Betty finds her freedom equally difficult to cope with, like a long-term prisoner just released from jail: 'I'll never be able to manage. If I can't even walk down the street by myself. Everything looks so fierce ... I do feel safer with a man. The park is so large the grass seems to tilt.'[60]

Churchill recognizes the problematic nature of contemporary relationships, knowing that, paradoxically, freedom too can be oppressive and disorientating: 'And it's upside down when you reach Cloud Nine.'[61] Contemporary freedoms may prove as confining as imperial morality. As John Peter has observed, being on Cloud Nine may feel good; but it is very easy to get vertigo.[62] Thus, Michelene Wandor has missed the point when she writes: 'The second half is merely a series of isolated portraits of more libertarian sexual relationships in the 1970s.'[63] Cloud Nine goes far beyond this, analysing at a personal level how society might be better organized to provide the opportunity for real freedom. Because this is a question which everyone faces, it is a genuinely political matter and not one that is confined to women. When the director of the premiere, Max Stafford-Clark, suggested to Churchill that he should resign in favour of a female director, Churchill responded by insisting that, as a man, he had as big a stake in sexual politics as she had.[64]

As the opening quotation to this chapter says, 'Playwrights don't give answers', and Churchill offers no glib solutions to our contemporary situation. Matriarchy and worship of the earth-goddess may exist as a putative past utopia, but here the yearning to restore it becomes little more than a bit of drunken fun in the park. The best hope is represented by the simple and gentle gesture of the two Bettys embracing as the play ends. Like the bath and communal meal in *Traps* or the final Ranters' meeting in *Light Shining in Buckinghamshire*, we are offered a glimpse of a better life, but equally an awareness that the road to it will be long and hard.

Churchill's considerable achievement in *Cloud Nine* is to have united the personal and the political in a wittily entertaining play: 'For the first time I brought together two preoccupations of mine – people's internal states of being and the external political structures which affect them, which make them insane.'[65] As Victoria expresses it more forcefully: 'You can't separate fucking and economics.'[66]

By combining emotional complexity with socio-economic concerns, Churchill has also presented new and interesting challenges for performance. Stanislavskian internalization has to go hand in hand with Brechtian demonstration. As Gillian Hanna of Monstrous Regiment expressed it:

> It doesn't work for me or for an audience, if I'm doing it just
> on the level of remembering some sort of pain that I've
> experienced...Nor does it work on the level of 'I'm showing
> the audience something here.' The nights it seems to work
> best are when there is, and on a level that I've not experienced
> before, a meshing of those two.[67]

Thus, in her playful approach to theatre, Churchill has succeeded not only in combining the personal with the political, but also in finding a way, as Brecht put it, of instructing entertainingly and entertaining instructively. And the lesson she conveys? That we can take responsibility for our own lives, that we can recognize oppression, whether colonial or sexual, and seek the means to free ourselves. As Briggs says in *Light Shining in Buckinghamshire*:

> All I've learnt how to get things done, that wasn't for nothing. I don't believe this is the last days. England will still be here in hundreds of years. And people working so hard they can't grasp how it happens and can't take hold of their own lives, like us till we had this chance, and we're losing it now, as we sit here, every minute.[68]

Conclusion

I don't think any particular play's going to effect a revolution.
I don't think one starts out with that premise at all, but if
there's a revolution it will have been partly prepared by the
cultural change that we're taking part in.

(Roger Howard)[1]

The plays of the nine writers we have been considering, although sep-
arated from us by mere decades, in some respects come down to us
like documents of a past age. The demand for radical political change
within Western capitalism now seems hopelessly optimistic, since
Margaret Thatcher succeeded in imposing a monetarist consensus
on both Conservative and Labour policies, and after the Communist
regimes of Eastern Europe have been replaced by frequently malfunc-
tioning free-market economies. Virtually world-wide, and even in still
nominally Communist countries like China, the tendency is less towards dispossessing the rich to provide for the poor as to encouraging the rich in their endeavours, so that notionally enough wealth is
created for poverty to be eradicated. As David Hare ruefully already
admitted in 1978: 'consciousness has been raised in this country for
a good many years now and we seem further from radical political
change than at any time in my life'.[2]

However, it would be a mistake to treat this body of British
political playwriting as a failure. While some of the plays we have
considered may be of interest mainly for the light they shed on specific
and topical concerns, most will stand the test of time. There are not
so many good plays of the recent past that British theatre would not be

considerably enriched by revivals of plays like Griffiths's *Comedians*, or, no doubt to his own dismay, of Howard Barker's *Stripwell*.

It will be noted that the continuing relevance of a play does not depend on its placing on the Reflectionist–Interventionist spectrum.[3] As stylized a piece as *The Cheviot, the Stag and the Black, Black Oil* may well not be suitable for revival (and John McGrath would surely have accepted that it would need to be considerably revised and updated, if it were to be performed again). By contrast, a realist play like *Roots*, with its emphasis on humanist values, can still find resonance almost half a century later. What is important is whether a given play is narrowly political and therefore of its time or whether it embraces wider political and social issues. This is where the strategy of Caryl Churchill's work, as exemplified in *Cloud Nine*, may be seen to have been particularly successful. In its playful and theatrical treatment of the personal dimension of politics, especially in the area of gender politics, Churchill explores issues that are both more immediate and more tractable than calls for a Marxist revolution. And, empirically, it may be seen that the agitation of Churchill and other feminists has resulted in a substantial amount of legislation to begin to put right the traditional injustices against women, and has had a far greater effect on public and private thinking than the unheeded clarion calls of male political revolutionaries.

Does this mean that British political theatre, at least in the form it has been considered in this volume, is dead? It would be no small wonder if it were so. The would-be political playwrights of today are deprived of socialist models to emulate, except for minor remnants like Cuba. They live in a political landscape, where, in order to get elected, the Labour Party has embraced such right-wing positions on issues like privatization and immigration control that it is now difficult for the Conservatives to establish a separate identity. In the economic recession of the 1980s and early 1990s it also became harder to adopt a revolutionary stance. For it is a sobering paradox that, in Europe at least, it is only when the populace feel economically secure that they can risk thinking of major political upheavals. Hence it was the boom period of the 1960s and 1970s that stimulated radical activity and thought, creating a perceived threat that eased Thatcher into power. As Hare commented:

> in my own estimate, European countries have been more unstable during times of affluence than times of depression. It is hard to believe in the historical inevitability of something which has so frequently not happened, or rather, often been nearest to happening in places and circumstances furthest away from those predicted by the man who first suggested it.[4]

Yet economic injustice persists. There are considerably more homeless in Britain now than when Shelter was set up in the wake of Jeremy Sandford's television play, *Cathy Come Home*, directed by Ken Loach in 1966. Statistics indicate that, while there is greater wealth in the nation, the gap between rich and poor has consistently widened. Looking beyond Britain, it is clear that there is a colossal and inexcusable disparity between the wealth of the developed nations and that of the so-called Third World. A need for economic and social restructuring has never seemed more acute, and yet it is hard for creative writers to find forms in which to express their disquiet with the status quo.

Howard Barker is one of those who, acknowledging 'the extinction of official socialism', speaks of the 'triumph of defeat': 'When the opposition loses its politics, it must root in art.'[5] He, together with others like Edward Bond, has adopted a new strategy by exploring the fragmentation and uncertainties of post-modernism, in order to challenge received modes of thinking. Even if these writers no longer propagate a political ideology, they at least continue to question the existing hegemony.

Another potential strategy is to limit political agitation to single issues, whether on stage or in reality. This at least accords well with the temper of the times. As Paddy Ashdown, the former leader of the Liberal Party, expressed it:

> We live in a curious age, an age in which all the 'isms' have died – conservatism, socialism, communism. These were the great pillars that dominated the twentieth century. They're

the things that people killed each other for. For what would you stand on the political barricade in this day and age? A single issue, yes. The live export of animals certainly, genetic foods, yes. But for a political creed? And we seem to be an age without creeds.[6]

Theatre will continue to be an effective medium for involving communities in agitating for specific improvements to their lives, and there is a growing use of drama for this purpose in developing nations. In Britain the Campaign for Nuclear Disarmament, which was probably the most significant single-issue protest movement in the history of Britain, once attracted the talents of writers like Edward Bond. It is, however, now hard to imagine a single issue like genetically modified foods having the power to impel a playwright to attempt a major piece of theatre. It is a sad comment on political agitation in Britain today that the major achievements of the May Day 'anti-capitalist' riot in 2000 were to deface the Cenotaph and to invade a branch of McDonald's.

A more attractive strategy is to recognize that television has appropriated political theatre, particularly in its soap operas.[7] As Stephen Lacey pointed out in his *British Realist Theatre*, the popular tradition in theatre 'contained . . . an image of the lower- and working-classes that official culture rigorously suppressed'.[8] It is certainly now the case that through soap operas the British public can nightly observe ordinary citizens operating within a recognizably realistic social framework, often facing dilemmas and situations of a broadly political nature. Thus the lawful but patently unfair imprisonment of a character in *Coronation Street* could lead to a national outcry and even to questions being asked in Parliament. Soap operas dealing with the police and the National Health Service repeatedly point to problems created by inadequate public expenditure, and promote generally liberal if not actually radical ideas. The discussions that follow some of the more dramatic episodes frequently generate debate that is not so very far removed from the Forum Theatre of Augusto Boal.

Of course, the question arises whether this daily diet of minor issues does not defuse a sense of outrage at the wider injustices in evidence in the world. By emoting over the fate of a character in a soap opera, we may, as Brecht argued many years ago, be dissipating our potential activity in emotion rather than in moving to correct the injustice. However, this is a danger that is not exclusive to television drama.

The other problem with television is the level of control, however benign, of commercial management. It is probably unthinkable that a piece like Frank Wedekind's *Spring Awakening* (1891) could be shown on television even today, almost a century after its stage premiere, containing as it does a scene of young men competing to see who can ejaculate soonest over a coin on the floor. The freedoms necessary for radical political opinion are more likely to be found in the live theatre.

It remains unclear when and how political theatre may re-emerge. That it will, given the continuing injustices of the world, I regard as inevitable. That, when it does, it will draw on the work of a group of remarkable British playwrights of the last century, I regard as highly desirable.

Notes

INTRODUCTION

1. David Edgar, 'Ten years of political theatre', *The Second Time as Farce: Reflections on the Drama of Mean Times*, London: Lawrence & Wishart, 1988, 16

2. Interview with Judith Thurman, *Ms*, May 1982, 54

3. David Hare, *Writing Left-Handed*, London, Faber & Faber, 1991, xi

4. Richard Seyd, 'The theatre of Red Ladder', *New Edinburgh Review*, August 1975; quoted in Edgar, *The Second Time as Farce*, 34

5. Interview with Ira Peck, *New York Times*, 10 April 1966, Section 2, p. 3

6. Simon Trussler, 'Alternative theatre – for what?', *Theatre Quarterly* 5 (19), September–November 1975, 11

7. 'Admittedly, Molière's *Miser* never cured a miser, nor Regnard's *Gambler* a gambler. We must accept that laughter cannot cure these fools; so much the worse for them, but not for comedy. It is enough that comedy, even if it cannot heal the desperately sick, strengthens the healthy in their health.' Gotthold Ephraim Lessing, *Die Hamburgische Dramaturgie*, 29. Stück, Leipzig: Reclam, n.d., 92

8. Irving Wardle, 'Introduction', *Theatre at Work*, ed. Charles Marowitz and Simon Trussler, London: Methuen, 1967, 14–15

I   STRATEGIES OF POLITICAL THEATRE:
A THEORETICAL OVERVIEW

1. Statistics taken from Stephen Lacey, *British Realist Theatre: The New Wave in its Context 1956–1965*, London: Routledge, 1995, 10

2. 'Die Übernahme des bürgerlichen Theaters', *Schriften zum Theater* 3, ed. W. Hecht, Frankfurt am Main: Suhrkamp, 1963, 121. My translation

3. David Edgar, 'Public theatre in a private age', *The Second Time as Farce: Reflections on the Drama of Mean Times*, London: Lawrence & Wishart, 1988, 168

4. *Brecht on Theatre*, trans. John Willett, London: Methuen, 1963, 190

5. Quoted in Edgar, *The Second Time as Farce*, 171

6. John Berger, *Art and Revolution: Ernst Neizvestny and the Role of the Artist in the USSR*, London: Weidenfeld & Nicolson, 1969, 51

7. Interview in *Theatre at Work*, ed. Charles Marowitz and Simon Trussler, London: Methuen, 1967, 51

8. *The Guardian*, 1 December 1986

9. Bertolt Brecht, quoted in Stanley Mitchell, 'From Shklovsky to Brecht: some preliminary remarks towards a history of the politicization of Russian formalism', *Screen* 15 (2), 1974, 78

10. *Brecht on Theatre*, 219

11. For some of the arguments and references about the Lukács–Brecht debate I am indebted to: Maria Germanou, 'The concept of realism and the aesthetics of Bertolt Brecht', unpublished MA thesis, University of Essex, October 1979

12. Quoted in Helga Gallas, 'Georg Lukács and the League of Revolutionary Proletarian Writers', *Cultural Studies*, ed. Richard Dyer, Birmingham: Centre for Contemporary Social Studies, 1973, 110

13. Fredric Jameson, *Beyond the Cave: Demystifying the Ideology of Modernism*, The Midwest Modern Language Association, 1974, 10; quoted in Germanou, 'The concept of realism', 10

14. Brecht, quoted in Mitchell, 'From Shklovsky to Brecht', 72

15. Georg Lukács, 'Realism in balance', Ernst Bloch et al., *Aesthetics and Politics*, London: Verso, 1980, 43

16. Bertolt Brecht, 'Die Not des Theaters', *Schriften zum Theater* 1, ed. W. Hecht, Frankfurt am Main: Suhrkamp, 1963, 116

17. Lukács, 'Realism in balance', 57

18. *Art and Revolution*, 53
19. John Peter, *Vladimir's Carrot: Modern Drama and the Modern Imagination*, London: André Deutsch, 1987, 19
20. Ibid., 308
21. Edgar, *The Second Time as Farce*, 40–1

2 THE 'REFLECTIONIST' STRATEGY: 'KITCHEN SINK' REALISM IN ARNOLD WESKER'S *ROOTS* (1959)

1. Arnold Wesker, 'Theatre, why?' (1967), *Fears of Fragmentation*, London: Jonathan Cape, 1970, 100
2. Arnold Wesker, 'A cretinue of critics', *Distinctions*, London: Jonathan Cape, 1985, 341
3. Quoted in John Russell Taylor, *Anger and After*, London: Methuen, 2nd edn, 1969, 147
4. Arnold Wesker, 'A sense of what should follow', *Distinctions*, 128 (originally published in *Theatre Quarterly* 7 (28), Winter 1977–8, 20)
5. Interview with Ronald Hayman (ca. 1969), R. Hayman, *Arnold Wesker*, London: Heinemann, 2nd edn, 1974, 2. See also Michael Patterson, 'The reception of Arnold Wesker's plays in Europe', *History of European Ideas* 20 (1–3), Oxford: Pergamon, 1995, 31–4
6. Interview with Maureen Cleave, *Observer Magazine*, 4 October 1981
7. 'A sense of what should follow', 101
8. Ibid., 114–15
9. Quoted in Glenda Leeming, *Wesker the Playwright*, London: Methuen, 1983, 10
10. Erwin Piscator, *Das politische Theater*, Schriften 1, Berlin: Henschelverlag, 1968, 245 (my translation)
11. 'Theatre, why?', 115
12. John McGrath, reviewing *The Friends* in *Black Dwarf* 15 (34), 1970; quoted in *Distinctions*, 301
13. *The Kitchen*, London: Jonathan Cape, 1961, 58
14. *The Wesker Trilogy*, London: Jonathan Cape, 1960, 41
15. Ibid., 71
16. *Chips with Everything*, London: Jonathan Cape, 1962, 65

17. *The Wesker Trilogy*, 167
18. Ibid., 149
19. 'A sense of what should follow', 115
20. 'Theatre, why?', 100
21. *The Wesker Trilogy*, 75
22. Ibid., 77
23. Ibid., 222
24. Ibid., 107
25. 'A sense of what should follow', 111
26. Interview with Ronald Hayman, 3
27. Ibid., 23
28. *The Wesker Trilogy*, 72
29. Taylor, *Anger and After*, 157
30. 'Miniautobiography in three acts and a prologue', *Contemporary Authors Autobiography Series* 7, Detroit: Gale Research, 1987, 249
31. Interview with Ronald Hayman, 15
32. *The Wesker Trilogy*, 92
33. Ibid., 140
34. Ibid., 146
35. Ibid., 102
36. Ibid., 109
37. Ibid., 128
38. Ibid., 113
39. Ibid., 147
40. Ibid., 130
41. Ibid., [6]
42. London: Writers and Readers Publishing Co-operative, 1976, reprinted in *Distinctions*, 209–22
43. *The Wesker Trilogy*, 83
44. 'Question and answer', *New Theatre Magazine*, 1 (3), 1960, 6
45. *The Wesker Trilogy*, 84
46. *Distinctions*, 9–10
47. *The Wesker Trilogy*, 90–1
48. Interview with Ronald Hayman, 10
49. *Distinctions*, 6

50. Ibid., 5
51. Quoted in Leeming, *Wesker the Playwright*, 47
52. Ibid., 48
53. Interview with Ronald Hayman, 98
54. Ibid.; see also the entry for February 1971 in 'From a writer's note-book', *Distinctions*, 23–4, where Wesker worries that Beatie's last speech may be mere 'wish-fulfilment' by the writer
55. C. W. E. Bigsby, 'The language of crisis in British theatre: the drama of cultural pathology', *Contemporary English Drama*, ed. C. W. E. Bigsby, Stratford-upon-Avon Studies 19, London: Arnold, 1981, 13
56. *The Wesker Trilogy*, 158

3 THE 'INTERVENTIONIST' STRATEGY: POETIC POLITICS IN JOHN ARDEN'S *SERJEANT MUSGRAVE'S DANCE* (1959)

1. *New Theatre Magazine* 1 (2), January 1960, 25
2. *The Best of Plays and Players*, ed. Peter Roberts, London: Methuen, 1987, 108
3. *Distinctions*, London: Jonathan Cape, 1985, 20–2
4. See Frances Gray, *John Arden*, London: Macmillan, 1982, 8
5. 'Who's for a revolution? Two interviews with John Arden', *Tulane Drama Review* 11 (2), T 34, 1966, 46
6. John Arden, *Plays: One*, London: Methuen, 1977, 15
7. Ibid., 11
8. Ibid., 19
9. Ibid., 106
10. Ibid., 82
11. See G. W. Brandt, 'Realism and parables (from Brecht to Arden)', *Contemporary Theatre*, ed. John Russell Brown and Bernard Harris, Stratford-upon-Avon Studies 4, London: Arnold, 1962, 53
12. E.g. by Gray, *John Arden*, 108ff.; John Russell Taylor, *Anger and After*, 2nd edn, London: Methuen, 1969, 93–4
13. *Plays: One*, 42
14. *Deutsche Dramaturgie der Sechziger Jahre*, ed. G. Wunberg, Tübingen: Max Niemeyer, 1974, 141 (my translation)

15. Albert Hunt, *Arden: A Study of his Plays*, London: Methuen, 1974, esp. 24ff.

16. 'Building the play: an interview', *Encore* 8 (4), July–August, 1961, 31; reprinted in *Theatre at Work*, ed. Charles Marowitz and Simon Trussler, London: Methuen, 1967, 44

17. Ronald Hayman, *British Theatre since 1955*, Oxford University Press, 1979, 23. Gray, *John Arden*, 12ff., also criticizes Hayman's misguided demand for conventional characterization with regard to the scene in the stable, where two of the soldiers reject Annie's sexual advances

18. *The Good Person of Szechwan, Collected Plays*, 6 (1), ed. J. Willett and R. Manheim, London: Methuen, 1985, 3

19. *Plays: One*, 27

20. Gray, *John Arden*, 115

21. *Schriften zum Theater* 5, ed. W. Hecht, Frankfurt am Main: Suhrkamp, 1963, 266 (my translation)

22. *Plays: One*, 15

23. *The Sunday Times*, 25 October 1959

24. *The New Statesman*, 31 October 1959, reprinted in *Plays in Review 1956–1980: British Drama and the Critics*, ed. Gareth and Barbara Lloyd Evans, London: Batsford, 1985, 89–90

25. *Plays: One*, 42

26. Ibid., 68

27. Ibid., 34–5

28. *The Independent*, 20 November 1991

29. *Plays: One*, 113

30. Ibid., 30

31. Ibid., 32

32. Ibid., 50

33. 'Telling a true tale', *Encore* 7 (3), May–June 1960, 25; reprinted in *The Encore Reader*, ed. Charles Marowitz, Tom Milne and Owen Hale, London: Methuen, 1965, 127

34. Ibid.

35. Preface to *The Bagman, Two Autobiographical Plays*, London: Methuen, 1971, 17

36. 'On comedy: John Arden talks to Albert Hunt', *Encore* 12 (5), September–October 1965, 16; quoted in Hunt, *Arden*, 148
37. 'Building the play', 31
38. *Plays: One*, 89
39. Ibid., 38
40. Ibid., 20
41. Ibid., 33
42. Ibid., 39
43. Ibid., 75 and 102
44. Ibid., 93
45. Ibid., 42
46. Ibid., 28
47. Paul Hadfield and Linda [= Lynda] Henderson, 'Getting time for adjustments', Interview with John Arden and Margaretta D'Arcy, *Writing Ulster*, Coleraine: University of Ulster 2/3, 1991–2, 88–9
48. *Plays: One*, 99
49. Notebook, 1 September 1920, *Schriften zum Theater* 2, 18–19 (my translation)
50. See 'On comedy', 17; Hunt, *Arden*, 25–6
51. *Plays: One*, 36
52. Ibid., 102
53. Ibid., 13
54. Ibid., 108
55. Ibid., 13
56. Ibid., 57
57. Ibid., 108
58. Ibid., 110
59. 'On comedy', 16
60. John Arden, 'Brecht and the British', *To Present the Pretence. Essays on the Theatre and its Public*, London: Methuen, 1977, 40

4 THE DIALECTICS OF COMEDY: TREVOR GRIFFITHS'S *COMEDIANS* (1975)

1. Trevor Griffiths, 'Transforming the husk of capitalism', *Theatre Quarterly* 6 (22), Summer 1976, 46
2. Trevor Griffiths, *Plays One*, London: Faber & Faber, 1996, 179

3. 'Transforming the husk of capitalism', 46
4. Interview in *The Leveller*, November 1976, 12; quoted in Catherine Itzin, *Stages in the Revolution*, London: Methuen, 1980, 169
5. Griffiths, *Plays One*, 151.
6. David Hare, 'A lecture given at King's College, Cambridge, March 5 1978', *Licking Hitler*, London: Faber & Faber, 1978, 61
7. Unpublished interview with Griffiths by Karin Gartzke, 'Alternative theatre in Britain', MA thesis, University of Manchester, quoted in Itzin, *Stages in the Revolution*, 167
8. Interview in *The Leveller*, November 1976, 12–13; quoted in Itzin, *Stages in the Revolution*, 165
9. Personal communication, Leeds, 1985
10. Griffiths, *Plays One*, 121
11. David Edgar, 'Political theatre', *Socialist Review*, April–May 1978
12. Derived from P. Willis, *Common Culture*, Milton Keynes: Open University Press, 1990, quoted in Graham Holderness (ed.), *The Politics of Theatre and Drama*, Basingstoke: Macmillan, 1992, 10
13. Griffiths, *Through the Night and Such Impossibilities: Two Plays for Television*, London: Faber & Faber, 1977, [10]
14. *Plays One*, vii
15. Ibid., 52
16. Ibid., 51
17. 'Countering consent: an interview with John Wyver', David Edgar et al., *Ah! Mischief: The Writer and Television*, ed. Frank Pike, London: Faber & Faber, 1982, 39
18. *Plays One*, 5
19. Ibid., 132
20. 'Transforming the husk of capitalism', 45
21. From an unpublished lecture given at King's College, Cambridge, Conference on Political Theatre, April 1978; quoted in Itzin, *Stages in the Revolution*, 168
22. *Times Educational Supplement*, 25 June 1976; quoted in John Bull, *New British Political Dramatists*, London: Macmillan, 1984, 118
23. Quoted in *Plays One*, 3
24. Interview with Catherine Itzin, *Stages in the Revolution*, 171
25. *Plays One*, 76–7

26. 'Transforming the husk', 37
27. *Plays One*, 45
28. Ibid., 44
29. Ibid., 43
30. Ibid., 151–5
31. *Plays One*, 4
32. Ibid., 14
33. Bull, *New British Political Dramatists*, 126
34. Ibid., 98. Since no actor is credited with the role in the cast-list of the premiere, this introduction may not have been used in the early stage-versions of the piece
35. *Plays One*, viii
36. Ibid., 193. Italics mine
37. Ibid., 211–12
38. Ibid., 229
39. Ibid., 237
40. Ibid., 214
41. Ibid., 262
42. Ibid., 247
43. Ibid., 248
44. Ibid., 250
45. Ibid., 266
46. Ibid., 267
47. Ibid., 269
48. Ibid., 270

5 APPROPRIATING MIDDLE-CLASS COMEDY: HOWARD BARKER'S *STRIPWELL* (1975)

1. Quoted in Catherine Itzin, *Stages in the Revolution*, London: Methuen, 1980, 250
2. Interview with Tony Dunn, *Gambit* 11 (41), 1984, 43
3. Quoted in Itzin, *Stages in the Revolution*, 252
4. Quoted in ibid., 250
5. Sandy Craig, *Dreams and Deconstructions*, Ambergate: Amber Lane, 1980, 139

6. 'Notes on the necessity for a version of Chekhov's *Uncle Vanya*', programme notes to *(Uncle) Vanya*, 1996

7. See Introduction, n. 7

8. Interview with Tony Dunn, 35

9. Ibid., 36

10. James Vinson (ed.), *Contemporary Dramatists*, 2nd edn, London: St James Press, 1977, 65

11. Stephen W. Gilbert, 'In and out of the box', *Plays and Players* 22 (6) March 1975, 12

12. Howard Barker, 'The redemptive power of desire', *The Times*, 6 February 1986

13. Interview with Tony Dunn, 35. The printed text actually reads '...the satricial element...'

14. Howard Barker, *Arguments for a Theatre*, London: Calder, 1989, 6

15. Barker, '49 asides for a tragic theatre', *The Guardian*, 10 February 1986, 11

16. *Arguments for a Theatre*, 34

17. Howard Barker, *Stripwell, Claw*, London: John Calder, 1977, 13

18. Ibid., 74

19. Ibid., 30–1

20. Ibid., 72

21. Ibid., 18

22. Ibid., 11

23. Ibid., 36

24. Ibid., 81

25. Ibid., 99

26. Ibid., 23

27. Ibid., 82–3

28. Ibid., 42

29. Ibid., 114

30. Ibid., 33

31. Ibid., 20

32. Ibid., 120

33. Ibid., 24

34. Quoted in Itzin, *Stages in the Revolution*, 252
35. *Stripwell*, 9
36. Ibid., 120
37. Ibid., 121–2

6 STAGING THE FUTURE: HOWARD BRENTON'S
THE CHURCHILL PLAY (1974)

1. 'Petrol bombs through the proscenium arch' [interview with Catherine Itzin and Simon Trussler] *Theatre Quarterly* 5 (17), March–May 1975, 20. Fourteen years later Brenton was still employing the same image, but having moved up-market from the tenement: 'Writing a political play is rather like drumming on the pipes in a small room in the hope that the rest of the housing estate can hear you, or at least pick up something you are saying' (Tariq Ali and Howard Brenton, 'On *Iranian Nights*', *Independent Magazine* 36, 13 May 1989, 14)
2. John Bull, *New British Political Dramatists: Howard Brenton, David Hare, Trevor Griffiths and David Edgar*, London: Macmillan, 1984, 29
3. Quoted in Richard Boon, *Brenton: The Playwright*, London: Methuen, 1991, 176
4. *The Guardian*, 19 March 1982; quoted in Boon, 176
5. 'Petrol bombs through the proscenium arch', 4
6. Ibid., 8
7. Ibid., 11
8. Ibid., 20
9. Boon, *Brenton: The Playwright*, 54–5; see also 317, n. 42, and Richard Boon, 'Politics and terror in the plays of Howard Brenton', *Terrorism and Modern Drama*, ed. John Orr and Dragan Klaić, Edinburgh University Press, 1990, 138–50
10. The subtitle of the revised 1978 version reads: 'As it will be performed...' but omits the specific reference to 1984 (*Plays One*, London: Methuen, 1986, 107), and the 1988 version refers to 'the century...winding down' (quoted in Boon, *Brenton: The Playwright*, 115)
11. 'Petrol bombs through the proscenium arch', 6

12. *Plays: One*, 111

13. Ibid., 111

14. Howard Brenton, *The Churchill Play*, London: Methuen, 1974, 10. The gusts of wind are cut in the 1978 version, although 'Furry' Keegan is still revealed operating a wind machine

15. *Plays: One*, 113

16. Ibid., 119

17. 'Petrol bombs through the proscenium arch', 8

18. Malcolm Hay and Philip Roberts, 'Howard Brenton: an introduction', *Performing Arts Journal* 3 (3), Winter 1979, 136

19. Preface to *Plays: One*, [xi]

20. 'Petrol bombs through the proscenium arch', 8, referring to *Christie in Love*. It is a metaphor he had already used in his play, *How Beautiful with Badges*, 1972, and was to use again in the 'Author's Production Note' to *Christie in Love*, *Plays: One*, 3

21. Boon, *Brenton: The Playwright*, 113

22. 'Petrol bombs through the proscenium arch', 14

23. *Plays: One*, 116

24. Ibid., 117

25. Angus Calder, *The People's War: Britain 1939–1945*, London: Jonathan Cape, 1969. See also Boon, *Brenton: The Playwright*, 104, and D. Keith Peacock, 'Chronicles of wasted time', *Themes in Drama*, ed. James Redmond, Cambridge University Press, 1986, 195–212

26. *Plays: One*, 170

27. Ibid., 164–5

28. Brenton, 'Taking liberties', *Marxism Today*, December 1988, 35

29. Boon, *Brenton: The Playwright*, 114–15

30. *Plays: One*, 129

31. Ibid., 157

32. *The Churchill Play*, London: Methuen, 1974, 90

33. *Plays: One*, 176–7

34. Quoted in Boon, *Brenton: The Playwright*, 116

35. *Plays: One*, 138

36. Quoted in Boon, *Brenton: The Playwright*, 116

37. Brenton, Interview with Hugh Herbert, *The Guardian*, 9 May 1974
38. 'Petrol bombs through the proscenium arch', 18

7 AGIT-PROP REVISITED: JOHN MCGRATH'S *THE CHEVIOT, THE STAG AND THE BLACK, BLACK OIL* (1973)

1. John McGrath, approvingly quoting Ferdinand Lassalle, quoted in C. W. E. Bigsby, 'The language of crisis in British theatre: the drama of cultural pathology', *Contemporary English Drama*, ed. C. W. E. Bigsby, Stratford-upon-Avon Studies 19, London: Arnold, 1981, 38
2. I discount Howard Barker's Wrestling School, which does not seek to identify itself as an activist political theatre group
3. John McGrath, 'Articles from the original programme', *The Cheviot, the Stag and the Black, Black Oil*, London: Methuen, 1981, 76
4. Quoted in Catherine Itzin, *Stages in the Revolution*, London: Methuen, 1980, 120
5. 'Better a bad night in Bootle...' [interview with Catherine Itzin], *Theatre Quarterly* 5 (19), September–November 1975, 43
6. Ibid., 43
7. *Events while Guarding the Bofors Gun*, London: Methuen, 1966, 56
8. Unpublished interview with John McGrath, Edinburgh, 10 November 1983
9. 'Better a bad night in Bootle...', 48
10. Ibid., 54
11. See David Edgar, 'Ten years of political theatre, 1968–78', *Theatre Quarterly* 8 (32), 1979, 25–33
12. 'Popular theatre and the changing perspective of the eighties' [interview with Tony Mitchell], *New Theatre Quarterly* 1 (4), November 1985, 394–5
13. *A Good Night Out*, London: Methuen, 1981, 25
14. 'New directions' [interview with Ramona Gibbs], *Plays and Players*, November 1972, xiv
15. The list is based on that given in 'The theory and practice of political theatre', *Theatre Quarterly* 9 (36), 1980, 51–3, which is reproduced almost verbatim in *A Good Night Out*, 54–9

16. 'The theory and practice of political theatre', 46
17. 'Popular theatre and the changing perspective of the eighties', 392
18. *The Moon Belongs to Everyone: Making Theatre with 7:84*, London: Methuen, 1990, 196
19. Unpublished interview with Colin Mortimer, 27 March 1980, p. 35 of the transcript
20. Colin Chambers and Mike Prior, *Playwrights' Progress: Patterns of Postwar British Drama*, Oxford: Amber Lane Press, 1987, 67
21. 'Popular theatre and the changing perspective of the eighties', 399
22. *The Moon Belongs to Everyone*, 49
23. Interview with Rudolf Bergmann, 1978; quoted in Michael Patterson, *Peter Stein*, Cambridge University Press, 1981, 56
24. 'Popular theatre and the changing perspective of the eighties', 396
25. *A Good Night Out*, 30; italics mine
26. Chambers and Prior, *Playwrights' Progress*, 73
27. Unpublished letter to the Scottish Arts Council, 5 March 1973
28. Ibid.
29. *The Cheviot, the Stag and the Black, Black Oil*, London: Methuen, 1981, 1
30. *A Good Night Out*, 54
31. *The Cheviot, the Stag...*, 26
32. Ibid., 38
33. Ibid., 14
34. Ibid., 29
35. Ibid., 73
36. Bernard Sharratt, 'The politics of the popular from melodrama to television', *Performance and Politics in Popular Drama*, ed. David Bradby; Louis James; Bernard Sharratt, Cambridge University Press, 1980, 287
37. 'The year of the Cheviot', *Plays and Players*, February 1974, 30; reprinted in *The Cheviot, the Stag...*, xxvii
38. Rick Rylance, 'Forms of dissent in contemporary drama and contemporary theory', *The Death of the Playwright?*, ed. Adrian Page, Basingstoke: Macmillan, 1992, 138

8 BRECHT REVISITED: DAVID HARE'S *FANSHEN* (1975)

1. 'A lecture given at King's College, Cambridge, March 5 1978', *Licking Hitler*, London: Faber & Faber, 1978, 60

2. 'Humanity and passion don't count', *Plays and Players* 19 (5), February 1972, 18

3. John Bull, *New British Political Dramatists*, London: Macmillan, 1984, 61

4. Ibid., 82

5. Ibid., 61; Catherine Itzin, *Stages in the Revolution*, London: Methuen, 1980, 330

6. John McGrath, unpublished interview with Colin Mortimer, 27 March 1980, p. 31 of the transcript

7. The first had been based on Heathcote Williams's book, *The Speakers*, London: Hutchinson, 1964

8. Quoted in Itzin, *Stages in the Revolution*, 223

9. Quoted in Ann McFerran, 'Fringe beneficiaries', *Time Out* 340, 24–30 September 1976, 11

10. William Hinton, *Fanshen*, New York: Monthly Review Press, 1966

11. Ibid., 609

12. 'From Portable Theatre to Joint Stock... via Shaftesbury Avenue' [interview with Catherine Itzin and Simon Trussler], *Theatre Quarterly* 5 (20), December 1975–February 1976, 114

13. David Hare, *Fanshen*, London: Faber & Faber, 1976, 7

14. Quoted in Itzin, *Stages in the Revolution*, 221

15. Reported in William Gaskill's unpublished lecture given at King's College, Cambridge, Conference on Political Theatre, April 1978, quoted in Itzin, *Stages in the Revolution*, 222

16. Bull, *New British Political Dramatists*, 94

17. Hare, *Fanshen*, 15

18. Ibid., 22

19. Ibid., 29

20. Ibid., 31. William Hinton's book refers to the death by beating of two landlords and a landlord's son, and also of Fu-wang, who was a rich peasant and not a landlord. It mentions the death by starvation of only one individual, a landlord's daughter-in-law. Hare's text does not record the fact that the families of several landlords

were permitted to live on in the village (Hinton, *Fanshen*, 138 and 142). When Hare discussed his script with Hinton, the latter was unhappy with what he regarded as Hare's 'liberal' attitude and with Hare's emphasis on 'justice'. As a result of their discussion, Hare revised his script slightly to reflect Hinton's more Marxist analysis

21. Ibid., 34. Based on a direct quotation from Hinton, *Fanshen*, 156
22. Ibid., 35
23. Hinton, *Fanshen*, 157ff.
24. *Fanshen*, 48
25. Hinton, *Fanshen*, 365
26. *Fanshen*, 79
27. 'A lecture', *Licking Hitler*, 62
28. Ibid., 84
29. Hinton, *Fanshen*, 135ff.
30. *Fanshen*, 41
31. 'A lecture', *Licking Hitler*, 69–70
32. 'From Portable Theatre to Joint Stock', 112
33. 'A lecture', *Licking Hitler*, 63

9 REWRITING SHAKESPEARE: EDWARD BOND'S
LEAR (1971)

1. Quoted in Malcolm Hay and Philip Roberts, *Edward Bond: A Companion to His Plays*, London: TQ Publications, 1978, 71
2. '*Lear*: saving our necks', programme note for Liverpool Everyman's production of *Lear*, 8 October 1975; quoted in Hay and Roberts, *Edward Bond: A Companion*, 52
3. 'Author's Preface' to *Lear*, *Plays: Two*, London: Methuen, 1978, 4
4. 'The memorandum', *The Worlds, with The Activists Papers*, London: Methuen, 1980, 91
5. 'Author's Preface' to *Lear*, *Plays: Two*, 11
6. 'Drama and the dialectics of violence: Edward Bond interviewed by the editors', *Theatre Quarterly* 2 (5), January–March 1972, 12
7. 'Author's Preface' to *Lear*, *Plays: Two*, 5
8. 'A discussion with [Harold Hobson et al.]', *Gambit* 5 (17), 1970, 24

9. Liverpool Everyman programme note, quoted in Hay and Roberts, *Edward Bond: A Companion*, 53

10. Interview with John Hall, *The Guardian*, 29 September 1971; quoted in Hay and Roberts, *Edward Bond: A Companion*, 18

11. 'The rational theatre', *Plays: Two*, ix

12. 'A discussion with [Harold Hobson et al.]', 24

13. 'Drama and the dialectics of violence', 8

14. For a fascinating account of these and many other adaptations of Shakespeare, see Ruby Cohn, *Modern Shakespeare Offshoots*, Princeton University Press, 1976

15. Gerd Stratmann, 'Edward Bond, "Lear"', *Anglo-amerikanische Shakespeare-Bearbeitungen des 20. Jahrhunderts*, ed. Horst Priessnitz, Darmstadt: Wissenschaftliche Buchgesellschaft, 1980, 353

16. Richard Scharine, *The Plays of Edward Bond*, Lewisburg: Bucknell University Press, 1976, 216

17. *Plays: Two*, 17–18

18. Ibid., 62

19. Letter to Katharine Worth, 24 October 1972. See Katharine Worth, *Revolutions in Modern English Drama*, London: Bell, 1973, 180, fn. 2

20. *Plays: Two*, 99

21. Bertolt Brecht, 'Der Messingkauf' ['The Messingkauf Dialogues'], *Schriften zum Theater* 5, Frankfurt am Main: Suhrkamp, 127–8

22. Letter to Patricia Hern, 4 March 1982; quoted in Edward Bond, *Lear*, ed. Patricia Hern, Methuen: London, 1983, xvii

23. Gregory Dark, 'Production Casebook no. 5: Edward Bond's *Lear* at the Royal Court', *Theatre Quarterly* 2 (5), January–March 1972, 31

24. Bond, *The Worlds, with The Activists Papers*, 99

25. Ibid., 27

26. Ibid., 27

27. *Plays: Two*, 73

28. Bond, 'On Brecht: a letter to Peter Holland', *Theatre Quarterly* 8 (30), Summer 1978, 35

29. *Plays: Two*, 29

30. Ibid., 77

31. H. Zapf, 'Two concepts of society in drama: Bertolt Brecht's *The Good Woman of Setzuan* and Edward Bond's *Lear*', *Modern Drama* 31 (3), September 1988, 357

32. P. Weiss, *Dramen I*, Frankfurt am Main: Suhrkamp, 179 [my translation]

33. 'On Brecht: a letter to Peter Holland', 34. The V-effect is a reference to Brecht's method of *Verfremdung* or distanciation (see p. 18)

34. Liverpool Everyman programme note; quoted in Hay and Roberts, *Edward Bond: A Companion*, 52

35. *Plays: Two*, 98

36. Letter to Malcolm Hay and Philip Roberts, 18 March 1977; quoted in Hay and Roberts, *Bond: A Study of his Plays*, London: Methuen, 1980, 129

37. *The Guardian*, 29 September 1971

38. Letter to David L. Hirst, 4 August 1984; quoted in David L. Hirst, *Edward Bond*, London: Macmillan, 1985, 140

39. *Plays: Two*, 95

40. James C. Bulman, 'Bond, Shakespeare and the Absurd', *Modern Drama* 29 (1), March 1986, 63

41. *Plays: Two*, 102

42. 'Drama and the dialectics of violence', 13

43. Letter to W. Gaskill, 18 May 1971; quoted in Hay and Roberts, *Bond: A Study of His Plays*, 65

44. *Plays: Two*, 18

45. B. Henrichs, 'Gute Gespenster, liebende Leichname', *Süddeutsche Zeitung*, 2 October 1972 (my translation)

46. W. Gaskill, *A Sense of Direction*, London: Faber & Faber, 1987, 122

47. See Introduction, pp. 22–3

48. John Peter, 'Political realism crushed by paranoia', *The Sunday Times*, 11 March 1990

49. Interview with David L. Hirst, 9 June 1984; quoted in Hirst, *Edward Bond*, 164–5

10 THE STRATEGY OF PLAY: CARYL CHURCHILL'S
CLOUD NINE (1979)

1. Caryl Churchill, 'Not ordinary, not safe', *The Twentieth Century*, November 1960, 448
2. Caryl Churchill, Interview with Kathleen Betsko and Rachel Koenig, *Interviews with Contemporary Women Playwrights*, New York: Beech Tree Books, 1987, 76; quoted in Linda Fitzsimmons, *File on Churchill*, London: Methuen, 1989, 90
3. Janelle Reinelt, 'Beyond Brecht: Britain's new feminist drama', *Feminist Theatre and Theory*, ed. Helene Keyssar, Basingstoke: Macmillan, 1996, 36. See also Helene Keyssar, *Feminist Theatre*, Basingstoke: Macmillan, 1984, 16–17
4. *Strike While the Iron Is Hot: Three Plays on Sexual Politics*, ed. Michelene Wandor, London: Journeyman Press, 1980, 60
5. Keyssar, *Feminist Theatre*, 19–20
6. Sue-Ellen Case provides a good overview of the history of women's playwriting in her *Feminism and Theatre*, Basingstoke: Macmillan, 1988
7. Well documented in works like: Joanna Russ, *How to Suppress Women's Writing*, London: The Women's Press, 1984; Dale Spender: *The Writing or the Sex? or Why You Don't Have to Read Women's Writing to Know It's No Good*, New York: Pergamon, 1989
8. See Virginia Woolf, *A Room of One's Own* (1929), London: Vintage, 1996, 44–5
9. Ibid., 72
10. Quoted in Dale Spender, *The Writing or the Sex?*, 51, fn. 5
11. Caryl Churchill, quoted in Linda Fitzsimmons, *File on Churchill*, London: Methuen, 1989, 90
12. Gillian Hanna, 'Feminism and theatre', *Theatre Papers*, 2nd series 8, 1978, 8; quoted in Sue-Ellen Case, *Feminism and Theatre*, 123
13. Ruby Cohn, *Retreats from Realism in Recent English Drama*, Cambridge University Press, 1991, 12
14. Caryl Churchill, Interview with Kathleen Betsko and Rachel Koenig, 76; quoted in Fitzsimmons, *File on Churchill*, 90

15. Frances Gray, 'Mirrors of Utopia: Caryl Churchill and Joint Stock', *British and Irish Drama Since 1960*, ed. James Acheson, Basingstoke: Macmillan, 1993, 51
16. Quoted in Catherine Itzin, *Stages in the Revolution*, London: Methuen, 1980, 279
17. Caryl Churchill, *Omnibus*, BBC1, November 1988
18. Quoted in Itzin, *Stages in the Revolution*, 279
19. Ibid., 279
20. Caryl Churchill, 'Making room at the top', *The Village Voice* 28 (9), 1 March 1983, 81
21. Quoted in Itzin, *Stages in the Revolution*, 281
22. Ibid., 279, 285
23. Caryl Churchill, interviewed by Emily Mann, *Interviews with Contemporary Women Playwrights*, ed. Betsko and Koenig, 81
24. *A Room of One's Own*, 68
25. John F. O'Malley, 'Caryl Churchill, David Mercer, and Tom Stoppard: a study of contemporary British dramatists who have written for radio, television and stage', unpublished dissertation, Florida State University, 1974, 50; quoted in Fitzsimmons, *File on Churchill*, 22
26. Friedrich Dürrenmatt, *Theaterprobleme*, Zurich: Arche, 1963, 28
27. O'Malley, 'Caryl Churchill...', 56; quoted in Amelia Howe Kritzer, *The Plays of Caryl Churchill*, Basingstoke: Macmillan, 1991, 45
28. Preface to *Traps*, London: Pluto Press, 1978
29. Kritzer, *Plays of Caryl Churchill*, 79
30. 'A note on the production', *Light Shining in Buckinghamshire*, London: Nick Hern Books, 1989, [viii]
31. Itzin, *Stages in the Revolution*, 286
32. Keyssar, *Feminist Theatre*, 93
33. *Omnibus*, November 1988
34. Ibid.
35. Ibid.

36. Interview with Geraldine Cousin, 'The common imagination and the individual voice', *New Theatre Quarterly* 4 (13), February 1988, 4
37. *Omnibus*, November 1988
38. Caryl Churchill, *Plays: One*, London: Methuen, 1985, 245
39. Churchill, quoted in Itzin, *Stages in the Revolution*, 286
40. Loren Kruger, 'The dis-play's the thing: gender and public sphere in contemporary British theatre', *Feminist Theatre and Theory*, ed. Keyssar, 54
41. John Peter, 'Imperial designs on the mind', *The Sunday Times*, *Culture* section, 30 March 1997, 14
42. Churchill, *Plays: One*, 246
43. Quoted in Itzin, *Stages in the Revolution*, 286–7
44. *Omnibus*, November 1988
45. Anne Herrmann: 'Travesty and transgression: transvestism in Shakespeare, Brecht, and Churchill', *Performing Feminisms*, ed. Sue-Ellen Case, Baltimore: Johns Hopkins University Press, 1990, 312
46. Letter to Richard Seyd, director of the production of *Cloud Nine* by the Eureka Theatre Company, San Francisco, 10 May 1983; quoted in Fitzsimmons, *File on Churchill*, 48
47. *Cloud Nine*, London: Nick Hern Books, 1989, 3
48. Ibid., 10
49. Ibid., 82–3
50. Ibid., 8
51. Ibid., 76
52. Ibid., 1
53. Ibid., 6
54. Ibid., 44
55. The phrase is Sue-Ellen Case's (*Feminism and Theatre*, 85)
56. Kruger, 'The dis-play's the thing', 54
57. *Cloud Nine*, 82–3
58. Gray, 'Mirrors of Utopia', 52
59. *Cloud Nine*, 61–3
60. Ibid., 60, 65
61. Ibid., 78

62. Peter, 'Imperial designs on the mind', 15
63. Michelene Wandor, 'The fifth column: feminism and theatre', *Drama* 152, 1984, 7
64. Judith Thurman, 'Caryl Churchill: the playwright who makes you laugh about orgasm, racism, class struggle, homophobia, woman-hating, the British Empire, and the irrepressible strangeness of the human heart', *Ms*, May 1982, 54
65. Quoted in Itzin, *Stages in the Revolution*, 287
66. *Cloud Nine*, 75
67. Hanna, 'Feminism and theatre', 6–7; quoted in Reinelt, 'Beyond Brecht', 46
68. *Light Shining in Buckinghamshire*, 53

CONCLUSION

1. Roger Howard, 'Gambit discussion: political theatre', *Gambit* 8 (31), 1977, 16
2. David Hare, 'A lecture given at King's College, Cambridge, March 5 1978', *Licking Hitler*, London: Faber & Faber, 1978, 61
3. See chapter 1, *passim*
4. 'A lecture', 62
5. '49 asides for a tragic theatre', *The Guardian*, 10 February 1986, 11
6. 'Analysis. The year zero', BBC Radio 4, 30 March 2000
7. For a fuller discussion of the following, see my article, 'The Good Woman of Holby: the appropriation of political theatre by television soap operas', *Whatever Happened to Political Theatre?*, to be published shortly by CONCEPTS
8. Stephen Lacey, *British Realist Theatre: The New Wave in Its Context 1956–1965*, London: Routledge, 1995

Select bibliography

GENERAL STUDIES

Acheson, James. *British and Irish Drama Since 1960*, Basingstoke: Macmillan, 1992

Adamov, Arthur. 'Theatre, money and politics', *Theatre Quarterly* 1 (4), October–December 1971, 83–8

Anderson, Michael. *Anger and Detachment: A Study of Arden, Osborne and Pinter*, London, 1976

Ansorge, Peter. *Disrupting the Spectacle: Five Years of Experimental and Fringe Theatre in Britain*, London: Pitman, 1975

'Underground explorations: no. 1, portable playwrights, David Hare, Howard Brenton, Trevor Griffiths, Snoo Wilson', *Plays and Players* 19 (5), February 1972, 14–23

Armstrong, William A. (ed.). *Experimental Drama*, London: Bell, 1963

Auslander, Philip. 'Toward a concept of the political in postmodern theatre', *Theatre Journal*, 39 (1), March 1987, 20–34

Barker, Clive. 'From fringe to alternative theatre', *Zeitschrift für Anglistik und Amerikanistik* 26 (1), 1978, 48–62

'The politicisation of British theatre', *Englisch Amerikanische Studien* 2 (2), June 1980, 267–78

Barnes, Philip. *A Companion to Post-War British Theatre*, Beckenham: Croom Helm, 1986

Bell, Leslie (ed.). *Contradictory Theatres: The Theatre Underground and the Essex University New Plays Scheme – Critical and Theoretical Essays*, Colchester: Theatre Action Press, 1984

Berger, John. *Art and Revolution: Ernst Neizvestny and the Role of the Artist in the USSR*, London: Weidenfeld & Nicolson, 1969

Berny, K. A., and N. G. Templeton. *Contemporary British Dramatists*, London: St James Press, 1994

Betsko, Kathleen, and Rachel Koenig (eds.). *Interviews with Contemporary Women Playwrights*, New York: Beech Tree Books, 1987

Bigsby, Christopher. 'The politics of anxiety: contemporary socialist theatre in England', *Modern Drama* 24 (4), December 1981, 393–403

Bigsby, C[hristopher] W. E. (ed.). *Contemporary English Drama*, Stratford-upon-Avon Studies 19, London: Arnold, 1981

Bloch, Ernst, et al. *Aesthetics and Politics*, London: Verso, 1980

Bock, Hedwig, and Albert Wertheim. *Essays on Contemporary British Drama*, Munich: Max Hueber Verlag, 1981

Boon, Richard, and Jane Plastow (eds.). *Politics, Culture and Performance*, Cambridge University Press, 1998

Bradby, David; Louis James; Bernard Sharratt (eds.). *Performance and Politics in Popular Drama: Aspects of Popular Entertainment in Theatre, Film and Television 1800–1976*, Cambridge University Press, 1980

Bradby, David, and John McCormick. *People's Theatre*, London: Croom Helm, 1978

Brater, Enoch (ed.). *Feminine Focus: The New Women Playwrights*, Oxford University Press, 1989

Brown, John Russell. *Theatre Language: A Study of Arden, Osborne, Pinter and Wesker*, London, 1972

A Short Guide to Modern English Drama, London: Heinemann, 1982

Brown, John Russell (ed.). *Modern British Dramatists*, Englewood Cliffs: Prentice-Hall, 1968

Brown, John Russell, and Bernard Harris (eds.). *Contemporary Theatre*, Stratford-upon-Avon Studies 4, London: Arnold, 1962, reprinted 1968

Browne, Terry. *Playwrights' Theatre: The English Stage Company at the Royal Court*, London: Pitman, 1975

Bull, John. *New British Political Dramatists: Howard Brenton, David Hare, Trevor Griffiths and David Edgar*, Basingstoke: Macmillan, 1984

Select bibliography

Calder, John. 'Political theatre in Britain today', *Gambit* 8 (31), 1977, 5–11

Campos, Christophe. 'Seven types of popular theatre', *Theatre Quarterly* 6 (23), Autumn 1976, 3–10

Carlson, Susan. 'Comic collisions: convention, rage and order', *New Theatre Quarterly* 3 (12), November 1987, 303–16

Case, Sue-Ellen. *Feminism and Theatre*, Basingstoke: Macmillan, 1988

Cave, Richard Allen. *New British Drama in Performance on the London Stage*, Gerrards Cross: Colin Smythe, 1987

Chambers, Colin. 'Socialist theatre and the ghetto mentality', *Marxism Today* 22 (8), August 1978, 245–50

Chambers, Colin, and Mike Prior. *Playwrights' Progress: Patterns of Postwar British Drama*, Oxford: Amber Lane Press, 1987

Cohn, Ruby. *Modern Shakespeare Offshoots*, Princeton University Press, 1976

Retreats from Realism in Recent English Drama, Cambridge University Press, 1991

'Modest proposals of modern socialists', *Modern Drama*, 25 (4), December 1982, 457–68

Craig, Sandy (ed.). *Dreams and Deconstructions: Alternative Theatre in Britain*, Ambergate: Amber Lane Press, 1980

Davies, Andrew. 'Political theatre in Britain since the 1960s', *Other Theatres: the Development of Alternative and Experimental Theatre in Britain*, London: Macmillan, 1987, 162–74

Davison, Peter. *Contemporary Drama and the Popular Dramatic Tradition in England*, London: Macmillan, 1982

Douglas, Reid. 'The failure of English realism', *Tulane Drama Review* 7, 1962–3, 180–3

Dunn, Tony. 'The play of politics', *Drama* 156 (2), 1985, 13–15

Edgar, David. *The Second Time as Farce: Reflections on the Drama of Mean Times*, London: Lawrence & Wishart, 1988

The Shape of the Table, London: Nick Hern, 1990

'Socialist theatre and the bourgeois author', *Workers and Writers*, ed. Wilfried van der Will, Birmingham: Department of German, Birmingham University, 1975

'Political theatre', *Socialist Review*, April–May 1978

'Ten years of political theatre, 1968–78', *Theatre Quarterly* 8 (32), 1979, 25–33; reprinted in Edgar, *The Second Time as Farce*

'Towards a theatre of dynamic ambiguities' [interview with Clive Barker and Simon Trussler], *Theatre Quarterly* 9 (33), Spring 1979, 3–23

Elsom, John. *Post-War British Theatre*, London: Routledge, 1976

Enkemann, Jürgen. 'Politisches Alternativtheater in Grossbritannien', *Englisch Amerikanische Studien* 2 (4), December 1980, 495–507

Findlater, Richard (ed.). *At the Royal Court: 25 Years of the English Stage Company*, Ambergate: Amber Lane Press, 1981

'Gambit discussion: political theatre', *Gambit* 8 (31), 1977, 13–43

Gaskill, William. *A Sense of Direction*, London: Faber & Faber, 1987

Gilbert, W. Stephen. 'In and out of the box', *Plays and Players* 22 (6), March 1975, 11–15

Gooch, Steve. *All Together Now: An Alternative View of Theatre and the Community*, London: Methuen, 1984

Goodman, Lizbeth. 'Feminist theatre in Britain: a survey and a prospect', *New Theatre Quarterly* 33, February 1993, 66–84

Gottlieb, Vera. 'Thatcher's theatre – or after *Equus*', *New Theatre Quarterly* 4 (14), May 1998, 99–104

Griffiths, Trevor R., and Margaret Llewellyn-Jones (eds.). *British and Irish Women Dramatists since 1958: A Critical Handbook*, London: Open University Press, 1993

Hall, Stuart. 'Beyond naturalism pure', *Encore* 8 (6), November–December 1961, 12–19

Hanna, Gillian. 'Feminism and theatre', *Theatre Papers*, 2nd series 8, 1978, 10–11

Hare, Carl. 'Creativity and commitment in the contemporary British theatre', *Humanities Association Bulletin* 16, Spring 1965, 21–8

Hayman, Ronald. *British Theatre Since 1955: A Reassessment*, Oxford University Press, 1979

The Set-Up: an Anatomy of the English Theatre Today, London, 1973

Hewison, Robert. *In Anger: Culture in the Cold War*, London: Methuen, 1988

Hinchcliffe, A. J. *British Theatre 1950–1970*, London: Blackwell, 1974

Höhne, Horst (ed.). *Political Developments on the British Stage in the Sixties and Seventies*, Rostock: Wilhelm-Pieck-Universität, 1977
  British Drama and Theatre from the Mid-Fifties to the Mid-Seventies, Rostock: Wilhelm-Pieck-Universität, 1978
Holderness, Graham. *The Politics of Theatre and Drama*, Basingstoke: Macmillan, 1992
Howard, Tony, and John Stokes. *Acts of War: The Representation of Military Conflicts on British Stage and Television Since 1945*, Aldershot: Scolar Press, 1996
Hudson, Roger. 'Towards a definition of people's theatre', *Theatre Quarterly* 1 (4), October–December 1971, 2 and 100–1
Hunt, Albert. 'Theatre of violence', *New Society*, 4 November 1976, 261–2
Innes, Christopher. *Modern British Drama 1890–1990*, Cambridge University Press, 1992
Itzin, Catherine. *Stages in the Revolution*, London: Methuen, 1980
  'Shakespeare's sisters: women in theatre in Britain in the seventies', *Englisch Amerikanische Studien* 2 (4), December 1980, 507–19
Kennedy, Andrew. *Six Dramatists in Search of a Language*, Cambridge University Press, 1975
Kerensky, Oleg. *The New British Drama: Fourteen Playwrights Since Osborne and Pinter*, London: Hamish Hamilton, 1977
Kershaw, Baz. *The Politics of Performance: Radical Theatre as Cultural Intervention*, London: Routledge, 1992
Keyssar, Helene. *Feminist Theatre*, London: Macmillan, 1984
  'Hauntings: gender and drama in contemporary English theatre', *Englisch Amerikanische Studien* 8 (3–4), December 1986, 449–68
Keyssar, Helene (ed.). *Feminist Theatre and Theory*, Basingstoke: Macmillan, 1996
King, Kimball. *Twenty Modern British Playwrights 1956 to 1976: A Bibliography*, New York: Garland, 1977
Kirby. Michael. 'On political theatre', *The Drama Review*, June 1975, 129–35
Kirkpatrick, D. L. (ed.). *Contemporary Dramatists*, London: St James Press, 1988

Kitchin, Laurence. *Drama in the Sixties: Form and Interpretations*, London: Faber & Faber, 1966

Klotz, Günther. *Alternativen im britischen Drama der Gegenwart*, Berlin: Akademie Verlag, 1978

Britische Dramatiker der Gegenwart, Berlin: Henschelverlag, 1982

'Alternatives in recent British drama', *Zeitschrift für Anglistik und Amerikanistik* 25 (2), 1977, 152–61

Kosok, Heinz. *Drama und Theater im England des 20. Jahrhunderts*, Düsseldorf: Bagel, 1980

Lacey, Stephen. *Theatre, Culture and Politics: British Theatre as Political Practice 1956–61*, Birmingham University Press, 1985

British Realist Theatre: The New Wave in its Context 1956–1965, London: Routledge, 1995

Lambert, J. W. *Drama in Britain 1964–1973*, London: Longman, 1974

Lambley, Dorrian. 'In search of a radical discourse for theatre', *New Theatre Quarterly* 8 (29), February 1992, 34–47

Lloyd Evans, Gareth and Barbara (eds.). *Plays in Review 1956–1980: British Drama and the Critics*, London: Batsford, 1985

Marowitz, Charles; Tom Milne; and Owen Hale (eds.). *Encore Reader: New Theatre Voices of the Fifties and Sixties*, London: Methuen, 1965

Marowitz, Charles, and Simon Trussler (eds.). *Theatre at Work: Playwrights and Productions in the Modern British Theatre*, London: Methuen, 1967

Merchant, Paul. 'The theatre poems of Bertolt Brecht, Edward Bond and Howard Brenton', *Theatre Quarterly* 9, Summer 1979, 49–51

'NTQ Symposium. Theatre in Thatcher's Britain: organising the opposition' [Simon Trussler, Vera Gottlieb, Colin Chambers, Clive Barker, John McGrath, Trevor Griffiths et al.], *New Theatre Quarterly* 5 (18), May 1989, 113–23

Page, Adrian (ed.). *The Death of the Playwright? Modern British Drama and Literary Theory*, Basingstoke: Macmillan, 1992

Peter, John. *Vladimir's Carrot: Modern Drama and the Modern Imagination*, London: André Deutsch, 1987

Plett, Heinrich F. (ed.). *Englisches Drama von Beckett bis Bond*, Munich: Fink, 1982

Rabey, David Ian. *British and Irish Political Drama in the Twentieth Century*, Basingstoke: Macmillan, 1986

'Images of terror in contemporary British drama: unlocking the world', *Terrorism and Modern Drama*, ed. John Orr and Dragan Klaić, Edinburgh University Press, 1990, 151–9

Rawlence, Chris. 'Political theatre and the working class', *Media, Politics and Culture: A Socialist View*, ed. Carl Gardner, London: Macmillan, 1979, 61–70

Rebellato, Dan. *1956 and All That: the Making of Modern British Drama*, London: Routledge, 1999

Reinelt, Janelle. *After Brecht: British Epic Theatre*, Ann Arbor: University of Michigan Press, 1994

Ritchie, Rob (ed.). *The Joint Stock Book: The Making of a Theatre Collective*, London: Methuen, 1987

Roberts, Peter (ed.). *The Best of Plays and Players*, London: Methuen, 1987

Roberts, Peter. *Theatre in Britain: A Playgoer's Guide*, London: Pitman, 1975

Rusinko, Susan. *British Drama 1950 to the Present: A Critical History*, Boston: Twayne, 1989

Sakellaridou, Elizabeth. 'New faces for British political theatre', *Studies in Theatre and Performance* 20 (1), 2000, 43–51

Shank, Theodore (ed.). *Contemporary British Theatre*, Basingstoke: Macmillan, 1994

Shank, Theodore. 'Political theatre in England', *Performing Arts Journal* 2 (3), Winter 1978, 48–62

Shaughnessy, Robert. *Three Socialist Plays: Lear, Roots, Serjeant Musgrave's Dance*, Buckingham: Open University Press, 1992

Shellard, Dominic. *British Theatre Since the War*, New Haven: Yale University Press, 1999

Stoll, Karl-Heinz. *The New British Drama: A Bibliography with Particular Reference to Arden, Bond, Osborne, Pinter, Wesker*, Bern: Lang, 1975

'Interviews with Edward Bond and Arnold Wesker', *Twentieth Century Literature* 22, December 1976, 411–32

Szanto, George H. *Theater and Propaganda*, Austin: University of Texas, 1978

Taylor, John Russell. *Anger and After: A Guide to the New British Drama*, 2nd edn, London: Methuen, 1969
The Second Wave: British Drama for the Seventies, London: Methuen, 1970

Tempera, Mariangela. 'Il rapporto autore/spettatore nel teatro di memoria colletiva: Peter Nichols, Arnold Wesker, Caryl Churchill', *Quaderni di Filologia Germanica* 3, 1984, 267–79

Thomsen, Christian W. *Das englische Theater der Gegenwart*, Düsseldorf: Bagel, 1980

'TQ symposium. Playwriting for the seventies: old theatres, new audiences, and the politics of revolution' [John Arden, Caryl Churchill, David Edgar, Arnold Wesker, et al.], *Theatre Quarterly* 6 (24), Winter 1976–77, 35–72

Trussler, Simon. 'Alternative theatre – for what?', *Theatre Quarterly* 5 (19), September–November 1975, 11–14
'British neo-naturalism', *Drama Review* 13, Winter 1968, 130–6

Trussler, Simon (ed.). *New Theatre Voices of the Seventies: Sixteen Interviews from Theatre Quarterly 1970–1980*, London: Methuen, 1981

Tschudin, Marcus. *A Writer's Theatre: George Devine and the English Stage Company at the Royal Court Theatre*, Bern: Lang, 1972

Tynan, Kenneth. *A View of the English Stage 1944–1965*, London: Methuen, 1984

Van Erven, Eugène. *Radical People's Theatre*, Bloomington: Indiana University Press, 1988

Vinson, James (ed.). *Contemporary Dramatists*, 2nd edn, London: St James Press, 1977

Wager, Walter (ed.). *The Playwrights Speak*, London: Longmans, 1969

Wandor, Michelene. *Carry On, Understudies: Theatre and Sexual Politics*, London: Routledge, 1986
Look Back in Gender: Sexuality and the Family in Post-War British Drama, London: Methuen, 1987

Drama Today: a Critical Guide to British Drama 1970–1990, London: Longman, 1993

'Sexual politics and the strategy of socialist theatre', *Theatre Quarterly* 9 (36), 1980, 28–30

'The fifth column: feminism and theatre', *Drama* 152, 1984, 7

Weintraub, Stanley (ed.). *British Dramatists since World War II, Dictionary of Literary Biography* 13, Detroit: Gale, 1982, 2 vols

Weise, Wolf-Dietrich. *Die "Neuen englischen Dramatiker" in ihrem Verhältnis zu Brecht*, Bad Homburg: Gehlen, 1969

Williams, Raymond. *Drama from Ibsen to Brecht*, London: Chatto & Windus, 1968

Marxism and Literature, Oxford University Press, 1977

Worth, Katharine. *Revolutions in Modern English Drama*, London: Bell, 1973

Wu, Duncan. *Six Contemporary Dramatists: Bennett, Potter, Gray, Brenton, Hare, Ayckbourn*, Basingstoke: Macmillan, 1994

Zeifman, Hersh, and Cynthia Zimmerman (eds.). *Contemporary British Drama 1970–90: Essays from 'Modern Drama'*, Basingstoke: Macmillan, 1993

INDIVIDUAL PLAYWRIGHTS

John Arden (1930–)

Primary literature

Serjeant Musgrave's Dance, London: Methuen, 1960; reprinted in *Plays One*, London: Methuen, 1977

To Present the Pretence: Essays on the Theatre and Its Public, London: Methuen, 1977

[With Margaretta D'Arcy] *Awkward Corners: Essays, Papers, Fragments*, London: Methuen, 1988

'Building the play: an interview', *Encore* 8 (4), July–August 1961, 22–41

'Delusions of grandeur', *Twentieth Century* 169, February 1961, 200–6

'Getting time for adjustments', Interview with John Arden and Margaretta D'Arcy by Paul Hadfield and Linda [= Lynda] Henderson, *Writing Ulster*, Coleraine: University of Ulster 2/3, 1991–2, 88–9

'On comedy: John Arden talks to Albert Hunt', *Encore* 12 (5), September–October 1965, 13–19

'The reps and new plays: a writer's viewpoint', *New Theatre Magazine* 1 (2), January 1960, 23–6

'Telling a true tale', *Encore* 7 (3), May–June 1960, 22–6

'Who's for a revolution? Two interviews with John Arden' [with Walter Wager and Simon Trussler], *Tulane Drama Review* 11 (2) (T 34), Winter 1966, 41–53

Secondary literature

Adler, Thomas P. 'Religious ritual in John Arden's *Serjeant Musgrave's Dance*', *Modern Drama* 16 (2), September 1973, 163–6

Blindheim, Joan Tindale. 'John Arden's use of the stage', *Modern Drama* 11 (3), December 1968, 306–16

Clinton, Craig. 'John Arden: the promise unfulfilled', *Modern Drama*, 21 (1), 1978, 47–58

Day, P. W. 'Individual and society in the early plays of John Arden', *Modern Drama* 18, 1975, 239–49

Gilman, Richard. 'Arden's unsteady ground', *Tulane Drama Review* 11 (2) (T 34), Winter 1966, 54–62

Gray, Frances. *John Arden*, London: Macmillan, 1982

Hayman, Ronald. *John Arden*, London: Heinemann, 1968

Hunt, Albert. *Arden: A Study of his Plays*, London: Methuen, 1974
  'Arden's stagecraft', *Encore* 12 (5), September–October 1965, 9–12
  'Serjeant Musgrave and the critics', *Encore* 7 (1), January–February 1960, 26–8

Jordan, Robert. 'Serjeant Musgrave's problem', *Modern Drama* 13, 1970, 54–62

Leeming, Glenda. *John Arden*, London: Longman, 1974

McMillan, Grant E. 'The bargee in *Serjeant Musgrave's Dance*', *Educational Theatre Journal* 25, 1973, 500–3

Mills, J. 'Love and anarchy in *Serjeant Musgrave's Dance*', *Drama Survey* 7, Winter 1968–9, 45–51

Milne, Tom. 'A study of John Arden's plays', *New Left Review*, January–February 1961, 21–3

O'Connell, Mary B. 'Ritual elements in *Serjeant Musgrave's Dance*', *Modern Drama* 13, 1971, 356–9

Page, Malcolm. *John Arden*, Boston: G. K. Hall, 1984

Page, Malcolm (ed.). *Arden on File*, London: Methuen, 1985

Trussler, Simon. *John Arden*, New York: Columbia University Press, 1973

   'Arden – an introduction', *Encore* 12 (5), September–October 1965, 4–8

Wike, Jonathan (ed.). *John Arden and Margaretta D'Arcy: A Casebook*, London: Garland, 1994

Howard Barker (1946–)

Primary literature

Stripwell, 1975, published with *Claw*, London: Calder, 1977

Arguments for a Theatre, London: Calder, 1989

'49 asides for a tragic theatre', *The Guardian*, 10 February 1986, 11

'Energy – and the small discovery of dignity' [interview with Malcolm Hay and Simon Trussler], *Theatre Quarterly* 10 (40), Autumn–Winter 1981, 3–14

'Oppression, resistance and the writer's testament' [interview with Finlay Donesky], *Theatre Quarterly* 2 (8), November 1986, 336–44

'The redemptive power of desire', *The Times*, 6 February 1986

Secondary literature

Gambit: Howard Barker Issue, 11 (41), 1984

Grant, Steve. 'Barker's bite', *Plays and Players* 23 (3), December 1975, 36–9

Klotz, Günther. 'Howard Barker: paradigm of postmodernism', *New Theatre Quarterly* 25, 1991

Rabey, David Ian. *Howard Barker: Politics and Desire. An Expository Study of His Drama and Poetry, 1969–1987*, Basingstoke: Macmillan, 1989

Thomas, Alan. 'Howard Barker: modern allegorist', *Modern Drama* 35 (3), 1992, 433–43

Thomson, Peter. 'Humanism and catastrophe: a note on Howard Barker's polarities', *Studies in Theatre Production* 10, 1994, 39

Tomlin, Liz. 'Building a Barker character: a methodology from *The Last Supper*', *Studies in Theatre Production* 12, 1995, 47–53

Edward Bond (1934–)
Primary literature

Lear. 1971, first publ., London: Methuen, 1972; reprinted in *Plays: Two*, London: Methuen, 1978; publ. with Commentary and Notes by Patricia Hern, London: Methuen Student Editions, 1983

The Worlds, with The Activists Papers, London: Methuen, 1980

'Creating what is normal' [interview with Tony Coult], *Plays and Players* 23 (3), 1975, 9–13

'A discussion' [with Harold Hobson et al.], *Gambit* 5 (17), 1970, 5–38

'Drama and the dialectics of violence: Edward Bond interviewed by the editors' [Roger Hudson, Catherine Itzin and Simon Trussler], *Theatre Quarterly* 2 (5), January–March 1972, 4–14

'Dramatist in a schizophrenic society: Edward Bond on the context of the ideas in his plays' [interview with W. Bachem and R. Tabbert], *anglistik & englischunterricht* 7, 1979, 121–32

'Edward Bond in conversation' [interview with D. Roper], *Gambit* 9 (36), 1980, 35–45

'The first circle' [interview with G. Loney], *Performing Arts Journal* 1, 1976, 37–45

'From rationalism to rhapsody' [interview with Christopher Innes], *Canadian Theatre Review* 23, 1979, 108–13

'An interview by Giles Gordon', *Transatlantic Review* 22, Autumn 1966, 7–15

'On Brecht: a letter to Peter Holland', *Theatre Quarterly* 8 (30), Summer 1978, 34–5

Secondary literature

Arnold, Arthur. 'Lines of development in Bond's plays', *Theatre Quarterly* 2 (5), 1972, 15–19

Buhmann, Detlef. *Edward Bond: Theater zwischen Psyche und Politik*, Frankfurt am Main: Lang, 1988

Bulman, James C. 'Bond, Shakespeare and the Absurd', *Modern Drama* 29 (1), March 1986, 63

Coult, Tony. *The Plays of Edward Bond*, London: Eyre Methuen, 1978

Dark, Gregory. 'Production Casebook no. 5: Edward Bond's *Lear* at the Royal Court', *Theatre Quarterly* 2 (5), January–March 1972, 20–31

Donahue, Delia. *Edward Bond: A Study of His Plays*, Rome: Bulzoni editore, 1979

Gross, Konrad. 'Darstellungsprinzipien im Drama Edward Bonds', *Die Neueren Sprachen* 22, 1973, 313–24

Hay, Malcolm, and Philip Roberts. *Bond: A Study of His Plays*, London: Methuen, 1980

  Edward Bond: A Companion to His Plays, London: TQ Publications, 1978

Hirst, David L. *Edward Bond*, London: Macmillan, 1985

Holland, Peter. 'Brecht, Bond, Gaskill and the practice of political theatre', *Theatre Quarterly* 8 (30), Summer 1978, 24–34

Iden, Peter. *Edward Bond*, Velber: Friedrich Verlag, 1973

Jones, Daniel K. 'Bond's "Rational Theatre"', *Theatre Journal* 32 (4), 505–17

Klotz, Günther. 'Erbezitat und zeitlose Gewalt: zu Edward Bonds Lear', *Weimarer Beiträge* 19 (10), 1973, 54–65

Lappin, Lou. *The Art and Politics of Edward Bond*, New York: Lang, 1987

Oppel, Horst, and Sandra Christenson. *Edward Bond's Lear and Shakespeare's King Lear*, *Abhandlungen der geistes- und sozialwissenschaftlichen Klasse*, 1974 (2), Mainz: Akademie der Wissenschaften und der Literatur, 1974

Peter, John. 'Edward Bond: violence and poetry', *Drama* 117, Autumn 1975, 28–32

  'Political realism crushed by paranoia', *The Sunday Times*, 11 March 1990

Restivo, Giuseppina. *La nuova scena inglese: Edward Bond*, Turin: Giulio Einaudi, 1977

Roberts, Philip. *File on Bond*, London: Methuen, 1985

Roberts, Philip. 'Political metaphors: the plays of Edward Bond', *New Edinburgh Review*, 30 August 1975, 34–5

' "Making the two worlds one": the plays of Edward Bond', *Critical Quarterly* 21 (4), 1979, 75–84

Scharine, Richard. *The Plays of Edward Bond*, Lewisburg: Bucknell University Press, 1976

Spencer, Jenny S. *Dramatic Strategies in the Plays of Edward Bond*, Cambridge University Press, 1992

Stratmann, Gerd. 'Edward Bond, "Lear"', *Anglo-amerikanische Shakespeare-Bearbeitungen des 20. Jahrhunderts*, ed. Horst Priessnitz, Darmstadt: Wissenschaftliche Buchgesellschaft, 1980

Taylor, John Russell. 'British dramatists: the new arrivals no. 5: Edward Bond', *Plays and Players* 17, August 1970, 16–18

Tener, Robert L. 'Edward Bond's dialectic: irony and dramatic metaphors', *Modern Drama* 25 (2), 1982, 423–34

Trussler, Simon. *Edward Bond*, London: Longman, 1976

Wheeler, David. 'Curing cultural madness: Edward Bond's *Lear* and *The Woman*', *Theatre Annual* 46, 1993, 13–27

Wolfensperger, Peter. *Edward Bond: Dialektik des Weltbildes und dramatische Gestaltung*, Bern: Francke Verlag, 1976

Zapf, Hubert. 'Two concepts of society in drama: Bertolt Brecht's *The Good Woman of Setzuan* and Edward Bond's *Lear*', *Modern Drama* 31 (3), September 1988, 357

Howard Brenton (1942–)
Primary literature

The Churchill Play, London: Methuen, 1974, revised version of 1978 publ. in *Plays One*, London: Methuen, 1986

Hot Irons, London: Nick Hern Books, 1995

'Howard Brenton: an introduction' [interview with Malcolm Hay and Philip Roberts], *Performing Arts Journal* 3 (3), Winter 1979, 134–41

Interview [with Hugh Herbert], *The Guardian*, 9 May 1974

'On *Iranian Nights*', Tariq Ali and Howard Brenton, *Independent Magazine* 36, 13 May 1989

'Petrol bombs through the proscenium arch' [interview with Catherine Itzin and Simon Trussler], *Theatre Quarterly*, 5 (17), March–May 1975, 4–20

Select bibliography

'The red theatre under the bed' [interview with Tony Mitchell], *New Theatre Quarterly* 3 (11), August 1987, 195–201

'Taking liberties', *Marxism Today*, December 1988, 35–7

'Writing for democratic laughter', *Drama* 157 (3), 1985, 9–11

Secondary literature

Boon, Richard. *Brenton: the Playwright*, London: Methuen, 1991

Boon, Richard. 'Politics and terror in the plays of Howard Brenton', *Terrorism and Modern Drama*, ed. John Orr and Dragan Klaić, Edinburgh University Press, 1990, 138–50

Mitchell, Tony. *File on Brenton*, London: Methuen, 1988

Sotto-Morettini, Donna. 'Disrupting the Spectacle: Brenton's *Magnificence*', *Theatre Journal* 38 (1), 1986, 82–96

Caryl Churchill (1938–)

Primary literature

Cloud Nine, 1979, London: Pluto Press, 1979, revised edn 1983

'The common imagination and the individual voice' [interview with Geraldine Cousin], *New Theatre Quarterly* 4 (13), February 1988, 3–16

Interview with Steve Gooch, *Plays and Players*, January 1973, 40–41

'Not ordinary, not safe', *The Twentieth Century*, November 1960, 443–51

Secondary literature

Aston, Elaine. *Caryl Churchill*, 2nd edn, Plymouth: Northcote House, 2001

Case, Sue-Ellen and Jeanie K. Forte. 'From formalism to feminism', *Theater* 16 (2), Spring, 1985, 62–5

Cousin, Geraldine. *Churchill: the Playwright*, London: Methuen, 1989

Diamond, Elin. '(In)visible bodies in Churchill's theatre', *Theatre Journal* 40 (2), 1988, 188–204

'Refusing the romanticism of identity: narrative interventions in Churchill, Benmussa, Duras', *Theatre Journal* 37 (3), October 1985, 273–86

Fitzsimmons, Linda. *File on Churchill*, London: Methuen, 1989

'I won't turn back for you or anyone: Caryl Churchill's socialist–feminist theatre', *Essays in Theatre* 6 (1), November 1987, 19–29

Howe Kritzer, Amelia. *The Plays of Caryl Churchill: Theatre of Empowerment*, Basingstoke: Macmillan, 1991

Klett, Renate and Reinhardt Stumm. 'Autorenportrait: Caryl Churchill', *Theater heute*, January 1984, 19–27

Mitchell, Tony. 'Churchill's mad forest: a polyphonic study of South Eastern Europe', *Modern Drama* 36 (4), 499–511

Randall, Phyllis (ed.). *Caryl Churchill: A Casebook*, New York: Garland, 1988

Stone, Laurie. 'Caryl Churchill: making room at the top', *The Village Voice* 28 (9), 1 March 1983, 80–1

Thurman, Judith. 'Caryl Churchill: the playwright who makes you laugh about orgasm, racism, class struggle, homophobia, woman-hating, the British Empire, and the irrepressible strangeness of the human heart', *Ms*, May 1982, 52–7

Wandor, Michelene. 'Free collective bargaining', *Time Out*, September 1976, 10–11

Griffiths, Trevor (1935–)

Primary literature

Comedians, London: Faber & Faber, 1976, revised version 1979

'Countering consent' [interview with John Wyver], in: David Edgar et al., *Ah! Mischief: The Writer and Television*, ed. Frank Pike, London: Faber & Faber, 1982, 30–40

'Current concerns' [interview with Peter Ansorge and David Hare], *Plays and Players*, July 1974, 18–22

Interview, *The Leveller*, November 1976, 12–13

Interview with Pat Silburn, *Gambit* 8 (29), 1976, 30–6

'Politics and populist culture' [interview with Alison Summers], *Canadian Theatre Review*, Summer 1980, 22–9

'Towards the mountain top' [interview with Robert Cushman], *Plays and Players* 21, August 1974, 14–19

'Transforming the husk of capitalism' [interview with Catherine Itzin and Simon Trussler], *Theatre Quarterly* 6 (22), Summer 1976, 25–46

Select bibliography

Secondary literature

Hay, Malcolm. 'Theatre Checklist no. 9: Trevor Griffiths', *Theatre Facts* 3 (1), 1976, 2–8

Nairn, Tom. ['Trevor Griffiths's Occupations'], *Seven Days*, 3 November 1971

Quigley, Austin. 'Creativity and commitment in Trevor Griffiths's *Comedians*', *Modern Drama* 24, December 1981, 404–23

Wolff, Janet, et al. 'Problems of radical drama: the plays and productions of Trevor Griffiths', *Literature, Society and the Sociology of Literature*, ed. Francis Barker et al., Colchester: University of Essex, 1977, 133–53

David Hare (1947–)

Primary literature

Fanshen 1975, London: Faber & Faber, 1976

Writing Left-Handed, London: Faber & Faber, 1991

'From Portable Theatre to Joint Stock ... via Shaftesbury Avenue' [interview with Catherine Itzin and Simon Trussler], *Theatre Quarterly* 5 (20), December 1975–February 1976, 108–15

'Humanity and passion don't count' [interview with Peter Ansorge], *Plays and Players* 19, February 1972, 14–24

Interview with Georg Gaston, *Theatre Journal* 45 (2), May 1993, 213–25

'A lecture given at King's College, Cambridge, March 5 1978', *Licking Hitler*, London: Faber & Faber, 1978, 57–71

Secondary literature

Ansorge, Peter. 'David Hare: a war on two fronts', *Plays and Players* 25, April 1978, 12–16

Cardullo, Bert. 'Brecht and *Fanshen*', *Studia Neophilologica* 58 (2), 1986, 225–30

'*Fanshen*, western drama and David Hare's œuvre', *San Jose Studies* 10, Spring 1984, 31–41

Dean, Joan FitzPatrick. *David Hare*, Boston: Twayne, 1990

Fraser, Scott. *A Politic Theatre: The Drama of David Hare*, Amsterdam: Rodopi, 1996

Haill, Lyn (ed.). *Asking Around: Background to the David Hare Trilogy*, London: Faber & Faber, 1993

Homden, Carol. *The Plays of David Hare*, Cambridge University Press, 1994

Ludlow, Colin. 'Hare and others', *London Magazine* 18, July 1978, 76–81

Myerson, Jonathan. 'David Hare: fringe graduate', *Drama* 149 (3), 1983 26–8

Oliva, Judy Lee. *David Hare: Theatricalizing Politics*, Ann Arbor: UMI Research Press, 1990

Page, Malcolm, and Ria Julian. 'David Hare checklist', *Theatrefacts* 2, 1975, 2–4, 10

Page, Malcolm. *File on Hare*, London: Methuen, 1990

Williams, Christopher, and Gaetano D'Elia, *La scrittura multimediale di David Hare*, Fasano: Schena, 1989

Zeifman, Hersh. *David Hare: A Casebook*, New York: Garland, 1994

McGrath, John (1935–2002)
Primary literature

The Cheviot, the Stag and the Black, Black Oil, first publ. Breakish: West Highland Publishing, 1974, revised edn, London: Methuen, 1981

A Good Night Out: Popular Theatre: Audience, Class and Form, London: Methuen, 1981

The Bone Won't Break: On Theatre and Hope in Hard Times, London: Methuen, 1990

'Better a bad night in Bootle...' [interview with Catherine Itzin and Simon Trussler], *Theatre Quarterly* 5 (19), September–November 1975, 39–54

'New directions' [interview with Ramona Gibbs], *Plays and Players*, November 1972, xiii–xiv

'Popular theatre and the changing perspective of the eighties' [interview with Tony Mitchell], *New Theatre Quarterly* 1 (4), November 1985, 390–9

'The theory and practice of political theatre', *Theatre Quarterly* 9 (36), 1980, 43–54

'The Year of the Cheviot', *Plays and Players*, February 1974, 24–30

Select bibliography

Secondary literature

Barker, Clive. 'Das Ensemble 7:84: über die Arbeit einer englischen Theatergruppe', *Theater der Zeit* 31 (2), 1976, 48–50

Boa, Elizabeth. 'Some versions of the pastoral in McGrath's *The Cheviot, the Stag and the Black, Black Oil* and Kroetz's *Stallerhof*', *Anglistentag 1984, Passau*, ed. M. Pfister, Giessen: Hoffmann, 1985, 219–30

Höhne, Horst. 'Political analysis, theatrical form, and popular language in the plays of Charles Wood, Henry Livings and John McGrath', *Zeitschrift für Anglistik und Amerikanistik* 25 (4), 1977, 332–50

Jäger, Andreas. *John McGrath und die 7:84 Company Scotland: Politik, Popularität und Regionalismus im Theater der siebziger Jahre in Schottland*, Amsterdam: Rodopi, 1986

MacLennan, Elizabeth. *The Moon Belongs to Everyone: Making Theatre with 7:84*, London: Methuen, 1990

Maguire, Tom. 'Under new management: the changing direction of 7:84 (Scotland)', *Theatre Research International* 17 (2), 1992, 132–7

McFerran, Ann. '7:84 six years on' (and response by John McGrath), *Time Out* 8–14 April 1977, 11 and 13; 29 April–5 May 1977, 3

Page, Malcolm. 'John McGrath' [checklist and bibliography], *New Theatre Quarterly* 1 (4), November 1985, 400–16

Schliephake, Bernd. 'Politisches Theater in Schottland: John McGrath und die Gruppe 7:84', *Englisch Amerikanische Studien* 2 (4), December 1980, 519–25

Arnold Wesker (1932–)

Primary literature

Roots, in: *The Wesker Trilogy*, London: Jonathan Cape, 1960

As Much as I Dare: Autobiography 1932–1959, London: Century, 1994

Distinctions, London: Jonathan Cape, 1985

Fears of Fragmentation, London: Jonathan Cape, 1970

'Art is not enough', *Twentieth Century*, February 1961, 190–4; reprinted in *English Dramatic Theories*, ed. P. Goetsch, 1972, 107–11

'Casual condemnations: a brief study of the critic as censor', *Theatre Quarterly* 1, April 1971, 16–30

Select bibliography

'From a writer's notebook', *Theatre Quarterly* 6, May–June 1972, 8–13
'His very own and golden city' [interview with Simon Trussler], *Tulane Drama Review* 11 (2), Winter 1966, 192–202
'An interview on Centre 42', *Encore* 9 (3), May–June 1962, 39–44
Interview with Maureen Cleave, *Observer Magazine*, 4 October 1981
'Let battle commence!', *Encore* 5 (4), November–December 1958, 18–24
'Miniautobiography in three acts and a prologue', *Contemporary Authors Autobiography Series* 7, Detroit: Gale Research, 1987, 227–63
'To react – to respond', *Encore* 6 (3), May–June 1959, 6–8

Secondary literature

Adler, T. P. 'The Wesker trilogy revisited: games to compensate for the inadequacy of words', *Quarterly Journal of Speech* 65, 1979, 429–38
Anderson, Michael. 'Arnold Wesker: the last humanist', *New Theatre Magazine* 8 (3), 1968, 10–27
Aylwin, A. M. *Notes on Arnold Wesker's 'Roots'*, London: Methuen Educational, 1975
Coppieters, Frank. 'Arnold Wesker's Centre Fortytwo: a cultural revolution betrayed', *Theatre Quarterly* 5 (18), June–August 1975, 37–51
Dornan, Reade. *Arnold Wesker Revisited*, New York: Twayne, 1994
Drabble, Margaret. 'Profile 10: Arnold Wesker', *New Review* 11, 1975, 25–30
Elsom, John. '*Roots*: Royal Court Theatre 30 June 1959' (reviews), *Post-War British Theatre Criticism*, London: Routledge, 1981, 91–7
Findlater, Richard. 'Plays and politics: Arnold Wesker's trilogy', *Twentieth Century* 168, September 1960, 235–42
Garforth, John. 'Arnold Wesker's mission', *Encore* 10 (3), May–June 1963, 38–43
Hayman, Ronald. *Arnold Wesker*, London: Heinemann, 2nd edn, 1974
Hughes, Ted. 'Arnold Wesker: "A Sort of Socialism"', *Nation*, 19 November 1960, 402–4
Hunt, Albert. 'Roots in Norfolk', *Encore* 7 (3), May–June 1960, 30–31

Jones, A. R. 'The theatre of Arnold Wesker', *Critical Quarterly* 2, Winter 1960, 366–70

Jones, Mervyn. 'Arnold Wesker's epic', *Encore* 7 (5), September–October 1960, 6–10

Latham, J. '*Roots*: a reassessment', *Modern Drama* 8, September 1965, 192–7

Leeming, Glenda. *Wesker the Playwright*, London: Methuen, 1983
  Wesker on File, London: Methuen, 1985

Leeming, Glenda, and Simon Trussler. *The Plays of Arnold Wesker: an Assessment*, London: Gollancz, 1971

Lindemann, Klaus and Valeska. *Arnold Wesker*, Munich: Fink, 1985

Mander, John. 'Arnold Wesker's *Roots*', *The Writer and Commitment*, London: Secker & Warburg, 1961, 194–211

Marland, Michael (ed.). *Arnold Wesker*, London: Times Newspapers, 1970

Patterson, Michael. 'The reception of Arnold Wesker's plays in Europe', *History of European Ideas* 20 (1–3), Oxford: Pergamon, 1995, 31–4

Ribalow, Harold U. *Arnold Wesker*, New York: Twayne, 1966

Wilcher, Robert. *Understanding Arnold Wesker*, Columbia, South Carolina: University of South Carolina Press, 1991

Zimmermann, Heiner O. 'Wesker and Utopia in the sixties', *Modern Drama* 29, 1986, 185–206

Index

Index

Lightning Source UK Ltd.
Milton Keynes UK
UKOW02f0852130116

266320UK00001B/55/P